CHILD OF THE STORM

CHILD OF THE STORM

The Adventures of a West Coast Kid

Lawrence Foort

Trafford Publishing

Order this book online at www.trafford.com
or email orders@trafford.com

Most Trafford titles are also available at major online book retailers.

Printed in Victoria, BC, Canada.

ISBN: 978-1-4269-1555-0 (sc)

*Our mission is to efficiently provide the world's finest, most comprehensive book publishing
service, enabling every author to experience success. To find out how to publish your book, your
way, and have it available worldwide, visit us online at www.trafford.com*

Trafford rev. 01/04/2010

 www.trafford.com

North America & international
toll-free: 1 888 232 4444 (USA & Canada)
phone: 250 383 6864 ♦ fax: 812 355 4082

For Frank ("Trapper") Nason, Lorne Carney,
Harvey Lancell, Carl Peterson, George Newson,
Billie Rapita, Bob Blaine and Sid Moss.
Lost at sea but not forgotten.

The Demand for a Sign

The Pharisees and Sadducees came along, and as a test asked Jesus to show them some sign in the sky. He gave them this reply: "In the evening you say, red sky at night, the day will be bright, but red sky in the morning, sailors take warning."

INTRODUCTION

October 9, 1940 dawned, I'm reliably informed, with a bright red sky, which is a sign to all mariners to beware of a rising storm.

Carl Johansonn was one of many rowboat fishermen who worked the Gulf of Georgia during the great Depression of the 1930s. He saw the blazing red sunrise and his thoughts turned towards his small one-room shack at Poverty Point on Quadra Island, just opposite Campbell River on the shore of Discovery Passage. Carl was fishing what became known as The Gap, the channel between Steep Island and Gowlland Island, just off the Quadra shore, as the ebb tide was due to turn to flood.

The fishing was poor that day because it was so late into the salmon fishing season. Most of the large Northern Coho salmon had already moved towards the rivers of their birth to spawn and die, as was their life cycle. The winter Chinook salmon wouldn't appear until the herring arrived in late November, so Carl felt a pang of sadness as yet another summer season of fishing was drawing rapidly to a close.

Mr. Johansonn was born in Sweden in 1885 and came to North America with his parents in 1897 to settle in Minnesota. He started work in the great northern forests at a young age, and had moved west as new timber was cut for the ever expanding growth of the nation. The spring of 1930 found him in Seattle,

Washington, with no prospect of work, due to the international economic downturn of that year.

So he and a couple of other unemployed loggers headed north to try their luck in Canada. After riding a freight train into Vancouver, they found their chances of finding work there about the same as they had been in Seattle, pretty poor.

As luck would have it though, one day they wandered down to the waterfront and there a Japanese fish buyer offered them a rowboat that they could have right away and pay him for it out of revenue derived from fish that they caught and delivered. Carl took up this offer, but his two friends decided to keep searching for a job in the forests falling timber. This was the start of many years of fishing that would last him for the rest of his life. Many hundreds of rowboats and putter boats were involved in the fishery at that time and during the remaining years of The Depression, as it held the land in its angry grasp.

Carl, with his newly acquired vessel, was towed out along with several others to the fishing grounds off Five Fingers Island, located near the town of Nanaimo on the east coast of Vancouver Island, directly across Georgia Strait from Vancouver.

The fleet of little boats would fish all day, then deliver their fish in the evening to a fish packing vessel, which would supply them with food, fishing gear and other necessities, along with a statement of account once a month. At night they would camp on the beach in Pipers Lagoon along with the many other people who found themselves in this same desperate situation. As blue back salmon fishing slowed in early June, the boats moved north to Hornby Island, then in early August further north still to Cape Mudge, located at the south tip of Quadra Island.

As the Great Depression faded into the war years at the end of the 1930's, Carl found that he was getting too old to be of much use in the forests as a logger, the career he had always intended to go back to. So he continued on as a rowboat fisherman for many more years, until old age caught up with him, as it does with all of us fortunate enough to live that long.

With the morning red sky as a warning of weather to come and the fishing very slow, he caught the first part of the flood tide down to Quadra Island's Quathiaski Cove, where he sold his few fish at the B.C. Packers fish camp.

With his earnings of $1.75 stashed in his pocket, he rowed north against the incoming tide back towards his shack on Poverty Point. Even after years of practice, rowing against the tide still was never easy. He hugged close to shore to take advantage of the back eddies that formed as the six-hour duration of the incoming tide wore on. The steadily rising southeast wind pushing from astern helped to propel his frail craft against the flooding tidal current though, and after much effort he was finally past 'Row And Be Damned', a well named rock and area just off shore where the rushing water would make one final unsuccessful effort to defeat the small boat, before the water gave way to a favourable back eddy which would take Carl safely back home to his hut.

The rough and ready one room cabin, if you could call it that, was made of split cedar planks. There was a wood burning stove, an old bed, a table and a couple of chairs. The earth floor was littered with fishing gear, wood for the stove, kerosene cans and unwashed clothes. Several other fishermen made this westerly facing point of Quadra Island shoreline their home. Upon arrival, Carl found that most of his rowboat colleagues had already pulled their little wooden craft well up the gravel beach, far beyond the high tide mark. All could tell that the angry looking red sunrise was a sure sign of an early winter storm.

Chapter 1

Quadra Island is the largest of the northern Gulf Islands at the top of Georgia Strait, located on the west coast of Canada about 100 miles north west from the city of Vancouver, British Columbia.

Captain George Vancouver originally named this Island Valdes Island during his exploration of the West Coast of Canada in the late 1700's. During this voyage of discovery, he met Senor Juan Francisco de la Bodega y Quadra at Nootka Sound in August of 1792, and the two navigator-explorers and mariners developed a mutual respect and friendship for each other.

Senor Quadra, to give him the usual shortening of his last name, had sailed north from San Blas, Mexico, in 1775 under orders from the Spanish Viceroy of Mexico to explore the west coast of North America and claim it for Spain. Captain Vancouver, in counterpoint to that, was under orders of the British Admiralty to chart the coast of what is now British Columbia and claim it instead for England, before the Spaniards could lay first claim. Most of the charts that Captain Vancouver produced are still used today, with remarkably little change from the originals. The name of the island, one of the larger ones in the area, was changed from the original Valdes to Quadra about 1903, to honour Senor Quadra and also to save confusion with another Valdes Island, located in the southern part of the coast.

Permanent settlement on Quadra by non-native people appears to have begun about 1882, with the first land purchase duly noted in the Land Registry records. In May of that year, the records show William Clarke purchased 144 acres located at Gowlland Harbour on the west coast of the island. The next year the property was transferred to William Sayward, who owned a sawmill in Victoria, and during that same year R.H. Pidcock purchased 150 acres in the island's Quathiaski Cove. These and other early purchases were on behalf of large timber companies: Quadra had some spectacular stands of timber and the sawmill operators, located mostly in Vancouver, were expanding up the coast. Timber and fishing was what interested most early settlers and companies, and in later years some farming took place on the areas where trees had been cleared.

Other settlers were recorded during the late 1800s, other than timber interests, but they're not part of our story. By about 1900 though, many new families were taking up land and settling at various places on Quadra, with Quathiaski Cove, Heriot Bay, Bold Point, Granite Bay and Gowlland Harbour being among the most popular places.

The year 1884 brought completion of the first native Indian school, with a second one built the next year. The spread out settlement and poor transportation saw several other small schools built at various locations during those bygone years.

The first Gowlland Harbour School, built in 1924, lasted just a year until it was burned by forest fire in 1925. So later that year, the next one was built and that operated until a stove exploded and it burned to the ground in 1935. For the remainder of the 1935/36 school year, our home was used as the Gowlland Harbour School.

The year after that, in 1936, the Cape Mudge School was built near the village on the south western tip of the island and that's where I was destined to take Grade 4 in 1949-50.

Finally the new Quadra United School was built at Quathiaski Cove in 1950, which had an impressive four rooms, and a gymnasium. This resulted in all the other one room schools, except Granite Bay, being permanently closed. I attended this new school for Grades 5 through 7. But I'm getting ahead of myself; we have a long way to go before then.

Chapter 2

My earliest memories of life on Quadra Island are of our old grey cat sitting on the back porch of the family home, and of my sister Ruth asking me to shake my head so that my long curls would flop around. Ruth seemed to delight in this and would often tell me to shake my head. I can remember her laughing every time I did so, and I loved to make her laugh, but my mother cut those curls off when I was three. So I guess those early memories must predate my third birthday.

The reason I tell you about the weather Carl faced that October morning is that I was born later that day, at about 10 p.m. October 9, 1940. My mother said later she tried to postpone my birth so I'd arrive the next day, which was her birthday, but it didn't pan out that way. Apparently I just couldn't wait any longer to get started on this whole huge and enjoyable adventure that has been my life.

The storm promised from the glorious red sky that morning broke later as predicted and was said afterwards to be one of the worst in many people's memories, blowing in that night to make it impossible for my mother to be taken by boat out from Gowlland Harbour across Discovery Passage to the hospital at Campbell River. My brother Bill, who is 18 years older than I am, was a crew member on the tug B.C Boy, which was sent out from Gowlland to go across Discovery Passage to pick up the doctor in Campbell River, but that didn't work either. The seas were so towering and fierce and the wind so fearsome that the tug couldn't land. Bill, who even at that age was already a seasoned sailor, said years later that he'd never seen such a savage storm. So skipper Ralph Hendrickson had no choice but to return to port on Quadra. The result of all this was that I was born at home, on the dining room table, with my father in attendance. Bill wrapped me up and put me in an apple box behind the kitchen stove to keep me warm. I have to admit I have no recollection of any of this, but I can say that I'm most grateful to all those who participated, especially Mum, who was just two hours short of turning 39 when all this took place.

I learned later that the great storm of the night of October 9-10, 1940 did considerable damage along the coast. Many of the fishermen's shacks were washed away at Cape Mudge and up at what was then Poverty Point, now April Point, just outside Gowlland Harbour, where I was involved in my own little drama. In those days there were still many men and some women who made their living rowboat fishing for salmon along the east coast of Vancouver Island, many of them living around the south end of Quadra Island in cabins and shacks that faced out into the teeth of the southeast storms and gales.

With winter approaching and the prevailing storm winds blowing out of a long fetch of the northern half of the Gulf of Georgia directly at them, the loss of these homes was a terrible hardship to their residents. There were no social services in those days to help people through difficult times, but everyone used to pitch in to help each other and in a very short time, all the homes would be rebuilt. Life carried on, as of course, it must.

At the time of my birth, World War II was raging across the Atlantic in Europe, and my oldest brother Jim had joined the Royal Canadian Air Force. As near as I can tell, he joined up more to get away from home and the trials of coastal living during the latter days of the Depression, than really from any sense of duty to King and Country. I'd certainly now agree with his decision, as he had grown up during those days of great financial hardship and deprivation for so many people, and life was pretty difficult for almost everyone during those terrible times.

As an amusing footnote, Jim had also let it be known he couldn't wait to get to Europe, into the action, and to see the rest of the world. But fate intervened; the first half of his war was spent in central Canada and the second half at Shearwater, just a short 200 miles up the coast from home. He was in the coastal patrol and was kept busy looking for Japanese submarines after Pearl Harbour was attacked in December 1941.

My sister Ruth is seven years older than I am as the baby of the family. Mum sent Ruth off to Victoria for most of her schooling, as she was determined to see that her only daughter was given the opportunity to get a better education than the one room, multi grade facilities at Quadra Island offered. Afterwards, Ruth trained as a nurse and graduated from the Jubilee Hospital in 1955.

I also had another older brother named David, but he died at the age of five, before I was born, and is buried at the old homestead on Quadra Island. Mum told me she thought of David every single day of the rest of her long life and Ruth's only boy is named after him. My wife and I also named our son John David, whose second name is after my late brother.

This completes my immediate family, but there are others, as Dad had a family of four boys before he married Mum. To fill you in on this, I must go back in history to the time of my ancestors and take us overseas to relate as best I can where we all came from.

My father was born in England on March 21, 1880. At an early age, he joined the British Army and spent a good deal of his life in India. He also fought in both the Boer War in South Africa and in World War I in Europe. He married first in November 1904, and it was that marriage which produced my four half brothers. His first wife, Fanny Louise Temple, died quite young, and he was faced with the not uncommon situation of having to live in a far off land, raise his four growing sons, and carry on with his army career all at the same time. Fortunately, domestic help was both available and affordable in India at the time, so he was able to continue in the army, and eventually retired with the rank of Major after the end of the WWI.

My father's parents owned a hotel in England and during the Boer War they were discriminated against due to the possibility that their ancestors were Dutch. This led to my grandparents going bankrupt and the early death of my grandfather. All this while, their son Fredrick, my father, was serving with the British Army against the Boers in South Africa. One of my English cousins, Rosemarie, has sent me something of a family tree. This information shows that the original Foorts were Amersforts, who had come to England with William and Mary in 1668. We have no real record of father's ancestors other than this information. I suppose we will have to go to England sometime to investigate old church records etc.

About 1920 father was stationed in Lebanon, where he met my mother, who was then working as an interpreter for the British Army. Dad was 22 years older than her, and I'm not completely sure why she married him. Though I asked Mum on many occasions, I never got any straight answers. She always said it was none of my business. I suspect Father was looking for a mother for his four boys so that he could afford to leave India; and maybe Mum was looking for a way out of her homeland, which had been devastated by the war.

One of my aunts told me later that my Lebanese grandfather gave his permission for the marriage only on the absolute assurance from Dad that he wouldn't leave Lebanon with his 'child bride'. But as soon as they were married, they left immediately by ship for India, where father had to finish up his term with the army. I don't even know if Mum was aware of my father's previous family, but she certainly found out as soon as they arrived in Bangalore in central India. Naturally there was apparently all hell to pay back in Lebanon. My grandfather was not amused!

At that time, most people in the Middle East were Muslim as the Turks of the Ottoman Empire had ruled the area for several centuries. My great-grandfather as a child was the sole survivor of a whole village that was massacred by the Turks about the middle of the 19th Century. An older sister had hidden him out of sight under a bed before she was slaughtered along with the rest of the village. He was found some days later by some American missionaries, and was raised and educated at a Christian school, which explains why Mum's family is Christian rather than Muslim. Unfortunately, we have no history at all of our family on Mum's side beyond my great grandfather.

After my father finished his duties with the army in India, Mum, Dad and the family, such as it was at that time, embarked once again by ship for China. Father had a pension of about $50 per month, which was quite adequate in the 1920s, and his plan was finally to move on to Canada with Mum and the four boys. They boarded the Canadian Pacific liner The Empress of Russia at Shanghai, and, after stops in Japan and Hawaii, landed in Vancouver on Labour Day, 1920. Father was 41 by then, with Mum still only 19. It's amazing how events in one's life seem to cross with the events in the lives of others. My wife's father, my business partner's father and my best friend Lance's father were all born in India about the same time Dad was serving there. It would be interesting to know if the families knew each other, but of course it's not very likely.

Another coincidence is that my wife's father was a doctor and his first job after graduating from medical school was as a ship's doctor - which happened to be on The Empress of Russia. My whole life seems to have been filled with similar coincidences, where I met people who had contact with family, business associates and friends prior to our meeting.

The Empress of Russia and her sister The Empress of Asia had very distinguished careers on several theatres of operation. Both served on the run from Vancouver to the Orient terminating in the Philippines, with stops at Hawaii, Japan and China. During both world wars, these vessels were used as troop carriers with the Asia being lost in the Second World War. The Russia survived only to be lost by fire while being refitted for civilian service after the end of the war in 1945.

One incident of interest happened on the Russia while in port at Newport News, Virginia. Both of theses vessels were among the last of the coal burning ships that had never been converted to oil. This, of course, presented problems with refuelling at various ports around the world. During their war service, the Chinese crews were supplied by the ship owners, the Canadian Pacific Railway. The officers were British Navy regulars and reservists. While at Newport News during August 1941, the crews walked off the ship and refused to load coal or return to regular duties. The owners arranged for a new crew to be sent east by rail from Vancouver to meet the ship at Halifax, Canada.

The Captain called for volunteers from amongst the officers to go below to the boiler room to shovel coal so the ship could proceed to Halifax. This duty was just about as low as it gets. The work was hot, heavy and dirty for long hours and done by what was known as The Black Gang. Several junior officers stepped forward to volunteer, one of them being Prince Phillip who was later to become the Duke of Edinburgh, husband and consort to Queen Elizabeth.

During my father's extensive travels as a British Army officer, he had traveled several times on various Empress Ships while serving in Hong Kong and the Far East. He became very good friends with one of the Chief Engineers who presented father with a ship's bell taken from The Empress of Japan when she was retired from service in 1922. This bell was mounted by the back door of our Quadra Island house to call us home when rung by mother. My brother Jim moved it to California during the ten years he lived at Berkley before returning it to Quadra Island after he moved back to Canada in 1963.

Chapter 3

On arriving in Canada, the family settled in Vancouver, where mother was evidently completely confused by all of the different customs and ways of life in Canada.

After a few years, with first Jim and then Bill added to the nucleus family, Dad bought a boat and took up travelling and fishing along the B.C. coast, introducing that ocean based way of life to the family. They first settled at Surge Narrows on Read Island on the eastern side of Quadra Island, where both my brothers started school.

From there the family moved to Quadra Island, first to Heriot Bay, and then on to Gowlland Harbour. They bought 100 plus acres at the north end of the harbour about 1932 and settled there for keeps. They built a five bedroom house, quite a substantial property for those days, and settled back to wait out the Depression.

Dad was reportedly never very good at fishing, but there were just so many fish in those days that he managed to catch enough to earn a small income, which, along with his army pension, gave the family enough finances to meet their needs. They did a lot of travelling along the coast, in a 36 foot launch by the name of Merrybelle. In later years, the vessel got a new engine and Bill used the old one as an auxiliary motor for a sawmill he built.

The west coast of Canada was a place of some prosperity

during the WW II and on into the 1950s. The pre-war Depression which so seriously affected much of the western world was over, and the war, with its demands on resources and manpower, brought a big increase in employment. After Japan attacked Pearl Harbour in late 1941, the whole North American west coast really came alive. Airports were built in the most unusual places, and the navy became very visible and strong. Our merchant marine was new, strong and efficient, and the coastal industries of lumber, mining and fishing were in full production, along with shipbuilding and manufacturing. Boys and girls too young for military service worked alongside their mothers in factories and shipyards. Men too old for the military were also employed in war-time production such as farming, fishing and other work critical to the war effort.

Dad was 60 years old when I was born just after the start of the war, but being a military man for so many years, he was very eager to volunteer for something in aid of the war effort. He of course was beyond the age of being much help to the military. Today older people are in demand because of their experience, but back in 1940 the world was different; dad wasn't called on to assist, and this inactivity made him more restless than usual. He started leaving home regularly and for longer and longer periods until, when I was about three, he left home more or less for good.

When he left, he took his pension with him. On the other side of the coin, the new financial prosperity which had come with the war also tended to have the more unfortunate effect of raising the cost of living, even though price controls and rationing were in effect. I think the only way we survived after Dad left Mum to raise me and Ruth as young children, was because of Bill, who was only 20 and had to support the whole family for several years.

Life on the British Columbia coast was very different during the 1940s from what it is today. Bill was in the Home Guard rather than the regular military, due to a problem with his feet, which prevented him from joining the regular army. He was also employed in the fishing industry on a fish packing vessel, which was deemed an essential service or industry, along with agriculture and other things like mining. I well remember him studying his navigation books so that he could obtain his captain's papers.

In 1944, after several years on tugs and fish packers, Bill finally got his first job as a captain on a medium sized fish packer. He and Mum had also started farming in a sizeable way, mainly to feed us but also resulting in sales of milk, eggs, butter, meat and various fruits and vegetables during the summer season, to supplement the family income. First Nations people used to come from all over the coast during the summer fishing season to pick berries at our place, and a good deal of the produce from our garden was sold to the native and non-native residents of Cape Mudge.

Mother had a strange relationship with our aboriginal neighbours. She seemed to distrust them as a whole, but at the same time some of her very best friends were First Nations women from all over the coast. It could be that it was men she distrusted after Dad left home, and native men were unfortunate to be included in this group at that time in her life. Strangely, Mum also had a certain strange attitude towards most of the other residents of Quadra Island as well, and this was evident in her refusing ever to allow Ruth to attend school on the island. During a few years when we couldn't afford to send her to school in Victoria, Ruth took her schooling by correspondence, as I did until Grade 4.

Our life really revolved around home, the ocean and its tides and winds, and at that time just about everyone along the coast had a boat of some kind. These boats ranged in size from small rowboats, which everyone seemed to have, to larger west coast trollers and the odd privately owned purse seine fishing boat. As an example, in our family Bill had a boat called Seabird. It was about 32 feet long, with a Buick car engine for a motor. Mum had a 14 foot Turner built boat with a 2.5 horsepower Briggs & Stratton engine. These types of boats were called 'putter boats', due I guess to the noise made by their engines. Everyone fished almost as soon as one was old enough to pull a line. Brother Jim was the best fisher in our family, and he worked his way through university after the war by fishing during the summer vacation.

Other vessels that had a tremendous influence on our and everyone else's lives were the ships of the Union Steamship Company, which brought mail and supplies every week; and if one had to travel to Vancouver for any reason, this was the best method of transportation.

Gowlland Harbour at that time was a storage area for logs, as it still is today. There were always large steam-powered tugs in the harbour making up tows of logs for sawmills in Vancouver. We'd row out to the tugs in the evening after they had finished their work for the day, and trade with the crews, bringing them fruit and fresh vegetables to trade for sugar, flour, kerosene and coal. Many of these aging vessels still burned coal in their boilers, and every sack of coal we could get replaced a large quantity of wood we otherwise had to collect and split for use for heating and cooking. All of our wood was cut by hand, so it was a welcome relief from this drudgery when we could get coal from the tugs. Many of the crew members became our good friends, and it was always a time of celebration when a tug came into the harbour fresh from the city with a new supply of goodies for us kids.

We didn't get electricity in our home until about 1958, 13 years after the war. Until then, kerosene was used in the lamps for lighting and we had no refrigeration of any kind. We did have two modern conveniences which Mum insisted on. One was proper hot and cold running water, heated by a coil in the wood stove, the other was a telephone. Turning a crank on the side of the large box which housed the ear and mouth piece used to charge the battery for the call, and everyone who had a telephone could, and usually did, listen in on your far from private conversation.

Eddy Joyce was the telephone linesman covering the area up as far as Alert Bay for a number of years. He had a phone company boat in which he ploughed up and down the coast, looking for trouble with the lines that ran mostly along the beach, stretching all the way from Campbell River to the northern end of Vancouver Island. Remains of these old lines can still be seen today along the shore north of Salmon River.

Joyce was a very large man of native extraction who had a wife of rare beauty from the Haida Nation, and it was amazing that for many years he was able to service such a large area almost entirely by himself. He was very clever, ingenious and inventive, and always seemed to be able come up with some innovative way to keep the system operating.

I'm told the Joyce family were early pioneers on Quadra, arriving there before the 20th Century. I can remember visiting with Granny Joyce and hearing stories of their early days on the island. They lived at the very end of Cape Mudge, farming and fishing for a living. When they first settled there, the nearest town from which to obtain supplies and mail was down to the south, across the northern part of Georgia Strait on Vancouver Island, in Comox, a distance of some 50 kms or more away. The Joyces travelled by rowboat to Comox twice a year to get their mail and supplies for the next six months.

On one trip they forgot to get matches, which were needed to light the fires to heat their home. With winter fast approaching, they only had two matches left in the house. Naturally Mrs. Joyce was very nervous about this and feared it could be a huge problem if an extra cold winter should set in. So she gave the boys strict instructions to make certain to keep the fires burning with extra care, so there'd be hot coals each morning to rekindle, to build up for that day. I can remember her telling Mum that the following spring, when it came time to launch the boats for the next trip to Comox, she still had both of those two matches hidden away in a safe place. It just shows how independent they were, and also how careful the boys were about ensuring the fire didn't go out that winter.

Arthur Joyce, one of the sons, later had a small salmon seine boat named Valdes Isle. He and his crew fished dogfish during the winter and salmon during the summer salmon season. My brother Bill was a crew member on this fine little vessel for part of one salmon season, during a September when the chum salmon were plentiful. Bill would bring home a large salmon each week, which we would put in the Queals' smoke house for curing.

Mum used to like to meet the Union Steamship company ships on their way north when they stopped at Quathiaski Cove. This meant mail from the outside world and perhaps some word from Jim or Dad. We'd go down to The Cove in her boat, and I can still remember vividly those trips, as other boats would also be making the same trip to greet the Union ship as it was coming up the channel. I recall the wake from the big ship resulting in such gigantic waves that I was terrified they would swamp us. That lasted right up until I was about six, and I used to howl my head off as we danced over the wake of the big ships in Mum's little boat. Ruth was quite the contrary to me, and the bigger the waves, the more she seemed to enjoy herself, looking at me all the time with total disgust and telling me what a big sissy I was.

Of course during the war certain items were rationed, and we were sent coupons that had to be presented at the B.C. Packers store before we could purchase certain commodities such as sugar, butter etc. Being classified as fishermen, we always had an endless supply of gasoline, even though it was rationed to all non-fishermen, but some things that weren't rationed were simply unavailable up the coast, ice cream being one of them. One day when I was about three, I was standing outside the store at Q Cove under the totem pole located there. Mum came out of the store with Ruth, and they had an ice-cream cone for me. I had never seen one before, and Ruth had to show me the proper way to eat it, so for reasons that haunt me to this day, I turned the cone upside-down to take a look at the bottom. To my great surprise, shock, horror and consternation, the wonderful, tasty ice cream instantly fell on the dock at my feet, where a big black dog promptly and happily licked it up. All I could do was to look on with dismay, and I howled even louder than I had when we went over the waves in our boat. Mum and Ruth both roared with laughter, and the big black dog must have thought I was his best friend, for he didn't leave my side again until we got into the boat for yet another of those terrifying return rides home.

Mail day was always something Mum looked forward to. Every so often she'd get a letter in Arabic from one of her sisters in Lebanon. The postmaster was Mr. Endersby and he looked very much like the pictures of King George that were on all the Canadian postage stamps. My fertile and active little mind quickly figured out that the man who very kindly gave us the mail was obviously King George, and it was difficult for Ruth to convince me otherwise.

Chapter 4

About six weeks after I was born, Mum received a call from Dad asking her to pack up Ruth and me and catch the steamer to Vancouver, then carry on by train to Los Angeles. This was the first of many trips I was to make to California over the years. There was supposed to be some kind of new life for Mum and Father in California, but apparently it didn't work out, and we wound up back on Quadra Island shortly after New Year in 1941.

Mum was not a good traveller and was always nervous about trying anything new. For many years after this trip she'd talk about how there had been a train wreck just south of us somewhere in Oregon, and our train had to back up for about 200 miles. These kinds of unknowns were always a severe trial for Mum, and she always advised us against going anywhere or trying anything new or risky, at least until she had tried it first.

Ruth, who was seven years old at the time and had a memory of it, related to me in later years that one of many noteworthy incidents that took place on the trip was Mum rushing to catch the train loaded down with bags containing my spare diapers and some feeding bottles for me. Just before we boarded the train, one of the bags containing my bottles fell to the platform and the bottles, all filled with milk for me for the ride to Seattle, shattered into thousands of pieces.

Mum, in her usual panic, was completely distraught and quite certain in her own mind that I'd be dead from starvation within a matter of minutes. Along came a black porter, who promised he would search the train for a baby bottle. This was the first black man Ruth had seen, so the incident was burned deep into her memory as she told me the story 60 years later.

This kind man did indeed search the train, but all he could find was an empty beer bottle. Mum immediately went into shock at the horrific thought of her tiny and precious baby being fed from a beer bottle of all things, but then the reality of the situation began to settle in, and it was found that the salvaged rubber nipples from the broken bottles fit the beer bottle perfectly. So, with a supply of warm milk from the kind and helpful porter, I was fed and happy as the train rumbled on southwards towards the border. Contrary to Mum's possible fears though, or maybe because of the event, I've never developed any liking for beer.

According to Mum's passport visa, we crossed the border into the United States on November 29, 1940. We lived with Dad somewhere in west Los Angeles for a time, but the stay was short lived. We returned to Canada less than three months later, re-crossing the border February 27, 1941. So my first Christmas was spent in the warm climate of California, the first of many Christmas vacations I was to spend in southern climates.

Upon our return to Gowlland Harbour, Mum planted a walnut tree next to our house with a nut she brought home with her, and a big tree, which is still standing today, grew from this planting in 1941. I still consider this to be my tree, and we will have to see who lives longer, the tree or me; but I think the tree will win, as it still looks healthy and produces a good crop each year.

Chapter 5

World War II was very much a part of our lives on the Canadian West Coast after the attack on Pearl Harbour; even mine at such a tender age.

Each evening Ruth and I had to keep very quiet while the British Broadcasting Corporation news from England was broadcast on the radio. We had a massive short wave radio which had been bought from Jim Spilsbury, one of the largest pioneering spirits on the coast, especially in those days. He was primarily in communications in its early years, but later branched out into the airlines business, as he put it in one or two of his excellent books, "by accident". He used aircraft to service the many radios he had helped sell and install all over the coast, finally putting in so many over such a wide distance and in so many remote areas, that he eventually found he couldn't keep up with servicing them by boat.

His subsequent use of aircraft developed into the establishment of Queen Charlotte Airlines, which in later years, after many changes in ownership and name, became Canadian Airlines International, the forerunner of the present Air Canada. Spilsbury's early years were reportedly spent on Savory Island, not far from Read Island, where our family had lived at one time.

The family radio was powered by two wet cell batteries of two volts each and one dry cell battery. The dry cell battery was not rechargeable and had to be replaced about every six months. Rob Yeatman, who lived at the southern end of Gowlland Harbour, had a small gasoline powered generator which he set up to recharge everyone's wet cell batteries, and I remember we made many trips in Mum's 'putter boat' to get the batteries recharged each month.

This was a special social occasion for Mum, as it gave her an opportunity to visit with Mrs. Yeatman and her three daughters. Peggy Yeatman was a schoolteacher, and my brother Jim credits her with helping him to finish his secondary schooling so that he was able to go on to university after he was discharged from the air force after the end of the war. These trips to the Yeatmans at the other end of the harbour were very pleasant for me, particularly compared to going out of the bay at that time, since the waters were sheltered and I didn't have to face the dreaded waves of Discovery Passage and its Union steamships.

It was always a dream of Peggy's and Mum's that one day one of my older brothers would marry one of the Yeatman girls, but this didn't happen, and it could perhaps be considered as a good basis for the principle of not putting too much faith in planning other people's lives for them. The Yeatmans later moved to Campbell River in the late 1940s, but always kept their home on Quadra. Peggy taught for many years at the Indian Reserve School in Campbell River, and was greatly cherished and admired by all for her teaching skills and the way she handled children. When she finally retired, the school was closed and the students were sent to the main school in Campbell River. There was a small residence for the teacher next to the Reserve school while it was open, and I can remember spending many happy evenings and sleepovers as guests of these warm and kindly people. After retirement, they moved back to Quadra and lived out their lives at their old family home.

In the meantime, the monthly trips to get our radio batteries recharged continued and also gave me the chance to see all the various tugs waiting for favourable weather to start their long journey back to Vancouver with their long tows of logs. These tows could only move at about 1.5 to two miles per hour, and could only be towed during calm weather. As a result, during poor weather spells, it would sometimes take these tugs several weeks to complete the journey from Gowlland to the lumber mills of Vancouver.

My exposure to these vessels and their crews at an early age had a great influence on my desire in later years to follow a sea faring lifestyle. Charlie Granholm was captain of one of the small tugs of about 40 feet that was permanently stationed in Gowlland Harbour. This tug was used to help the larger vessels make up their tows and to generally assist as needed. The Granholms lived in a float house that was tied up to the pier leading out to the Government wharf in front of Yeatmans' place.

Float houses were a common sight along the coast in those days, and there were even some under the Second Narrows (Steelworkers) Bridge in Vancouver up until the 1960s. Mum always used to stop in to say hello to Mrs. Granholm as we walked up the dock to deliver our batteries to Rob Yeatman. Mrs. Granholm was always jovial and usually had a large wash hanging out on a clothesline to dry.

The war was always part of the background of our lives until its end in 1945, even though of course we were far from the action. I learned later that the day I was born, a Canadian cruiser arrived in port after arresting the German merchant ship Weser off the West Coast of Mexico. The Weser was lying in Manzanillo, Mexico, and was making ready for sea. The converted Canadian National passenger-ship Prince Robert had sailed from Victoria September 12, 1940 for Manzanillo. Under cover of darkness on September 25, the Prince Robert sighted the Weser leaving Manzanillo harbour. The 'cat and mouse' chase was on. The master of the German vessel said later that he had mistaken the Prince Robert for a small island. The Canadian ship steered in behind the Weser to cut it off from returning to port, and stalked it until it was clear of Mexican waters. Then there was little the German crew could do as they watched the Prince Robert closing in. They had prepared their ship for scuttling in case of capture, but the Canadians acted too quickly for them to carry out the plan. The Weser was escorted into Victoria on the day of my birth, flying the Canadian Navy white ensign above the swastika on her flagstaff, an important prize of war. The Weser was renamed the Vancouver Island and made several trips under Canadian colours before finally being lost to a torpedo in the Atlantic. Also, after Pearl Harbour in 1941, a Japanese submarine shelled the lighthouse on Estavan Point on the west coast of Canada. But I was too young to remember that

These actions and others prompted the creation of what became known as The Gumboot Navy, and other civil defence measures. The Gumboot Navy consisted of larger fishing vessels and yachts, taken over by the government and crewed by local fishermen and tugboat crews to patrol the coast. Households with men capable of firing a gun were also issued small arms and ammunition for self defence. I recall long after the war was over we still had boxes full of ammunition at home.

Another shameful aspect of this time was the transporting of Japanese Canadians from the coast to interior camps. Several families were uprooted from Quadra and shipped out. The Atagies, Matsunagas and Sacatas were all among the many thousands of unfortunate families who were sent away from their homes to be held in internment camps for the duration of the war, a sad episode in Canada's sometimes glorious history.

Chapter 6

The year that I was four years old, we attended the wedding of my brother Jim to Rosemary Darville in Victoria. Trips to Victoria and Vancouver were always a major adventure at that time and travelling to the wedding was no exception.

We went by boat to Campbell River where Bill dropped us off, and then someone kindly drove us over the rough gravel road to Courtenay, where we caught the train to Victoria. This train consisted of a very old steam locomotive which was followed by a couple of equally ancient cars. The journey was in July, and I can still remember being thirsty and hot during the whole trip. What a surprise to arrive in Victoria as a four year old boy who had never seen the modern life of a city before! Everywhere were Streetcars, electric lights, telephones without cranks, cars, and houses without end.

The Darville family lived on Olive Street, a short distance from the Dallas Road waterfront. Mrs. Darville and Mum became instant friends and we used to go for walks together along the Victoria waterfront. My father arrived for this exciting event and I can remember him and Mr. Darville playing in a band in Beacon Hill Park on a Sunday.

The wedding took place in a huge church downtown and that was the first and last I saw of brother Jim until after the war was over. Jim and David, Rosemary's brother, were in uniform and they all drove off in a car, not to be seen again for over a year.

Mother and I visited with Ruth who was in school at St Ann's Academy, while we stayed with Rosemary's parents. After a week or so we caught the midnight C.P.R. ferry to Vancouver. The Princess Joan and The Princess Elizabeth were the ships on the midnight run from both cities. What a wonderful and wondrous way to travel. We were snug in our bunks as the ship traveled the 70 miles across southern Georgia Strait. Arrival time was about 5 a.m., but we didn't leave the ship until we had arisen and dressed at about 8 a.m. Then it was up to the St. Francis Hotel located on the corner of Cordova and Seymour Streets.

Walking up from the ship via the Granville Street overpass, we could look down on the railway tracks below. What a sight for a young boy. Huge steam locomotives parked at the C.P.R. train station, hissing away like big angry animals. I had never imagined anything so fascinating. Mum finally had to drag me along, as I just wanted to stand there all day looking over the railing at the monsters below.

After checking into our hotel room, it was off to Spencer's Department Store for some shopping. What a drag. Why do women always take so long to buy anything! As far as I was concerned it was time wasted when I could have been watching the trains.

Then lunch upstairs at the store where Mum always ordered shepherd's pie. What an excitement and a novelty the big city was for us. This was my first visit to Vancouver and it was burned into my memory.

After we got back to the hotel completely exhausted we met up with Dad. "Where did he come from?" Dad was only a faint memory from some previous life. Anyway, at last there was someone to take me to see the trains again. Mum said to go ahead, as trains weren't exactly her idea of a good time. As Dad and I crossed Cordova Street he took out a small gold case that looked like a pocket watch on a chain. He popped open the lid and inside were some tiny strong-flavoured mints: this city life was certainly all right! I couldn't help but wonder what would be next.

After a sleepless night with all the noise from the trains switching cars across the street, it was up early and off to breakfast and goodbye to Dad. Another day of shopping at Woodward's for supplies to be shipped home to Quadra Island, and then we were off to catch the Union Steamship vessel for home.

The S.S Chelohsin was due to sail late that evening. To reach.the dock at the foot of Carroll Street, we had to walk down through what is now called Gastown. At that time it was more of a warehouse district, very dark and lonely, and Mum was already more than a little nervous when someone suddenly whistled at her out of the dark. She clutched my hand tightly as we crossed the railway tracks to the safety of the Steamship ticket office. Soon we were on the ship and I was tucked into my bunk and quickly fell asleep, as the grey ship glided through the night and my dreams.

Early the next morning, I was awakened by the steward ringing the breakfast gong. Before long we were in the dining room and being waited on in royal fashion. Around mid-morning we made a stop at Vananda, a small port on the east coast of Texada Island, to off load some passengers and supplies. The Chelohsin had huge steam winches right in front of the main cabin, for operating her freight lifting gear. This big main winch scared me, as we had to pass right in front of it as we boarded the vessel. And now this steel monster was in operation with all its hissing fury. It was just too much noise and clatter for me and I remained scared of it for as many years as the vessel was still afloat. Captain Wilson was in command of the ship this trip. He was a good friend of our family and came to visit with Mum and me for a few minutes while the ship was unloading freight.

We arrived at Campbell River after dark. Alex Thompson was the freight agent and wharfinger, and he had a real peg leg, which just consisted of a large wooden handle somehow attached to the stump of his left leg. It amazed me to see him get around so well on this devise. It's worth mentioning here that in later years my brother Jim became one of the world's foremost designers of artificial legs. This peg leg of Alex's of 1944 vintage certainly needed some improvement. Alex was a huge, tough looking man who, with his scary wooden leg, always reminded me of a pirate, without his parrot.

We got a ride from Campbell River to Q Cove on someone's fish boat; there was always someone meeting the steamers no matter the time of night. George Mitchell picked us up at the cove with his model T Ford truck and took us home to their place, where Granny Mitchell put us up for the night. The Mitchell's had several large dogs that came out to meet us, their eyes shining brightly in the lights of the old truck as we pulled into the orchard outside the house. The next day Bill came to meet us and we hiked over the trail to our home, as we did not have road access until a few years later.

It had been a great adventure for me at such a young age, but life soon got back to normal, with many days playing around the beaches and watching the activities out on the ocean. Our house had a commanding view of the inside passage to Alaska, and during the war, the marine traffic was steady and varied. Large warships would pass by at high speed throwing out a huge wake behind them. This increased my fear of going out in Mum's little boat, as these waves were large by anyone's standard.

All the passenger and freight ships were painted wartime grey, as were the vessels of the gumboot navy. Many of our family friends and neighbours were employed on the various vessels used to move freight and service personnel to Alaska after the attack on the Aleutian Islands by Japan. We'd always keep a watch for vessels that had people aboard as crew members we knew. Sometimes they would blow the ship's whistle in greeting as they passed by.

In the meantime, the war escalated in the Pacific and in Europe, and while I was celebrating my third year of life, Canadian soldiers crossed the Straits of Messina from Sicily to Italy. This was the start of many Canadians' long and bitter fight for Italy that was to last until well into the next year.

Dad had a sister who lived in England for the duration of the war. Aunt Aggie had been out to Canada to visit us shortly before I was born. Mum would send parcels of foods that were readily available here but were very difficult to obtain in England during wartime. We always had a good supply of home canned salmon and this was always included in her parcels. We also sent canned butter, sweetened condensed milk and honey. Mum would sew the parcels up tightly inside an old flour sack and it usually took the parcels about three months to reach England, but they were apparently greatly appreciated by Aunt Aggie. Sometimes they were opened and some of the contents were missing, but most of them arrived safely and intact

Our neighbours to the north were Dick and Mrs. Queal. Their daughter Mary had a house on the same property. Mary's husband, Bob Blaine, worked with his boat transporting freight and supplies for the wartime effort to remove Ripple Rock from Seymour Narrows. The Narrows are a constriction of the 'Inside Passage' to the north coast and Alaska, which is the only passage between Vancouver Island and the B.C. Mainland that is wide and deep enough to handle large ships going to and from Alaska. The alternate route is on "the outside" in the open Pacific Ocean, where the threat of ocean storms and Japanese submarines were a constant fear.

On the inside though, Ripple Rock was located almost mid-channel in Seymour Narrows and was only about nine feet under the surface at low tide, a constant hazard to the larger vessels. It claimed many ships and lives over the years. Later in the war and afterwards, action was taken again to lower the height of the underwater mountain's twin peaks, but we'll come back to that later. I do recall though that during an attempt to drill into the rock from a barge that was anchored in place by overhead cables, our neighbour, Bob Blaine, was drowned along with some other workers when his boat capsized in the strong tidal currents that are common to this stretch of water.

I can still remember seeing his boat tied up to the float in front of their house. It gave me a very lonely feeling as a child knowing that his children, Ricky and Isobel, would never see their father again, even though the boat seemed to have survived. Ricky and Isobel were about my age and they were the only playmates I had up until that time.

Shortly after this sad event, some men arrived with a large log float and Mary's house was taken away to Campbell River. The family lived in the same house for many years at its new location on 10ᵗʰ Avenue. I was to reunite with my early childhood playmates when students from Quadra Island attended high school in Campbell River in 1954. Mary supported her mother and family by hard work and plain strong determination after her husband was drowned. She started a janitorial business and I remember her working for many years, until after her children had left home.

Chapter 7

The excitement of life increases with each passing month when one is growing up. The year 1945 brought many new developments for the family and me.

Mrs. Queal sold the 140 acres she owned to Bill and Katy Howell, who lived in Seattle. She had asked Mum what she thought about selling for $1,500, after her husband Dick passed away from a heart attack. Mum said she thought it was a good price and that Mrs Queal would be much better off living with her daughter Mary in Campbell River. So Mrs Queal left. Fortunately for me though, the Howells had two children, Barbara and Johnny. They were older than I was, but just about the right age for my sister Ruth, and they came to Quadra for a short time to complete the purchase of the property, promising to return the following August. I missed Mrs. Queal, as she used to always give me little treats whenever I walked over the trail to her house.

The property consisted of a house with numerous outbuildings suitable for woodsheds, chicken houses and barns, and we kept our chickens in one of these buildings, as Mum never liked chickens too close to where she lived. One of my chores was to keep the chickens fed and to collect the eggs each day. It was about a quarter mile walk on a trail through the woods to the chicken house. Even at this early age, I was used to being by myself in the forest, and it gave me a good understanding of direction and survival in the outdoors.

Ruth and I used to swim every day if we could, during the summer months. One day we came home from swimming and Mum told us the war was over. It didn't mean a lot to me at the time of course, but it did later, and I recall Mum and Ruth were both quite excited. Mum had a large bottle of poison she kept to put in the water supply, in case we were forced out of our homes by the threatened Japanese invasion that never came. She disposed of this poison the very day the war ended, and not much was ever said about it afterwards.

Jim and Rose came home for a visit early that summer of 1945. By then Bill was skipper on the fish packer Adolfina, with Rose's brother David as his deckhand. Bill, Jim and David worked together around home on numerous projects that summer, one of which was building a pier and float to which we could tie our boats. Before that, our boats had to be anchored out in the bay and we'd come ashore in a dinghy which was small enough to pull up on the beach.

The end of the war, with Jim and Bill safely home, seemed to stimulate a lot of activity around the property. The next project was an outbuilding, built with lumber cut at Brunsguard's mill, which was located around the other side of the island, on Read Island. The Seabird was put to work hauling lumber, and Jim used this faithful vessel also to fish for lingcod. He was planning to attend Victoria College for one year, then go on to the University of Toronto for a degree in engineering. The lingcod had to be kept alive until the day each week that a fish packing boat came out from B.C. Packers at Quathiaski Cove to collect everyone's fish.

Several families fished for cod in those days. They all worked together and built a herring pond to keep their bait alive on the south boundary of our property, next to a sheer cliff that gave it good protection from wind and waves. The fishermen used to club together to catch herring, so that the holding pond was always full of fish for bait. Each boat had a 'live' well to keep both the bait and the cod alive. Jim used to keep ginger ale in the cold water of the tanks, and it was always a special treat to pull one out nice and cold, to be shared with any other co-conspirator who happened to be present.

For those who fished for salmon, the fish packing boat came by every day to collect the catch. Each family had a fish storage box on their float, and if there was fish to sell, a white flag was hoisted. If there was nobody around at the time, after weighing and grading the fish, the packer boat would leave the cash in a bottle on the dock, for the family to collect. This was also a handy way to get supplies. Reg Pidcock was usually the skipper of the packing boat, and he would bring orders from the store at Quathiaski Cove upon request. Ruth and I used to fish for rock cod and Reg always bought them from us for a copper nickel each. Today these same fish sell for about $5 a pound.

The Pidcocks were a pioneer family on Quadra Island, and at one time owned the cannery at Q Cove. They had a beautiful grey house nearby, at the north end of the cove. In later years when I was in the fish-processing business, it was my turn to buy fish from Reg. He retired about 1970 and spent his golden years happily fishing for ling cod the old-fashioned way.

That year also brought a new rowboat into the family. This was known as Ruth's boat, and had been built at Chappell Boat Works near the Oak Street Bridge in Vancouver. It was a little beauty and it served the family very well for about 30 years, opening up a whole new world for Ruth and me. We could now easily go swimming at the north end of the harbour, where the water was much warmer. Ruth taught me how to handle the oars, and I don't believe she ever rowed again if I was with her.

Bill was always torn between being a sailor and being a farmer; I've long found it amazing how many people I know who make their living from the ocean live happily on a small farm when not at sea. I think it must be the contrast that appeals to them, though I've never shared their love of the land. My thoughts have always returned to the ocean whenever I have been ashore for very long.

Mum was always able to come up with some spare cash

at this time of her life. I have no idea where it came from, but probably some sort of financial settlement with Dad. The Seabird had been added to the family a couple of years earlier, at a cost of $600, which compared to the new rowboat at $125. The shop, float, and now a property for Bill, all cost $1,500 and there was some talk of selling our place for $5,000, as property values were increasing with the end of the war. It just goes to show how prices have changed. There was several hundred acres for sale near Morte Lake, inland on the island, and some thought was given to purchasing this for Jim and Rose.

We always kept livestock to supplement our income and food supply. There was a never ending stream of cows, sheep, chickens and pigs coming and going. Then a horse named Dolly was added. She was used as an added worker to haul wood, clear land and plough fields. Mum never thought much of the horse though, and considered her a drain on the winter food supply needed for the other animals.

Bill had three pigs he kept strictly as pets. One of them used to swim out to meet him whenever he came home on the Seabird. He had them all trained so that when he fed them, they wouldn't start eating until a bell was rung. As soon as it rang, they'd all dive into the food, squealing and pushing each other for the best position. But then one day one of them got the idea he'd lie down in the food trough as soon as the food was put in, before the bell was rung. I guess he reckoned that this way he could eat lying down and prevent the others from getting their share. This went on for a short time with the other two looking askance at Bill and complaining bitterly about this injustice and insult, squealing as loudly as possible to make sure they had his attention. Finally, Bill decided they all had to be fed separately to prevent further discord on Animal Farm. After that it was always amusing to see the three pigs each standing at a different pile of food, All waiting for Bill to ring the bell.

It was about this time that we had a visit from Dad, some friends of his and my half brother George. George had three children, Dolores, Moira and George Jr., and they all stayed with us for a few weeks. The girls were about Ruth's age and not of much interest to me, as they were so much older.

Mum also had a brother called Ted who lived with his family in Detroit, Michigan. Uncle Ted called Mum one day to see if she would come to Detroit to help his wife Josephine after the birth of their third child. Mum hadn't seen her brother since she left Lebanon 25 years earlier, so of course this was a huge and welcome surprise for her and she left as soon as her tickets arrived from Uncle Ted. The trip required the usual voyage down to Vancouver by Union Steamship, then train to Toronto, and on to Windsor, Ontario. Mum's Uncle Ameen lived in Windsor, so she also stayed with them for a few days. Then Uncle Ted picked her up for the short trip by car to Detroit.

I stayed home with Dad, his friends and Bill while Mum was away. It was the longest time I can ever remember being with Dad, and we did a lot of visiting with neighbours and friends. We went as far as Read Island to see the Robsons, Moulds, Masons and other people Dad knew there from when our family lived at Surge Narrows.

Eventually Mum came home from Detroit in the spring and brought me two books that I learned to read from. One was about the Canadian Rockies, and the other was called Paddle to The Sea, about how a carved native Indian wooden canoe toy managed to make its way down from a snow bank at the top of Lake Superior, through the Great Lakes and the St. Lawrence Ship Canal, out to the open Atlantic Ocean. It was a great book and excitingly and richly illustrated with many explanatory pictures, and helped me learn about geography and all the different kinds of logging and industry along the route. I kept these books for years and they helped me learn about this huge country of Canada.

It was a prosperous time with Jim being home from the war. Bill and Mum were able to accomplish more with the extra help they now had from family members, friends and of course Dolly the horse. A start was made on a road to our property. This was a distance of about half a mile, and was mostly built by hand. This original road is the base for the present one, which was upgraded in the early 1960s. Until the road was finally finished, there was just a trail which led to the Mitchells' place, where the public road ended.

Cutting wood for heating and cooking fuel was a constant chore for all members of the family. By the time I became an adult, I had cut, split and hauled all the wood I ever wanted to see in an entire lifetime. Back then this work had a dual purpose, as the trees that were felled to clear the land for crops also supplied fuel. This cutting was achieved with the large hand powered cross cut saws. I can still picture Mum on one end of the saw, with my limited strength on the other end, pulling and pushing with all my might. The work kept you warm twice, once when the wood was cut and hauled, and a second time when it was consumed in the kitchen stove and living room heater.

It is necessary perhaps to be remembered that our house lacked insulation of any sort, and none of the many windows were airtight. This resulted in us always being freezing cold in winter, especially in the morning before the stoves were lit for the day. A huge step forward was achieved when Bill finally bought a gasoline powered drag saw. These big saws were used in the logging industry for cutting felled trees into sizes suitable for milling, and were known as Wee McGregors.

Bill tried out this new saw on a huge fir tree that had blown down in a windstorm. What a treat it was to see this machine working away under its own power, while we split the cut blocks and loaded them on to a sled for Dolly the horse to pull home. I wasn't big enough yet to be of much help, it's true, but I always kept a lively chatter of questions that kept Bill busy finding answers until finally he would tell me to be quiet for a while.

Chapter 8

The year 1946 brought Jim, Rose and their new daughter Heather home to us for the summer, so I was an uncle at the great age of five. We all celebrated Heather's first birthday that summer with Sharon Beech and some other young ones in attendance. I remember Rosemary packing Heather up to the house for the first time, after disembarking from the Seabird. Heather was such a cute little girl and I was Rosemary's and Heather's constant companion during that summer.

Bill had built a sawmill on the waterfront of our property, and besides also being a new source of income for the family, the mill was a wonderfully novel place for me to hang out, explore and start learning about working for a living. The machinery was shipped from Heaps Engineering of New Westminster by freight boat then transferred to a float for delivery up to us at the site. The Wee McGregor saw Bill had bought was installed on a float, and logs were cut to length there before being pulled up on to the mill deck for milling into lumber.

At that time there seemed to be a never ending supply of logs to be had, as logging was in full production all along the coastline. First of all though, the felled logs were rafted together for towing to Vancouver, and this method of transport resulted in considerable loss due to tides and weather conditions. After a storm, drifting logs that had escaped from booms would be found in large numbers all up and down the coast. Bill would go out with the Seabird to gather them up and tow them home.

The summer of 1946 is remembered by many for the strong earthquake that struck the region, with an epicentre that wasn't far from southern Quadra. Rosemary, Heather and I were at home alone at the time, while Jim and Mum were busy doing some work on Seabird. The whole house started to shake and rattle wildly, and Rosemary grabbed Heather and held my hand tightly, while we looked out of the living-room window. Rosemary kept telling us two children not to be scared, but I think the truth is she was the one who was scared, as Heather and I thought it was all great fun. I recall seeing Mum come running up towards the house from the boat, as her only thought was for the safety of the children. She was even more excited than Rosemary, but it was all over almost before it began, and no serious damage was done to our property.

The same couldn't be said for other areas in the general vicinity around the northern half of Georgia Strait. A large part of Rebecca Spit sheered off and dropped down into the ocean, and some really serious damage was done to various properties on nearby Read Island. Later we learned a 40 foot high wave had raced down Comox Lake some 50 kilometres to the south on Vancouver Island, and a man who was out on the lake in a small rowboat was engulfed and lost. Also, the end of Mapleguard Spit at Deep Bay, south of Courtenay on Vancouver Island, slipped away, forming part of a large underwater reef that now guards the approach to this fine harbour.

Bill was skipper on the fish packer Adolfina at the time, and was on the west side of Read Island when the quake struck. He said afterwards that the boat started to bounce around as though the seas were really rough, when in fact they were flat calm at the time. That made him think they must have run over a floating log or something else below the surface. He stopped the vessel and reversed the engine. Everything seemed to be in order though, so the voyage just continued without further incident.

Another major happening in our immediate neighbourhood

that summer was the total destruction of the Beech family home by fire. Jack and Ma Beech lived only about half a mile from us at the extreme north end of Gowlland Harbour. I recall Jack told me at one time that in his early years he was a fireman in Victoria, at a time when the fire engines were still pulled with horses.

The flames apparently swept through the Beeches' house very quickly, as they very often did in wooden houses in those days, and, although no one was hurt, they lost all of their personal belongings. After that they moved temporarily into a house owned by the Hall family just a short distance to the east of the Beech homestead. Jack Beach gathered some logs for Bill to cut in his sawmill; and all the neighbours pitched in and helped them build a new but smaller house.

The Hall family were also early settlers on Quadra, arriving, as I understand it, about 1888. Bill Hall, one of the sons, later became quite well known as an officer on the crew of the RCMP vessel St. Roch. This vessel was the first ship to navigate the famed Northwest Passage and also circumnavigate the continent of North America. She now rests in the Maritime Museum in Vancouver. Bill later was the owner of the first Quadra Island passenger ferry, which started service between the island and Campbell River in 1949. Perhaps not entirely by coincidence, his brother Tom later became captain of the first vehicle ferry, beginning in 1960 and holding the post until his retirement.

It was about this time in 1946 that we met the Mitchell family, not related to the Mitchells who lived south of us in Gowlland Harbour. Alex, Rhoda and their two daughters Joan and Judy lived on Grouse Island, which is located in the mouth of Quathiaski Cove, just outside the harbour. Alexander Malcolm Mitchell, who was born in Regina, Saskatchewan, and was only about 26 by this time, had a marine fuel station and machine shop which he operated for several years before turning his talents to logging on Read Island.

Alex spent the war years as a marine engineer on the M.V. General Lake, a former army vessel which was previously used to supply York Island and other army gun emplacements along the coast during the war. His brother Eric was a fighter pilot in the war and took part in the Battle of Britain. I understand he was an incredible pilot. He was certainly an excellent storyteller, and I remember him telling numerous exciting stories of his wartime exploits. Daughter Joan was about four and her sister Judy was about two when we first met. I was so much older, at almost six, but I recall many good times of us all hanging about together over the next few years.

The kids' grandparents came to live with Mum and me a few years later, in 1949, and Grampa Mitchell was very much a part of my early training. I look back with very fond memories on the six years he and his wife spent with us.

In later years, the vessel General Lake became the tug Black Bird and was part of the Gulf of Georgia Towing fleet. One stormy night a good number of years later, in 1970, I was called out with a tug I owned to help keep Black Bird and the chlorine barge she was towing off the beach just north of Willow Point. The tug's towline had become fouled in her propeller and parted. The task was given to me to tow both tug and barge to safety before the barge became stranded on the beach in heavy seas and her cargo of chlorine spilled on to the shoreline. Thankfully for all concerned, and particularly those blissfully and ignorantly asleep in their beds down wind. It all turned out well, and we were successful before anything serious occurred, but it could have caused a major disaster.

The year 1946 continued to be an exciting period as the year progressed. Sheila Mackay appeared as brother Bill's future wife. She was just about 18 at the time, although I must say some controversy about her age has raged over all the years ever since. Mum had always been very secretive about her own age, and the speculation was enlivened from time to time by her trying to confuse other people's ages so we couldn't use those as reference points. One of her favourite ways of talking about other ladies on Quadra was to say, "She's about my age". Mum passed away at the age of 85, we think, on October 31, 1987. Interestingly, some of the other island women whom she always referred to as being "about my age" are still with us and would now have to be over 100 years old, *if* what Mum said was true.

My sister-in-law Sheila was great fun and used to pack me around on her back wherever we went. One evening when the Mitchell family was visiting, I saw her whisper something to Joan. With further whisperings from her mother Rhoda, Joan finally came over and planted me with a great big kiss. This was a great outrage to me as a tough young boy of six in that era, and was about as bad as Mum's lady friends wanting to hug me all the time. Uuuugh!

During August that year, the Howell family arrived from Seattle for their annual summer vacation. Barbara, Ruth and Sheila had great times together. They were of course so much older than Johnny and I, but they included us in their adventures once in a while, when Johnny and I weren't busy re-fighting all the battles of World War II. We spent huge amounts of time doing that, defending every bay, beach and alder flat, as well as conducting some always very well placed counter attacks against heavily entrenched Japanese armies hiding out in caves and forests. We also made amphibious landings to capture the small islands and rocks which the enemy held just offshore. It's hardly a wonder that the older girls didn't want anything much to do with us, they were interested in much more peaceful and gentle pursuits.

We always had easy access to loads of salmon in those post war days. Jim was fishing again that summer to fund his studies at the University of Toronto, and Bill Howell brought us a more scientific way to catch salmon. We were unendingly amazed that somehow he was always able to catch so many more fish much more easily than we could. He made small wooden plugs that had thin white rubber tails to hide the hooks, and those plugs managed to catch more fish than our wonderful fresh herring bait, which really surprised everyone. Probably part of the real reason was that we were careless and carefree in our fishing, allowing our bait to get stale and not caring much about keeping our gear clean and free of bits of seaweed. There were so many fish around at that time that we were slow to adapt to new methods. Bill changed all that with his remarkable new gear though, and eventually we took on his methods, which increased our catches greatly.

Bill Howell had worked for the telephone company in Seattle and he was extremely inventive, always coming up with new ideas, which was a source of great amazement and awe to my young and formative mind.

Bill had built a 12 foot plywood boat powered by a small Lawson outboard motor, which was air-cooled. Each evening, he'd remove the motor from the boat and take it to the boat shed to fit it up to power a 110 volt generator, which provided electricity for their house. An electric pump also quickly replaced their previous water supply pump at the kitchen sink, which had to be operated by hand. As the new pump could only run while the generator was being powered, Bill decided to devise a way to keep Katy supplied with a constant flow of water to the kitchen when the motor had been put back on the boat. He did this by installing a holding tank above the well. Each evening when the generator was running, the pump would fill the holding tank with water to provide enough volume and gravity feed to meet the family's water needs during the next day, while the motor was off serving other duties.

Other new wonders kept appearing from Seattle that were too numerous for me to mention here. This had a great influence on me and taught me always to look for a better way to do things. In later years I found myself able to come up with some neat inventions of my own that were very useful to my business and to others in the same industry. As we didn't have electricity at our house or anywhere on Quadra Island in those days, I was often surprised at how easily all this was accomplished.

One day we were surprised by a large floatplane which could be heard and seen circling overhead. The aircraft landed and taxied up to the floats in front of the Beeches' place. We all jumped into a couple of boats and raced over there as quickly as we could. The passengers were a couple of geologists who were going to hike in to visit some claims Bill Hall had staked. This was going to take several hours, so Ruth suggested to

Mum that we ask the pilot how much it would cost to go for a ride. Mum of course wasn't at all in favour of that idea and the serious risk and danger this new adventure would pose to us. No amount of coaxing could convince her to climb aboard. So Mum and I stayed on the float while Ruth, Bill, Sheila, Jack and Ma Beech all went aboard for a half hour joyride. Naturally, Mum was absolutely and utterly positive this would be the last we would ever see of any of them, as the Norseman roared along the water and then climbed into the air. None of us had ever flown up to that time, and Mum was convinced that every flight would inevitably end up as a pile of wreckage, with everyone killed outright in the thunderous crash. Soon though, we heard them returning and Ruth most of all was so excited by this first flight. Mum still wasn't to be persuaded and she was only ever to fly once in her life, but that's a story for later.

The lazy days of summer, with fishing, swimming, and pleasant good times, come to an end all too soon on the West Coast of Canada, as I suppose they do for others elsewhere. September brought shorter days as always, with Jim, Rose and Heather returning to Toronto loaded with canned food that Mum had sent with them on the long train ride back the east. The Howells also returned to Seattle for another year, and our southern neighbours Bill Walsh and family returned to Alberta.

One good thing was that Jim left Mum's putter boat fully rigged and ready for fishing, so off we'd go. Each evening we'd be at Copper Cliffs, just north of Gowlland Harbour, often along with most of the other residents of 'The Harbour', trying our skills for late run Coho salmon.

We still weren't very good at fishing as yet, but we learned quite quickly and each morning we'd hang out our white flag to let the fish buyer know to stop and take our fish. We didn't have that many, but it was all great fun and it added some extra income for the family. The competition was keen between us all for the biggest catch. Ma Beech usually out fished the rest of us, catching more fish even than her husband Jack with his big trolling boat.

I seem to recall that Mrs. Naknakim, another resident of the island, in her Indian dugout canoe, also caught more fish than her husband with his larger boat. She'd tie up to a small fir tree that grew out from the cliff, and would use a hand line with herring as bait. I remember her as a very large lady who managed to fill the canoe with her great bulk, right from side to side. She laughed with delight over each and every fish she landed, and sometimes had to paddle out to Jack's larger boat to hand over her catch, as her canoe was becoming overloaded with salmon. I was at Copper Cliffs a few years ago, and there can still be seen the remains of her tie up rope hanging from the tree half a century later.

September also brought another big surprise for me, or maybe it would be more accurate to call it a shock. It was called school. Ruth was sent off to Victoria again to attend school, but I stayed at home to take Grade 1 by correspondence, with Mum acting as my teacher. It was about a three kilometre walk to catch a ride to the school at Q Cove, and Mum decided that at this time that would be too much for me and my young legs, at least until I got a little older, so I stayed home to learn. Poor Mum, did we ever have some disputes over that schooling! I was used to the carefree and easy life, running around all over the place, and this having to stay in the house and learn most of the day was most certainly not my idea of having a good time. Mum persisted and did her best though, and I suppose I must have learned something from it all, because when I finally did go to school at Cape Mudge from Grade 4 on, I found I was ahead of the class in most subjects.

The cool weather that autumn, brought fog to the coast from late August onwards. It was during one of those fog shrouded nights that Bill was travelling home on Seabird, when he collided with Bill Beech outward bound on his boat. The damage was mostly to the Beeches' vessel and all luckily above the water line, so the two skippers were both able to get home safely. That was of course in the days before radar and modern electronics were available for even small craft, so travelling at night or with reduced visibility was extremely dangerous.

Larger vessels, such as the Union Steamships, were fitted with radar after the end of the war, but before that they navigated by blowing their whistle at frequent intervals and listening for the echo to return to the ship. The time for the sound to travel at 760 miles per hour from the ship to shore and return was then roughly calculated in the mind and from experience, to give the navigator the approximate distance from shore. The skill of these men is difficult for us to appreciate today with all the up to date and new navigational equipment we have at our disposal, some of it so small you can hold it in the palm of your hand.

On one trip to Quathiaski Cove on Seabird, we were moored at the main dock and the Island King was unloading freight and was getting ready to leave. I was sitting on the stern of Seabird looking up at the captain on the bridge of the Island King. The captain warned the deckhands to be careful letting the heavy mooring lines go and to watch out for the young man sitting on the boat down below. I recall feeling very excited and not a little honoured that he was concerned for my safety, as I gazed up at him in his smart, carefully pressed uniform, giving commands from his lofty position.

Many years later I towed the Island King with my tug Monarch II from the Northland Dock to Vancouver Shipyard, on the sad occasion of her last voyage across Vancouver Harbour. She had grounded on the west coast of Vancouver Island and was written off by the insurance company as a total loss. It was a terrible end to my long standing relation and a great fondness for the old ship.

It was also during 1946 in Campbell River that the Bickle family of Courtenay extended their chain of movie theatres to the Van Isle Theatre, later renamed the Tidemark, with a grand opening of this new facility and service for the community. Not too long afterwards, Bill, Mum and I climbed aboard Seabird one winter's evening for a trip across to Campbell River to see a movie. This was all super new to me, as I had never seen or been to a movie before. We tied up at the nearby dock and walked up to the theatre. I don't remember the movie or what it was called, but I was surprised to see Mrs. Blaine and her mother sitting in the lobby. Mum had a great time talking with our old neighbours, as we had not seen them since they had moved away the year before.

After the movie, of course, we returned to the boat for the trip home. There was no harbour as such at Campbell River at that time, so all the small craft had to moor on the inside of the steamer dock. When we got back to the dock, we found two other boats had rafted up on the outside of us, on the shoreward side, and the tide had dropped while we were in the theatre, leaving the boats nearest the shore firmly aground. So we were stuck and had to wait for the tide to rise before we could leave. In the meantime, the Union Steamship Coquitlam made a stop at the dock, which provided some welcome diversion and entertainment. She was one of three new vessels in the fleet which had been converted for passenger and freight service along the coast after the end of the war. They were very pretty little ships, and were all painted up in new colors that were a pleasant change from the usual drab war time diet of grey.

It was always exciting when a ship arrived, and even though it was already about 10 p.m., there were plenty of people still milling around, with Alex Thompson the wharfinger hobbling and hopping about on his peg leg. By the time the ship left, the water had returned enough for us to cast our boat off for the long trip home against the incoming tide.

Winter sometimes tends to be slow to retreat along much of the southern B.C. coast, but it seldom gets cold for longer than two weeks at most, before a southeast wind blows in from across the Pacific and brings with it mild, wet weather. The warm Japanese current that flows along the coast tends to keep the cold Arctic air from engulfing us for long. Although the winter weather is mild, it's also very damp, and the days can be short, due to our northern latitude. If there were a single word to describe our winters, it would be grey. But spring comes at last and brings with it longer days, warm weather and less firewood requirements. Mum and Bill, with the aid of poor Dolly the draughthorse, would start getting the land ready for the planting of crops.

We grew a lot of strawberries as a cash crop in those years, along with vegetables for our own use. A cold storage plant had been built by Alvin Parkin in Campbell River where we could rent storage space for freezing fruit, vegetables and meat for future use. This reduced our dependence on canning, while greatly improving the quality. We'd go across in Mum's little boat, which was small and shallow enough to navigate up the main stem of the Campbell River to within just a few blocks of the freezing plant.

This was a real adventure for me, as we had to cross the main channel of Discovery Passage to the mouth of the Campbell. From there, the trip up the river took us past the Elk River Timber logging camp, with its steam-powered train dumping logs into the water with a huge splash. The railway tracks ran right down in front of Shelby's Barber Shop, where one could get a hair cut with the train shunting noisily backwards and forwards in the background just a few feet away. This was great adventure and lots of fun, and I think I'd still enjoy it today.

Inside the freezer plant where we'd take our produce to be put away for the future, the temperature was always right down about minus 20 degrees Fahrenheit, so we didn't hang around inside there too long! On the way home we'd usually try to catch a fish for supper, so these trips were very much looked forward to.

Another traditional annual celebration and time of excitement on Quadra Island was the birthday of Queen Victoria, always celebrated on May 24. Bill had an old Ford truck we used to pile into for the ride to Drew Harbour on the other side of the island, for the yearly community picnic held there. It was great fun and great excitement, with races and sports for all the kids. This was truly a major social event of the Quadra calendar, with a dance held in the evening at the community hall. Beer flowed freely at these dances and was usually hidden somewhere outside, for reasons that don't seem to be too imaginable today. As we younger kids grew older, we used to hang out in gangs of boys outside the hall looking for these hidden stashes. When we found some of this liquid treasure, which we always did, a great time was had by all, with competition to see who could drink the most the fastest, before we got caught. The picnic grounds at Drew Harbour were on property owned by the Glendening family, who had a small shipyard and machine shop on the east side of the bay. They were very gracious in letting the community use their land for various events over many years, and the property was finally donated to the provincial government as a park. It's still maintained today as a very beautiful, scenic and much used campground and picnic area. It boasts stunning panoramic vistas out over the northern end of Georgia Strait to the nearby islands and the B.C Mainland, with its Coastal Range of mountains, often snow capped and gleaming against clear blue skies.

During 1946, we started to notice that there were new people starting to move into the general area. Work was started that year on the John Hart Dam above the Campbell River on Vancouver Island, and also on a new hydro generating plant to be located just below Elk Falls on the Campbell. A new dock was built just a little farther north at Duncan Bay, to off load supplies for this project. Before that, Duncan Bay had only a few fishermen's shacks, and the bay was much more noticeable as a coastal feature than it is today. The various projects brought many workers to live in Campbell River while the construction was in progress.

Quadra's well known Peterson family also moved to April Point, which until then had been known as Poverty Point, at about this time. They came from Vancouver for their vacation for several years and then, after buying a large piece of waterfront property on and adjoining the point, started the April Point Fishing Resort. Mr. P. became a very good friend of mine over the years, and we had some good times together. Mrs. P was a very beautiful and gracious lady, who always looked to me like a fashion model, even when she could be seen working away in the kitchen preparing meals for their guests.

The Peterson children consisted of Warren, who was

serving in the U.S. Navy, Thor and Eric, all of whom were a little older than me, and a younger sister Joy, who was my age. We all attended school together and the Peterson family became very well recognized and respected in the community. Bill cut most of the lumber that was used to build the original lodge, which is still very much in use, though now greatly altered, as a long standing, classy and classic fishing resort today. Previously, as Poverty Point, the site had been the home of several rowboat fishermen who had settled there during the pre war Depression years. Some of their shacks were very well built and with remodelling, formed the basis for some of the tourist cabins still in use today at April Point.

I didn't meet Warren until after he retired from the navy, but I do remember Joy bringing a wonderful collection of sea shells to school one day when we were in Grade 4. Warren had sent these shells home from somewhere in the South Pacific and we were all amazed at how different they were from the shells of our coast. It certainly opened our eyes in a small way to other parts of the world.

During the first few years April Point was being developed, the Petersons would go back to Vancouver each winter, returning each spring to open up the resort for the summer season. Bill used to keep watch on the place in their absence, to make sure no damage was done to the buildings and wharfs during the winter storms.

The Schoenfeldt family were American tourists who also built a large summer home at the south end of Gowlland Island. They appeared to be very wealthy, and we were amazed at all the expensive boats they had, as well as the beautiful modern home. Terry had a boat with a 22 horsepower Johnson outboard that was faster than anything we'd ever even dreamed of. He used to come by to take Barbara Howell for rides, and somehow we couldn't interest him into taking the rest of us along. The Schoenfeldts also had a boat with a large in board engine, which was a great departure from the little putter boats we had that could only do about five knots at best.

The spring of 1946 was also when I was given my first

dog. Bill brought him home to me as a little pup and I called him Pete. He and I had the most wonderful time growing up together that summer. We'd hang about at the sawmill playing and wrestling on the moss covered slopes, as Bill worked at cutting lumber. Mum used to get wool from our sheep and make it into sweaters and socks for us, and when Pete and I came home after a long day of rolling and playing, playing and rolling, my sweater would be covered with moss. Mum would be most displeased and scold me, but of course it didn't make a difference; it didn't stop me from doing it all over again the next time.

Bill also started to build a house just above where his sawmill was located. This didn't mean much to me, but Ruth knew right away that Bill and Sheila would be getting married soon. She was very excited and asked Bill if she could be the bridesmaid. That of course was fine with him, as Sheila didn't have any sisters or other close female relatives. Ruth and Mum got busy right away on a dress for her, and there was much excitement and talk flowing between them that I didn't understand.

Mum's Uncle Jack came to visit with us from his home in Rawdon, Quebec. He rode out west from Montreal on the train then, took the Union Steamship from Vancouver to Quathiaski Cove, where he was picked up by one of our boats and brought home to Gowlland Harbour.

Uncle Jack was one of my grandfather's younger brothers. Grandfather had sent him and most of the family out of Lebanon to avoid World War I. I believe he had intended eventually to come to Canada himself, but had exhausted his meagre resources by sending four brothers and two sisters to Canada, and a nephew to Argentina. Added to this, he also sent his two sons out of the country, Uncle Ted to Canada and Uncle Mofed to Argentina. Uncle Ted served in the U.S. Army during World War II and settled in Detroit, Michigan, while Mofed stayed in Argentina, never to be seen again by any of his immediate family.

Great Uncle Jack had a store and barber shop in Rawdon,

which he operated with his two sons and daughter named Pauline.

Bill was growing a beard at the time of his arrival, for showing off at a special dance to be held at the community hall. Jack and Bill spent a great deal of time trimming and coaching this beard into being. The two of them had also convinced Mum that Ruth should attend this dance, as she was almost 14 years old at the time. Mum was naturally firmly very much opposed to this, as to any such new adventure, and this type of social occasion was also not to her liking. But in the end Bill and Jack finally prevailed and Ruth was allowed to go. The result wasn't amusing for either Ruth or Mum. It seems that sometime during the evening Tommy Macklin either tried to or did indeed manage to kiss young and shy Ruth in a dark corner of the dance hall. I guess this started a great kafuffle and the uttering of all kinds of words in defence of my sister's betrayed and bedraggled honour, and I remember to this day that it was hotly discussed for months afterwards. As an aside, I think I might say that from my point of view as a young male at that time, to kiss my sister at that time of her life could well be compared to trying to kiss a wild cougar after the way she'd been brought up with me. Anyway, Tommy managed to escape by the skin of his teeth with his hide still just intact and of course Mum never ever allowed Ruth to go anywhere near any of these horrible and rowdy affairs again.

This was also about the time that one day we walked along the lower trail to visit Granny Mitchell, who lived with her two sons, Cecil and George, at the head of a small government dock that was built for the resident fishing fleet. There were usually lots of fishermen visiting the Mitchells, and a card game nearly always seemed in progress. On the day of our visit, Uncle Jack commented that it all looked very much like a saloon scene out of the old west. He wasn't too far out with his observation, as the Mitchells had come to Canada from Texas. Cecil, with his long moustache, cowboy hat and droopy eyes, looked like a natural to be a sheriff in a western movie. It was always great to visit with Granny Mitchell, as she was very entertaining and gracious with us each time we came to visit. Unfortunately, shortly after this visit she passed away at a very old age, and this was the last time I saw her. George had a son, Teddy, who was a little older than Ruth, and we used to play together whenever George came to visit us. Both of the Mitchells fished for a living. George had a boat named the Cherryland III, while Cecil's boat was Peachland.

We all enjoyed the visit of Great Uncle Jack very much, and it was great for Mum and everyone around the harbour to have our hair cut by a professional for a change. Jim and Rose didn't come home from Toronto that year, as Jim had managed to get a summer job in Ontario on a highway project.

Chapter 9

The summer of 1947 was capped off with the wedding of Bill and Sheila over on Read Island. We walked then rode the old Ford truck to Heriot Bay where Seabird was waiting for us. Once we had loaded all the things needed, the voyage out past Viner Point to anchor in front of Lambert's store took us about an hour. We rowed ashore in the rowboat and then hiked the half mile up a trail to Mrs. Mackay's house. Sheila had a brother Ian who was a little older than I was, and we had a great time together. The only drawback I can remember was that we had to wear good clothes and were firmly instructed to, "Stay clean!" What a drag!

The Rev. Canon Alan Greene, who ran the Columbia Coast Mission boat in the region for many years until 1959, finally arrived to conduct the ceremony, after which a wedding lunch concluded the festivities. The lunch was definitely the best part of course for Ian and me, and I recollect telling Mrs. McKay how much I was looking forward to the bright red Jell-o she had prepared as one of the desserts. But when dessert time came, she forgot to give me any and this caused her to feel very badly, so when she realised it, she gave me the biggest bowl possible, all topped off with whipped cream! Delicious!

The Rev. Greene could only stay for a short time before heading off in his boat to a funeral to be held next day on one of the other islands. Afterwards we all got on board our boat for the trip back to Heriot Bay, where Mum, Ruth and I were left for the walk home. I was really surprised to see Bill and Sheila weren't coming with us and was a little sad to see them going off in the boat for their honeymoon. It was a fun day though, and we were sure tired when we finally arrived back at home well after dark. Pete came out to meet us and after much tail wagging and kisses I could finally get out my good clothes and climb into bed for a sound sleep and much needed rest. I quickly fell asleep, totally exhausted from all the activity and excitement of the day.

After the honeymoon, Bill and Sheila moved into their new house they had built from lumber cut at the sawmill. It was great to have them home again and I spent a lot of time playing with Pete around the mill in the great piles of sawdust.

The Howells also arrived again for their annual month long visit in August that lasted until Labour Day weekend. Mr. H had built a new boat over the winter and was it ever a beauty! Sixteen feet long, it had the most pleasing lines I ever remember seeing, on a boat that is. He had built it out of plywood and fastened it with screws, which was much different from the heavy planked boats we were used to having. It was powered by a new Mercury outboard, which drove it along at about 20 knots with two people on board. This left the old air cooled Lawson outboard for full time duty at the generator so that Katy could have electricity during the day if she wanted.

I spent a lot of time that August fishing with the Howells. They had brought me an Air Force inflatable life preserver, which got the most reluctant approval from Mum, so I could go out fishing with them. Somehow though I managed to lose the new life preserver before the summer was over, and never ever wore one again during my childhood years. Not a good example for today's kids!

It was always sad to say farewell to the Howells when they left each September, but this year was to be different. Uncle Ted had again asked Mum to come to Detroit to help him and Josephine with a new baby that was due to be born soon, and this time I was going with her. We were going to stop in Seattle to visit with the Howells on our way south down into the United States, and was I ever excited about this whole trip, especially since it was the only way I was going to be able to escape my studies. So September and October were spent doing double duty at the Grade 2 schoolwork, as we wouldn't be able to keep up while travelling in November

This naturally cut down on the amount of time I had to play with Pete, as well as other outdoor activities, so was much resented by both Pete and me. Pete was growing up to be a wonderful dog and companion, and I was going to miss him very much while we were away. During that lead up time to the trip, we were seldom out of each other's sight and spent many happy hours together roaming the island hills, forests and beaches.

As the time of our departure drew near, I started to have severe regrets about leaving Pete for such a long time, and I know he felt the same way; as Mum and I left home on our boat for the first leg of the trip, he tried to swim after us. Naturally he soon had to give up, as he realized we weren't about to turn around to come back for him, and he could be seen swimming frantically for shore and then racing along the shoreline trying in vain to keep us in sight.

So it was a sad trip to Campbell River and I felt very cold, but Mum tried to keep my spirits up by remarking how lovely the autumn colours looked along the shoreline. At The Gap between Steep and Gowlland Islands, a large boulder had broken away from the cliff and fallen to the beach below. Each time I pass that way ever since that day this large boulder on the beach reminds me of that heart breaking departure that day in late October 1947.

The S.S Chelohsin was unloading freight and passengers at the dock in Campbell River when we got there, so we said our goodbyes to Bill and boarded the ship, walking fearfully past that awful, dreaded steam winch again. As usual at dock, it was working at full speed unloading freight and supplies at the time and the operator could see I was scared, so he kindly stopped it while Mum and I walked hesitantly past the hissing giant. Mum stopped in at the purser's office to buy our tickets as I was watching Bill pull away from the dock on Seabird and head for home.

Captain Robert "Bob" Wilson was in command of the ship that day. He was a great friend of the family, and it was always a pleasure to be with this kind and thorough gentleman. I think as a navigator he was the best there was in a family of fine officers that served the Union Steamship line. If I recall correctly, he was born in 1882 in the Shetland Islands, off the coast of Scotland, and went to sea in 1899 at the age of 17, joining Union Steamships in 1910. Captain Bob, as he was known all up and down the B.C. coast, gathered high praise from all who knew him. He was senior captain with the company and was close to retirement after 37 years of service when we went aboard that day.

Little did we know that this was to be the last time we'd see him. Two months later, on December 21, he was master of the S.S. Cardena picking up loggers heading home for Christmas from the camps when he collapsed on the bridge just as the vessel was passing Q Cove. The Coquitlam, under command of Captain Jack Boden, was northbound at the time and saw the Cardena apparently drifting sideways into mid channel in Discovery Passage. The officer of the watch on the Cardena saw the Coquitlam approaching and quickly contacted her by radio to inform them of Captain Bob's collapse. The Cardena then proceeded at full speed to Campbell River to get him to hospital and medical care there, but their efforts were too late; the coast had lost one of the great navigators and pioneers of the area to a massive heart attack.

For us, the voyage from Campbell River to Vancouver that day with Captain Bob was as pleasant as it always was on these comfortable ships. Some of the women travelling on the Chelohsin had the added luxury of having a private sitting room on the aft boat deck, which was strictly off limits to the area's rugged loggers and was regularly patrolled to keep them away. Being only just seven at the time, I was allowed to stay with the women, when I wasn't off roaming and exploring the ship thoroughly from stem to stern as usual.

We arrived in Vancouver after dark that same evening. The disembarking deck up forward was crowded with the usual collection of well oiled loggers who had been drinking and gambling most of the voyage. Mum clutched my hand tightly; the disembarking amid these characters was always a distasteful part of the trip for her. We gathered our baggage from the attendant then, took a taxi from the Union Docks to the St. Francis Hotel, where we stayed the night. Next day it was off to the Main Street railway station to board the train for Seattle.

The city of Seattle is the largest in Washington State, and a very busy seaport, lying on the east shore of Puget Sound about 125 miles from the open Pacific Ocean, which is reached via the Strait of Juan de Fuca below the southern end of Vancouver Island. Over the years the city's location has made it a regular gateway from that part of the United States to both Alaska and the Far East, and vice-versa. It is truly a large and metropolitan city, with a large per cent of the state population living there, which made it a very exciting place for a small boy.

I had ridden on a train once before, but this one was much more modern than the aged one on Vancouver Island. We had scarcely settled safely on board before the train started with a sudden great jolt, which scared me about as much as riding those huge steamer waves had in Mum's small boat, but I soon settled down and we had a wonderful ride to Seattle, where the Howells took us to their home for a couple of days. The house was set high up and commanded a panoramic view of the city and harbour. It was great to see our friends again and their hospitality was much enjoyed.

All too soon though, our visit was over and we boarded the overnight train to Portland. This was something quite new for me, actually sleeping on a train for the first time. The rumble and rhythmic sound of the big steel wheels rolling over the tracks soon put me to sleep and I awoke in Portland next morning. There we boarded the daylight train for Oakland, California. Travel is quite common for small children these days, but it wasn't when I was young, so the whole trip was a great excitement and a tremendous adventure.

The train ride from Portland to Oakland is spectacular: I've taken this trip several times since and have always come away wanting more. The journey starts off through the Willamette Valley to Eugene, and then slowly climbs up through the rolling hills past Roseberg and on to Grant's Pass. The valley land from Portland south is flat and green, and the farms were populated with cud chewing cattle and contented looking sheep, with the cities of Salem and Albany spaced out and leading to Eugene at the end of the valley. The land is so flat and the railway tracks were so straight that the train reached what seemed to me to be unimaginable speeds. I must say they also made me pretty nervous at first, having grown accustomed to churning slowly along in a boat was no preparation for a train racing along at times at close to 80 m.p.h. The mountain passes through southern Oregon and the northern part of California were of course a whole new experience for me, and deer and bears could be seen looking at us as the train rumbled noisily past. Mount Shasta looked like a looming giant ready to leap on us.

We finally reached the station in Berkley, where Ed Aboumrad and his mother, my great aunt Sarah, met us and took us to their home on 61st Street in Oakland. Uncle Ted and Great Uncle Sam were already there waiting for us, and we spent about a week visiting Mum and Uncle Ted's cousins. The Aboumrad family were to remain very much in my life over the years. Mr. Aboumrad took me for a number of walks and sadly this was the only time that I ever saw him, as he too, like Captain Bob passed away shortly after our visit.

Great Aunt Sarah was my grandfather's sister, one of the family members he sent out to Canada during World War I, and I recall she suffered all her life from a severe case of asthma. So, shortly after their arrival in Canada, the family moved from Winnipeg to California, with the hope that the warmer climate would help her condition, which I'm glad to say it did to some degree. Mum and Ted, along with great Uncle Sam, had the most wonderful time reuniting with their long lost family. But all too soon that too was over and we had to leave for the long journey ahead of us, by car to Detroit via Los Angeles.

Early one morning, after tearful goodbyes, Ted, Sam, Mum and I packed our belongings into Ted's impressive new green 1948 Lincoln and headed south. I had never ridden in such an automobile before, having lived in the wilderness as we did, so it took me some time to keep from getting car sick. Despite that, the trip from Oakland to Los Angeles by road was a journey I'll never forget, and what a paradise southern California was! Even today, if one takes the old highways instead of the freeways, the trip can be unforgettable. I've made this journey many times over the years, and it always brings back many memories of places previously visited and people that I have met in the towns along the way.

San Jose, just a small town at that time, made a big impression, and so did Monterrey, San Simeon, Moro Bay, Santa Barbara and finally Los Angeles. I was surprised to see all the outdoor markets along the road and I wondered aloud how they made out in the winter. Mum promptly reminded me that of course it was already winter now and they seemed to being just fine.

Finally, after a very long day, we arrived at Olga's home - or should I say, mansion. I had never seen such a huge and beautiful home. Olga was either a friend or distant relative; I can't really remember which for sure. Her husband seemed to be extremely wealthy, and as they had no children of their own, they wanted Mum and me to come to live with them. I remember how good they were to us. They took us to see the Mount Wilson Observatory and for a drive through Hollywood and Pacific Palisades. Then, just for something to do, one day we drove to Palm Springs so I could have a date milkshake, something I suspect many people have never even heard of.

Mum could see, though, that if we went to live with these people, I would be pampered and spoiled beyond anything that could be considered half reasonable or normal. This city life was so new to me that, although the street Olga lived on was comparatively very quiet, I was still nervous about crossing it.

I used to stop at the sidewalk and look both ways to see if any cars were coming, and there never were, then I'd run across as fast as I could.

So in the end, the family's kind offer to live with them was gently but firmly declined, and after a few days more we were heading east. Los Angeles and the other 84 surrounding cities make up a very large metropolitan area today. Back in 1947, the area was huge in population compared to most other North American cities but still quite small compared to its size today, and these big outlying cities still had plenty of open space and farms between them. Of course one also has to remember that that area was settled by the Spanish explorers something like two and a half centuries before 'civilization' came to much of the B.C. coast where I lived.

Chapter 10

One of my main memories of that trip is passing herd after large herd of cattle grazing on grass alongside the track on the way to Oklahoma City, and my spending lots of time alone with Uncle Ted there while Mum and Sam did some shopping and exploring. This was the first time my uncle and I had had some time together alone, so I took full advantage of the opportunity to ask all sorts of questions about all the new sights and sounds of this fascinating city.

As we were travelling through Tulsa, it was decided we needed a break from driving. Uncle Ted suggested we visit the caves at Merrimac. Needless to say, Mum was far from keen on this and had more than a few reservations, as she always did with anything new and unknown, always something to be avoided like the plague. After much persuasion though, we toured Fisher's Cave, the biggest and most spacious section of which is called "The Ballroom" because in 1865 Thomas Fletcher, after being elected governor of the state, held his inaugural ball there. Strangely, Mum was so intrigued and enjoyed it so much that she talked about this big adventure for years afterwards.

The weather was starting to get colder as we worked our way back north and up the Mississippi River. This is some river: It's so wide it reminded me of the salt water inlets back home. Then it was on to Detroit.

Uncle Ted and wife Josephine lived at 20147 Norwood

Street with their three children, Anthony, the oldest at about five, followed by Bonnie and then Jean, who was still a baby born just the previous year. They had a modern house in a new district where each house looked the same as the one next to it. All were constructed of brick and had modern kitchen appliances and laundry rooms. Uncle Ted's had one bedroom downstairs, where Mum and I slept, with three more upstairs. Uncle Sam had caught the bus to Windsor, Ontario, just across the river, to visit his brother Ameen and family who lived there.

We were to spend several months off and on in Detroit between visits to see Great Uncle Ameen in Windsor, my brother Jim near Toronto, attending university and Great Uncle Jack in Rawdon, Quebec. Everywhere we went that winter we were greeted by snow and cold weather. It was just plain winter for months on end, something quite new to us. Winters on the west coast of Canada tend mostly to be wet and dull but for the most part quite mild. If the temperatures do sink below freezing on the coast, it never usually lasts more than a couple of weeks or so. Only rarely do we get a prolonged spell of really hard freezing weather. The winter of 1949-50 was an exception, but we'll come to that later.

Even to this day, Detroit is a huge industrial city dominated by the Ford Motor Company and its major plant. The weather in that region of North America can certainly be bitterly cold during the winter, especially compared to the wet coast with chill days of sunshine between the storms. As a whole though, the area isn't usually nearly as gloomy as our west coast cloud and rain. I spent a good deal of time outside with my cousins Anthony and Bonnie, playing in the snow. Josephine and Mum were getting ready for the new baby now, expected to arrive quite soon. Christmas was a time for the entertaining of friends and family, with much housework and baking to be done.

After we'd settled in at Uncle Ted's house, he drove Mum and me through the tunnel under the Detroit River to Windsor, to see Mum's Uncle Ameen and his family. There were three children in the family, Loraine, Janet and Cameel. They were all teenagers at the time and worked after school and on weekends in the family grocery store. Mum was delighted to see her cousins again and grew very close with her Aunt Victoria.

Another day Uncle Ted took Mum and me to look at a hotel and summer resort he was going to purchase, located on an island in Lake St Claire. We rode out to the island on a small car ferry through an ice clogged river. Except for the ice, this was just like home being on the water again, but Mum's advice to her brother was not to buy this business, based, you'll have guessed, on her own never ending trepidation about stepping out into something new. Despite that, he did eventually buy the property, after we had left for home, and it turned out to be a great success for him.

On another trip to spend a few days with Uncle Ameen, Mum had her own unexpected adventure though. At Canada Customs on the way south across the border, we were asked if we had any purchases from the United States to declare. "Oh, no," said Mum, "nothing I can remember." That wasn't nearly enough of an assurance for the inspector, and he told us to open our bags for him. There, upon searching our baggage, he found a new hot water bottle Mum had bought in Detroit. This resulted in us being detained for several hours and a full interrogation for Mum. She resented this very much, and from that time on always had a great dislike for Canada Customs. I have to admit that those nasty, mean looking men in their uniforms, who finally reduced Mum to tears, scared me pretty badly too.

Jim was attending the University of Toronto at the Ajax Campus at the time. He and Rose had a small house they found quite comfortable and spacious after having lived in a trailer for a couple of years. Rose was teaching at a kindergarten and I helped her with the little kids. My job was to assist the children with their heavy winter clothing and boots. I can't say it was exactly inspiring work, but that was the penalty I had to pay for being only a couple of years older than the rest of the class. The afternoons were spent riding sleds down the steep hill in front of the house, which was much more to my liking, and it was great fun being with kids my own age, of which there seemed to be many in the neighbourhood.

Some friends of Jim and Rose came to stay, and one day Freddie asked me if I'd like to go to Oshawa with her on the bus to do some shopping. This sounded like an opportunity for another great adventure, besides being a valuable chance to escape the dressing room at kindergarten. The bus ride was scenic and interesting; farmers in southern Ontario still used horses to work the land, and a blanket of snow stretched far and wide around us gleaming over the fields and everything. I sat glued to the bus window for the whole trip, watching the farmers with their teams of horses and their sleds spreading out hay on the snow for the dairy cattle to eat. I was also impressed with all the new cars and noisy traffic, which was so different from quiet, peaceful Ajax.

Later we went for a visit to Rawdon, Quebec, where Uncle Jack lived with his family in a large building on the main street. Unfortunately, Jack's wife only spoke Arabic and French, which meant I didn't have much dialogue with her. She was very kind though, and we had a wonderful time with them. There was a lake out behind their property, where men with saws would cut large blocks of ice. The blocks were then loaded onto sleds, to be hauled away by teams of horses to well insulated storage, facilities for use as refrigeration during the next summer.

There was also an outdoor skating rink across the street from their store, where I saw my first hockey game. I recall young people would ski up and down the main street, pulled behind a car up to three at a time. This looked like great fun, but I was much too young to be allowed to take part in this highly dangerous sport.

Finally though, came the day when we were loaded on to the train for the journey back to Vancouver, which took us four days and four nights of constant travel. I recall I enjoyed this train trip very much. Northern Ontario was desolate and empty along the shore of Lake Superior, looking much like home on the B.C. coast, and the trip through the Rocky Mountains was spectacular, as usual. I could tell from the alder trees instead of the birch of Eastern Canada when we were finally close to home.

A couple of days were spent shopping in Vancouver for supplies to send home, then we took the Princess Elizabeth overnight boat to Victoria to visit with Ruth, who was staying with the Darvilles while going to school in the city. We all went to a photographer to have a family picture taken, and then Mum and I caught the bus one morning, for the long ride home. We were met in Campbell River by Bill and the Seabird for the last leg of our journey, back to Quadra Island. Home again! But where was my dog Pete? I had thought of him often during the past five months while I was away. But where was he? It seems that Pete missed me very much and took to wandering farther and farther from home. He eventually became a stray and was finally shot by Teddy Johnston, who lived at the south end of Gowlland Harbour, next door to Yeatmans. This was very sad for me, and it still brings back memories of all the good times he and I shared together, in the mill sawdust and roaming the slopes and wooded shorelines of Quadra Island. "Bye, Pete. You were a good dog and a great buddy."

Chapter 11

The next year, 1948, stands out in my memory as a year of a great many excitements. After Mum and I returned from our travels, I had to buckle down to some serious school studies, but there was also an above-normal abundance of fish that year, which was probably the outstanding event of the year for me. We could catch herring in great numbers off the end of our dock, and salmon were jumping everywhere as they fed on the enormous schools of baby shrimp and herring. Gulls and ducks were also getting in on this great feast and feeding frenzy, and could be seen chasing each other for their share of the wealth.

One day, when I was trying to rake some herring for bait, I hit a salmon. I wasn't able to land it, but it was certainly a tremendous thrill and an indication of the huge abundance of fish that summer. On another day, Jim and Bill were doing some work on our dock when a big octopus swam by. Ruth, who happened to be there, also became very excited at this and attempted to catch the slippery giant. Fortunately though, it was able to evade her, swimming off at great speed into deep water.

Mum and I started to do some serious fishing together that summer, but as usual, even with the amount of fish available, we weren't very successful. This was also a banner fishing year for the Howells. They really "cleaned up", with their superior fishing gear and methods. I was able to go fishing with them quite often and learned a great deal from both Bill and Johnny.

That summer Jim McPherson asked Mum if he could anchor a herring and cod box in front of our property. Jim was primarily a cod fisherman and needed a place to keep both his bait and his cod catch alive. This was done by storing the catch each day in a floating cage, with the bait in a separate pen to prevent the cod from eating them. Each week one of the fishing companies would send a fish packing boat by to kill, dress and buy the cod from the various fishermen in the area. Mum readily agreed to Jim's request, as she was a good friend of his and his wife Grace.

Jim, I believe, was born and raised in Scotland and came to Canada with his family just before the war. He and his brothers became lifelong friends of mine. They were always kind, cheerful, happy people with a ready smile, and always willing to help out anyone in need. Jim had one daughter named Arlette, who was in school with me and by chance we happened to share the same birthday.

When she was home, Ruth and I used to row in her boat to the north end of the harbour to go swimming. I did the rowing of course. The water was much warmer in this inner bay due to the long flat beach. During the summer the low tides are during the morning, often in the range of about 16 feet. When the tide is out during the early part of the day, the hot summer sun heats up the exposed beach and that warms the water when it starts to rise back over the beach in the afternoon. This results in much warmer water than usual and makes for very pleasant swimming.

One day that summer Ruth and I rowed up to the north end early while the tide was still dropping. As I was rowing, Ruth was looking down over the side into the water to the sea bottom, and saw a very large crab about three feet down. She immediately jumped into the shallow water and captured this giant before it knew what had hit it. Until then we hadn't even been aware these large crabs existed, and decided to hurry home to show off our catch. The crab wasn't at all happy at this turn of events though and kept trying to nip me with its large claws. I had to lift my bare feet off the bottom of the boat several times to avoid being clamped and that didn't help with the rowing. Up to the house we raced with our prize. Sheila of course knew exactly how to handle this situation and immediately put on water to boil in one of Mum's milking buckets. The poor unfortunate crab was doomed. It was promptly dunked into boiling water for 20 minutes, after which we sat down to sample the results. Even Mum, in her terror of anything new, had to admit it was very tasty. After this new discovery of a source of big crabs at the north end of the harbour, Ruth and I fished there regularly for them with a dip net, and would often bring home some for supper. In later years, when Bill was fishing crabs commercially, he found all of Gowlland Harbour to be a highly productive area for this particular species of Dungeness crabs.

We often had visits from our various neighbours at the house, as they came by to obtain some fresh milk or produce from us. On one occasion we were all working on a new ramp leading to a float that Bill was mooring near his sawmill, when Mr. Britenbach came by in his rowboat to get some milk. Mum sent me up to the house to get a quart from the cooler where it was kept, and of course I ran back to the waterfront as quickly as I could with the filled container. But just as I started down the sloping new ramp, it slipped off the float, and into the water I fell. Mum instantly went into a state of complete panic, of course, but Jim just jumped into the water to grab me and save me from certain instantaneous drowning, at least in Mum's eyes. Jim quickly hauled me over to where Bill could pull me out of the water. Mum was still jumping up and down and screaming blue murder when I handed Mr. Britenbach his sealed quart container of milk. I had kept it still clutched in my hand throughout the escapade! Everyone laughed except Mum, who must have still thought I was sure to drown, even after I was back on dry land again, wet but quite safe.

Bill and Jim were finding there wasn't enough revenue from the sawmill to support the two of them and their financial needs, so Jim went back to fishing to earn the extra money he would need for university. During one of our vegetable deliveries to Painter's world famous Fishing Resort on the Campbell River side, he was offered a job there as a fishing guide. This would be a more assured way for him to earn some money, as he was guaranteed the princely sum of $8 per day, so he took the job. Among his many guests, Jim guided Dr. Campbell, who visited Painter's each year from his home in California and was an avid fisherman. Much of the sport fishing was conducted at that time from rowboats, quite a number of which were designed and then built by lodge owner and operator Ned Painter.

These boats, which eventually became the basis for today's fleet of rowboats in the internationally cherished and respected Tyee Club, were a marvel of marine architecture. Their design makes them very stable, as well as easy to row in tides and currents. As still happens today, the guide took one or sometimes a maximum of two people out fishing at a time, and it was his job to row the boat, get them into the best place to catch big Chinook salmon, and try to ensure the guests caught some fish. Of course there was never any guarantee.

Jim used to use Mum's boat to tow several rowboats from Painter's at the mouth of the Campbell River, across Discovery Passage to April Point, to fish there. From there guests would fish all day from the boats, which would then finally be towed home again back to Painter's in time for dinner. In later years, outboard motors would be introduced and guiding became much easier and better paid, but that was after the advent of the 1950s.

This was the start of a long and mutually beneficial relationship between my family and Painter's Lodge that was to last for more than a decade. Each one of my family, except Dad, worked there at some time in the years to follow.

Ned and June Painter founded Painter's from very humble beginnings, starting with a small tent village or camp on the end of the Tyee Spit, on the opposite side of the Campbell River Estuary from the eventual site of the world famous lodge. Sport fishing by well heeled international guests from overseas was already well established in our area by 1920. One of the first recorded visitors was a Mr. Binsac, who made the journey from England to camp fish for one month in 1890. According to records, Mr. Binsac was a guest of area pioneer Fred Nunns, who charged him the sum of $2 a day, and that covered shelter, board and even guiding services!

Ned Painter moved to Campbell River in 1922 to construct rowboats for this growing industry. He built a fleet of 20 or more boats each year, for sale to local residents or for rent to guests. The ones he kept for renting out he sold at the end of the season and would replace with new ones before the start of the next season.

Over the years, Ned Painter also built a group of 12 cabins on the property north of the river mouth, which is where, in 1940, the main lodge was built. That caused business to really start to boom. The rich and famous began to come to Painter's Lodge in droves from all over the world, to fish for the famous Tyee, the name given to Chinook Pacific Salmon weighing 30 pounds or more. They still come, though in smaller numbers now.

After Jim and Rose went back to school in Toronto that autumn, Mum and I took up fishing with renewed interest. Jim had left Mum's boat well rigged and prepared, and we had a good supply of herring from McPherson's bait boxes. We enjoyed those days together, but we still didn't catch all that many fish, though we were able to make a little bit of extra money. That was always a great help, as Dad had not been heard from for some time.

There were so many salmon that year that it's still amazing to me now that we were so poor at catching them. This was brought home to us one day when we were at the south end of May Island and stripping off our old and well used bait before heading for home. I was watching over the side of the boat as Mum was throwing away the old herring. To my surprise, several salmon would chase after each piece of herring as it sank in the water. This immediately renewed our interest in continuing our fishing a little longer, but it also proved to us that our gear was so out of date and obsolete that the salmon would rather take our bait when it wasn't on our lines than pay any attention to it when it was! We started taking some lessons from Bill Howell, and soon our fishing improved, by using gear that was more difficult for the fish to see.

During July that summer there was also a new member added to the family. Bill and Sheila had a baby girl named Kathy. Mum was delighted as grandmothers usually are, particularly with the three members of the family so close by in their house located near the sawmill. The new arrival prompted a steady stream of visitors from around Quadra Island to see the baby, and these visitors added new excitement to my life, as the visits often brought me into contact with other kids my own age. Two of these new friends were Neil Watson and Percy Beech, who were to be close friends for many years.

Bill bought a new 1948 Ford flat deck truck that year, which was kept at Campbell River and used to deliver lumber from the sawmill. The lumber was first loaded onto a barge then, towed by the Seabird to Campbell River, where it was transferred onto Bill's truck. All this was done by hand and was slow and difficult work, but usually someone would happen by to lend a hand.

We had some great times using the truck for family travel and exploring. One time we loaded up all the Howells and the rest of the family and went on a picnic to Elk Falls, now a provincial park just north of Campbell River. What a great day filled with fine weather, swimming, exploring and adventure. Bill Howell, Johnny, Ruth, Barbara and I rode on the back on the flat deck, with the other five, Mum, Katy Howell, Bill, Sheila and baby, all jammed together in the cab up front.

Sheila had an aunt and uncle who lived on Denman Island near the present ferry dock, so one time Bill, Sheila, Kathy and I all took the opportunity to go south with a load of lumber. We stopped at the Big Rock Store and at Black Creek to deliver the lumber, then went on down to visit the Ford dealer in Courtenay, to have the new truck checked over. The next stop was at Buckley Bay, where we loaded the truck onto a small ferry for the short ride over to Denman Island. The ferry was owned by the well known Baikie family and consisted of a small barge pushed by a 36 foot tug named the Billy B. In later years, the first tug I bought was the sister ship to the Billy B, which I bought from Jack Baikie for $12,000.

We stayed overnight with Sheila's aunt and uncle, who were delighted to see her and her new addition to the family. Bill and I used the time to inspect the new boat they had just bought, a 14-foot Turner with a Briggs & Stratton in board engine. Next day it was back on to the ferry, for the drive to Campbell River and then the ride aboard the Seabird home to Gowlland Harbour.

Autumn brought yet another call from Uncle Ted for Mum to come back to Detroit to help Josephine with their ever growing family. Before that could happen though, I had to do a fast unit of Grade 3. This was a real drag for both Mum and me, and we had more than a few disagreements. She regularly scolded me for spending too much time staring out of the window and daydreaming longingly for summer. But we did manage to complete most of the Grade 3 curriculum for the year before she left for the east in early December. This time she didn't take me with her and Bill, Sheila and Kathy moved into the family house to look after me during Mum's absence.

The winter of 1948-49 is still remembered by many for its solid and exceptionally cold weather and several heavy snowfalls that caused high drifts on the coast. Bill kept busy at the sawmill, while Sheila looked after Kathy, the house and me. I packed wood to keep the hungry home fires burning and also fed the cattle and chickens. For me it was freedom all over again, after the intense schooling with Mum.

Sheila taught me to play cards and I used to watch her roll her cigarettes, which started me wanting to smoke. Sheila answered that with a flat "No!", but after much persistent pestering from me, she finally gave in and said I could smoke, but only if I rolled my own. After watching her so often, it took me only about 10 minutes to master this fine art, and Sheila was shocked when she came back into the kitchen, only to find me puffing away at a cigarette. She immediately put a stop to this eight year old's new bad habit by hiding her tobacco and we eventually reached a compromise. I was so adept at rolling smokes that she kept me busy rolling them for her. Fortunately, I found this far more interesting and enjoyable than smoking, but I enjoyed keeping her well supplied all that winter.

Often in the evening we'd climb aboard the Seabird for the short ride over to visit Rusty and Pat Beech. Their son Percy was just a couple of years younger than I was and we all had great evenings together. We'd start off by playing cards, then, after we tired of this, we'd go sleigh riding. When I think back over all the fun things I've done in my life, few can compare with those sleigh rides. Rusty had built a very large wooden sleigh that could hold all of us at one time. They lived at the top of a very long hill that ended up down by the ocean. On moonlit nights we'd spend hours riding down this hill at terrific speeds, coming to a snowy halt at the bottom. Then we'd hike back up to the top to start all over again. With the weight of four adults, and a couple of kids thrown into the bargain, the sled reached unimaginable speeds. Rusty would always ride at the back to steer and keep control. As we got close to the bottom, he'd jump off and quickly wrap a rope attached to the back of the sleigh around an old tree stump. This would bring us to a very sudden stop before we all ended up in the ocean, and usually resulted in us all ending up a pile of laughing bodies at the bottom of the run.

Sometimes that winter, when the tide was at its lowest, which is always at night at that time of year, we'd go shrimping along the beach. To catch the shrimp we'd use a flashlight and a small dip net. The eyes of the shrimp would glow when the light was on them, and it was simply a matter of scooping them up with the net. We'd return home with a bucketful of shrimp where Pat and Sheila would have a nice pot of boiling water ready to cook them. We'd feast on the shrimp, then go back to either playing cards or some more sleigh rides until about 2 a.m., when we tired visitors would head for home on the boat.

One night on the way home, Sheila fell into the freezing

cold water as we walked out on the snow covered floats to board the boat. Bill and I managed to pull her out quickly, and her first words were, "Where's Kathy?"

Bill had been ahead of us and had quickly laid Kathy down in the snow while we hauled Sheila out of the water. But the little one seemed at that moment to have vanished and in panic we started to search frantically for her in the dark. Finally, we came across her lying quietly in the snow, still fast asleep exactly where she'd been laid down. We proceeded home on the boat with Sheila giving Bill and me a very sharp talking to for our carelessness through her chattering teeth.

Another frigid winter day, Rusty, Bill and I travelled north through Seymour Narrows, past Ripple Rock, to Deep Water Bay to pick up some logs for the sawmill. This was my first trip through the churning waters of the notorious Narrows, where the rock had claimed so many lives, and Rusty showed me how to steer his boat safely through the turbulent tidal streams on the way north, going with the strong ebb tide. This was an exciting experience, and the knowledge gained then and later was to serve me well for the rest of my lengthy seafaring life.

As mentioned earlier, Seymour Narrows is a constriction in what is referred to by the commercial and freighter traffic as The Inside Passage, which runs 'inside' Vancouver Island, between the Island and the B.C. Mainland, from Puget Sound in the south, to Skagway, Alaska, in the north. This is a distance of well over 1,000 miles of spectacularly scenic waterways and stunning coastline. The Inside Passage is well protected from the gales of North Pacific Ocean blowing across from Hawaii and Japan. As a result, the passage, which has its own share of storms and adverse water conditions as well as navigational hazards, has been in constant use by seafarers since people began populating the coast, coming from Asia several thousand years ago. At the narrowest point of Seymour Narrows, which is only about half a mile wide, in those days lay the ferocious, ship consuming hazard of Ripple Rock.

We'll come back to that later, but suffice it to say now that, as Rusty, Bill and I travelled through the Narrows that winter's day, the huge overhead cables used to try to hold a drilling barge in place over the underwater mountain were still there, and so of course so was Ripple Rock and its fearsome eddies and flows. We spent the night anchored in Deep Water Bay waiting for daylight and favourable tides to start towing the logs through the narrows to Gowlland Harbour.

Rusty's boat was a former Japanese cod boat with a small stern cabin known as a 'doghouse', which was the living quarters, with the engine and pilothouse located in the forward part of the vessel. This resulted in very comfortable living space separated from the noisy and smelly Easthope engine.

We spent a warm and comfortable night sleeping in our bunks beside the glowing oil stove that was used for cooking and for heat. The next day we left with our tow of logs early enough so we could be at the entrance of the narrows, where the rock was, as the tide changed from ebb to flood. This resulted in a safe and speedy passage back through the Narrows and a fair tide to help us along on the way back down south to our final destination. I was to repeat this passage through the Narrows many hundreds of times over the coming years, but this first two way trip is always the one that stands out in my memory. It showed me this still hazardous stretch of water could even then be navigated with safety; if it was done properly and with due regard for the dangers the waters can hold. I owe a big debt of gratitude to Rusty and Bill for teaching me at an early age to appreciate the perils of this spot, as well as how to navigate the Narrows at virtually any time with relative safety.

That winter, Bill started to select fir timbers and planking to build a barge to transport lumber more efficiently. The timbers were cut from No. 1 or prime fir logs, and the barge frame soon started to take shape. The vessel was built upside down to make it easier to plank, and generous amounts of wood preservative were used.

Soon the whole bottom was caulked, copper-painted and ready to be turned right side up. Rusty and Bill tried to flip the barge over by towing it sideways with their two boats, and this is a method that will work, but only if the towing vessels have sufficient power. Theirs didn't, and several attempts were made without success. So, with the usual coastal know how, at high tide they secured the barge sideways to a couple of large trees at the top of a steep rock bluff. After the water level had dropped enough, they cut the lines and pulled on the topside with one of the boats. The barge promptly slipped back into the water right side up.

The upper parts of the sides were then added and the top deck finished, and Bill decided to install an engine on the vessel. A heavy duty two cylinder Vivian gas engine was located and bought. These Vivian engines were manufactured in Vancouver by Bill Vivian in a plant on West Georgia Street across from where the Bayshore Inn is today. Vivian was a brilliant engineer who manufactured big powerful diesel engines that were used all over the eastern Pacific shoreline, down as far south as the country of Chile.

Bill paid $100 for the whole engine, shaft and propeller included. This meant that the vessel was slow but could transport sizable loads of lumber with ease. Buford Haines, another groundbreaker on the coast, built a comfortable wheelhouse and living quarters for the boat with his usual expertise, and this craft replaced the Seabird, which was then sold to someone on Read Island. I can remember her being anchored in White Rock Pass for many years after that, and then working as a gulf troller out of Campbell River until comparatively recently.

Another major event that winter was the arrival of the Pacific Coast Children's Mission to Quadra Island. Before 1949, this organization consisted of young missionaries who travelled the coast by boat visiting and ministering to the many tiny clusters of homes scattered the length of B.C.'s fjord riven coastline. That year Mr. R.J. Walker and his wife donated some of their land for a permanent base ashore on Quadra, and Alf and Margaret Bayne started what was to become the Camp Homewood centre we know today, beginning with a Sunday school at the Walker home for the children who lived in the area.

The Walkers were among the early pioneers on Quadra Island, arriving at the Cape Mudge Indian Village in 1894.

Resident missionaries and teachers at the village school, they moved to a substantial acreage at the south end of Gowlland Harbour 10 years later, where they took up farming. They were both very community minded, with Mr. Walker serving on the local school board, as Justice of the Peace or magistrate on Quadra and in Campbell River, and also as chairman of the first Campbell River Hospital Board.

During the early part of the 1900's, several forest fires raged through the southern end of Quadra. Mr. Walker survived one of these fires by hiding under a hollowed out cedar stump for several days while the fire burned out its fury all around him. Afterwards he emerged from his hideout, tired and hungry and very thirsty but otherwise unscathed. Later he used to tell how, as he started walking towards his home, he came across a grouse that had been perfectly cooked by the fire. He used to joke that it "could have used a little salt, but other than that it was quite delicious!"

Chapter 12

One day in late January of 1949, Neil Watson invited me to come to Sunday school with him. He had been a couple of times before and thought it would be fun for us to go together. The next Sunday was a fine day, with some old snow on the ground and the sun shining brightly, so I started off along the trail and met Neil where their trail meets the Gowlland Harbour Road, about a mile south of our place. We walked on together, with Neil's dog Nipper jumping ahead and leading the way. As I hadn't been attending school at all yet, it was a whole new experience for me to be with a whole bunch of other kids. I didn't know most of them, but Neil introduced me as his guest and this was the first time I met Alf and Margaret Bayne.

The Sunday school was held in the living room of the Walkers house, with Mrs. Walker leading us in the singing of 'Jesus Loves Me' and other songs that I didn't know the words to. Mrs. Walker's false teeth would rattle as she sang and I was always kind of waiting for them to fall out onto the floor, which of course they didn't. Big disappointment! I soon learned to mumble along with the rest of the kids and felt it was a great time.

Strangely enough, Neil never ever came to Sunday school again, but I attended every Sunday for quite a few years. Alf would make the rounds of the area with the mission boat Goforth picking up all the kids from our various homes. In summer I'd use Ruth's rowboat, tying it up at Dewey Vaughn's float next door to Homewood.

When Ruth came home from school that year, she attended Homewood girls' camp and she and her family went on to a lifelong association with the summer camp which is still held there each year. She met her husband Ron at Homewood, and in 1958 they were married at the camp's small chapel.

Spring came at last in 1949, with warmer weather and Mum returning from her long winter in Detroit with her brother and family. It was good to see her again, but for me it was back to schoolwork right away, and we finished off the rest of Grade 3 in record time.

Bill, Sheila and Kathy moved back down to their own house by the waterfront, and were replaced by the father and mother of Alex and Rhoda Mitchell. The Mitchells came to live with us to help Mum with trying to make a living from the livestock and to aid with the farm produce we grew on the property. Mr. Mitchell was 60 years old at that time, and they were both at loose ends as to their retirement, so this seemed to be a good arrangement for both parties. They stayed with us yearly for the next five years, until the spring of 1954.

William Ajeet Singh Mitchell was born in 1890 in Bombay, India. His father and his mother were Salvation Army missionaries who served in India until 1896. W.A. followed in his father's footsteps by returning to India with the Salvation Army in 1913. There he met and married Hulda Johansson, also a missionary. Mrs. Mitchell was born in 1887 in Vahmanlands, Sweden. The couple served together at various locations in India and Hawaii and were to be a great influence on my early life.

Much of my training on how to behave properly came from W.A and his wife. They tried to make me conform to rules and regulations they felt were in my best interests in society, but met with only limited success I'm afraid. By the time I was eight, my ways were pretty firmly set as thoroughly non-conformist, and I have to admit I remain that way to this day well over 50 years later. I always rebelled against political and social conformity that is taught in school, and sometimes by society.

When Mr. and Mrs. Mitchell came to live with us, we had about 10 head of cattle, Dolly the horse, numerous chickens, a variety of fruit trees and a sizable strawberry patch. We kept the chickens at the Howells' place, where they had numerous out buildings they never used. One of my jobs was to collect the eggs each day and feed these chickens. It was about a 10 minute walk over a trail to the chicken house. I used to enjoy this time and take full advantage of the opportunity to waste an hour or more with the chickens each day.

When Mum was away the previous winter, I had also helped Bill feed the cows and I carried on with this after she returned. W.A. had been with us for about a month when it was decided to start reducing the size of the herd. Many other changes were to take place over the next year, affecting the operation of the property and my young life too.

This might be a good time to mention some of the many fishermen who lived and worked in our area during the 1940's. Things were starting to change in the local fishing scene as I approached my ninth birthday, though of course the two events weren't connected. Many of the men who fished for a living came to the area during the pre-war Depression years. Some of them bought property, some were squatters who built shacks on any available land, and still others lived on their boats. The ones who lived on their boats were the most prosperous, with bigger vessels up to 40 feet in length.

It was certainly possible to make a steady living fishing in those times. One wouldn't become wealthy by any means, but with some effort, a decent living just above the poverty line could be scratched out. Most fishing was for salmon and lingcod as the season and markets dictated. Fishing was done close to home in what is known as the Gulf, the Gulf of Georgia, which stretches from Victoria north to Seymour Narrows, north of Campbell River. The primary method of fishing this area at the time was by trolling with hook and line. Net fishing boats were much larger and tended to roam the coast more extensively. The trollers' fishing lines were pulled in by hand, unlike the practice of today which uses power lines, and the majority of the boats were rowboats. This was a very difficult way to fish, and I think I may still have calluses on my hands from the summers I rowed my sister's boat in the strong tidal currents.

The rowboat fishermen that worked the first half of the century were a tough lot though. I can remember one story of a man named Carman. He had fished the Gulf for many years, and decided one day he'd row to Vancouver to buy an outboard motor. Pre-war outboards weren't at all like the modern day, reliable marvels we have now. They sometimes took as much energy and patience to start as it took to row, and this turned out to be the case with Carman. After rowing all the way from Quadra to Vancouver, a distance of some 100 miles, he bought his new motor for the quite princely sum of $50. But after working on the rope starter for two days without success, he unbolted it from the back of the boat and dumped it into the ocean. He then proceeded to row the 100 miles home again, $50 poorer.

As we make a tour from Cape Mudge along the shore of Quadra to Seymour Narrows, then down the Vancouver Island shore to Campbell River, it might be amusing to try to remember some of the activities in each area and people who fished and lived there.

At Francisco Point, on the south eastern tip of Quadra Island there was a collection of shacks with boat launch skids, where the rowboats would be pulled up out of harm's way. This was and still is a very exposed area to the southeast winds that blast rain drenched storms up from the southern Gulf of Georgia, picking up speed and moisture as they drive towards the northwest over a long stretch of the Gulf. At times though the fishing in the shallows off the point could be spectacular, and that general area was a very popular sport fishing spot right into the late 1980s.

As we move westward and around 'The Cape' (Cape Mudge), past the lighthouse on the south western point of Quadra, we come to a little bay where B.C. Packers used to moor a fish buying barge during the summer season. These barges were very common and usually had a crew of a man, wife and deckhand, with living quarters for the crew, limited storage area for groceries and fishing gear, and an ice room for storing the fish.

The fishermen usually delivered their catch each day. The fish were graded for quality, weighed and either paid for in cash on the spot or booked for future payment at season's end. The fish were iced into boxes which were picked up by a large packer vessel two or three times a week and delivered to Vancouver, which was later to become my job.

At this particular spot, there was a seasonal village at this fish camp that was used mostly by Indian people from Cowichan and other southern villages. Many of these Cowichan people were good friends with Mum, as they always liked to come to our place to pick berries.

Next up along the coast was the main Cape Mudge Village, with several hundred permanent residents, a church and primary grade school. Almost everyone who lived there fished for a living. Many of them had quite sizable purse seine boats that travelled the entire coast fishing for salmon, herring and pilchards as the season permitted.

The next port and the major population centre of Quadra was Quathiaski Cove (Q Cove), in a fairly sheltered little bay almost directly across Discovery Passage from downtown Campbell River. There was a cannery there until 1941, when it was destroyed by fire. That particular cannery wasn't rebuilt, but Q Cove, as it's always been known, remained a major fishing centre for many years, with spacious net lofts, stores, a shipyard, post office and marine fuel stations. The post office and some of the stores have now moved up the hill behind the cove out of sight from the water, but at that time, as mentioned earlier, this was an important port of call for the Union Steamships Company for many years.

Each day, a small fish collecting boat would make the rounds as far north as Seymour Narrows, to pick up fish from residents and deliver these fish back to Q Cove for storage. The fish would then be transferred on to the fish packing boat sent out from Vancouver with ice and supplies for the various camps.

Next up along the coast was Poverty Point, now known by the name of April Point, which now sports a fairly well appointed tourist resort for visitors to the island, with a dining room and bar connected by small fast ferry passenger vessel to the famous Painter's Lodge, also owned now by Bob Wright's Oak Bay Marine Group out of Victoria. In 1949, the Peterson family had just bought the property three years before and set up the April Point Resort, changing the name of the point in the process.

Tucked away behind and just round the corner is Gowlland Harbour, where we lived, which had many residents who lived and fished from their homes there. Virtually everyone in the sheltered bay had a dock in front of their property, and there were also two government docks. This very sheltered little bay always attracted a sizable fleet of boats.

Most of the fishermen I remember from my childhood were interesting but ruggedly independent individuals who had mostly come up the coast from parts unknown. I am sure a book could be written about each one of them, and I'll relate some of their stories later as I remember them in my growing up years.

At the south end of Gowlland Harbour lived Frank Miller with a boat named Copper Cliffs, named after the once renowned fishing spot just to the north of Gowlland on the Quadra shore, which glows green with copper in the summer's evening sun.

Another fisherman from those days was Bill Law, with his beautiful Western Shore II. Bill kept his boat like a yacht, perfectly painted and shining inside and out. Then there was Stan Gardiner and Mrs. Smith. They lived together in separate houses immediately next to each other, and fished with a small putter boat. They always struck me as a strange pair, but Mrs. Smith took on the care and feeding of Stan in fine fashion, cooking all the meals, washing clothes and house cleaning. This all seemed very strange to me even as a child, as they lived in their separate little homes right next to each other.

Dewey Vaughn had a large troller and his son Lloyd owned a very big fishing vessel he used with great success until retirement a few years ago now.

Next on the Gowlland circuit was Slim Watson, with his two sons Hugh and Neil. Neil was my age and we spent a lot of time together as kids. Hugh followed his father into the fishing industry and owned several boats over the years.

Next around were George and Cecil Mitchell, whom I've mentioned earlier. They had a government dock right in front of their place, and this attracted quite a few non-resident boats that fished the area. Ed Sackville was among the transients. He had a beautiful big troller named the Henry Bay, which came complete with a wood burning stove.

The Beech family lived about a mile north of us, and the Britenbachs were out on the point. At a place called Missing Link lived Bill Navid senior and son Bill junior. They had a large troller named the Elk Falls.

At Race Point, over on the Campbell River side north of the town lived Joe Currie. The main thing I remember about him was his long pigtail. Joe continued to live in his shack at the point for many years after the heyday of the fishing era came to a close in the mid-1950's. He could be seen every month or so rowing to Campbell River for supplies.

On Gowlland Island lived Gus Norlander, who at one time owned the property where the Watson family lived. My family lived for a short time on this property before finally settling at our present location.

Another real interesting character was Axel Borin, who had the noisiest one cylinder Easthope engine I ever remember. Ruth and I always knew when he was coming, as we could hear his engine at least an hour before the boat came into view.

I mention the names of these people, as most of them were to be a part of my childhood memories, but there were many more that came before my time, during the old time fishing era. That was coming to an end and most of the fishermen from those early days had passed on by the end of the war.

These people, along with our neighbours mentioned

previously, were the rough and tumble, tough, hard scrabble individuals I grew up with. I mention that because when the Mitchells came to live with us, they were completely different from just about everyone I had known up until that time. They set out to present me with good examples and lessons in good manners, proper dress, more refined language, and some of the myriad of other social behaviour skills not evident among most of the logging and fishing community I was used to. Though I think I did manage to absorb a small assortment of some of these new social graces, I'm sorry to say most of them were totally lost on me.

In my defence, I have to say that other than the short term travel Mum and I did, all my time was spent on the waterfront and I still hadn't been to school as yet. As a result, any organized rules of behaviour were really quite foreign to me, particularly since my time with others my age was also very limited. The Mitchells set out with much vigour to try to catch up on this flaw in my young life and upbringing, and, to their credit, they did have some limited success, but that seemed to last pretty much only until I entered school in September 1949, just before my ninth birthday, and little changed in my manners and relationships with other kids.

After the Mitchells had prevailed on us to reduce the number of cows on the property, it was time also for Dolly the horse to go. Mum had never had any great affection for the horse, and made arrangements to send her to live with Mr. Marcoux, who had a sizable property at Quathiaski Cove. There she spent many happy years. We kept one cow by the name of Queenie, who, as can be guessed from the name, was the cow of cows, with turned down horns that had been cut off, which always reminded me of a water buffalo.

Queenie could open our garden gate no matter how well it was lashed with rope or wire, and she and Mum had a long running battle over the garden, which ended with Bill installing a battery operated electric fence. Queenie had a good look at this as Bill was installing it around the garden to keep her out. When it was finally ready for activation, Bill hit the switch and we all waited to see how Queenie would react to this new barrier. First of all, she opened the outer gate with her horns then, she approached the new electric fence. We all held our breath as she looked at it quietly for a few minutes. Then she put out her tongue to lick at one of the insulators to see what it tasted like. The shock sent Queenie leaping into the air like a rodeo bull, and she promptly ran off into the forest to get away from such a nasty experience. After she received this one first jolt of electricity, we never had to turn it on again, as she kept a healthy and respectful distance from both fence and garden.

That wasn't the end of Queenie's rebellion against authority though. She constantly tested Mum with new ways to disrupt our daily lives. One morning after milking, Mum went to the dock to check on the boats. She had left the pail of milk unattended, and upon her return, she discovered Queenie had drunk it all. Mum flew into a rage and used some new words I hadn't even heard from the fishermen. Bill tried to calm her down by suggesting she shouldn't worry about it too much, since now she'd get twice as much milk the next day! Whereupon Mum promptly threw the empty milk bucket at him and used a whole bunch more of these new words. The Mitchells were horrified! Their years on the mission field with the Salvation Army hadn't prepared them at all for this kind of wild behaviour and florid language. W.A. decided Queenie had to be put down after that, as she was continually devising new ways of disrupting our quite pastoral life. Strangely though, Mum dug in her heels and defended her with all her might, and in the end Queenie received her reprieve from death row, for the time being at least.

After the crops were planted for the year, the Mitchells went off to Banff, where they had summer jobs at one of the resorts. As the strawberries ripened in June, Ruth came home from school to help out with the harvest. It always seems to be raining on the west coast in June, and the summer of 1949 was unusually wet. The strawberries suffered along with us, but by picking some every day and drying them on towels spread out on the floor, we were able to save the crop. We'd pack them into small boxes of 24 to a master box then, ship them by boat to the B.C. Packers store at Q Cove. Jack Barfield was the manager and he'd advance us some cash, with the balance kept on account for our future use. On a good year we'd accumulate as much as $1,000 to be used over the rest of the year for other goods we bought at the store. The berries sold very well and were highly prized, especially by the local Indian population.

After the strawberries were finished, we'd start harvesting the raspberries, which were more difficult to sell, but also provided some income. Any surplus berries were canned or taken to the cold storage lockers for our own future use.

Chapter 13

The summer of 1949 was the first year there was a summer camp held at Homewood. I was really too young, by a few months, for the age limit, but Alf and Margaret let me attend anyway. This turned out to be one of the best times I had ever had in my life. We slept in the Walkers' barn, on a haystack, and there were no more berries to pick, and I made many new friends from all over the coast.

Looking back, I think it was all very primitive compared to the modern facility which Homewood has grown into today. The cost then was about $8 for two weeks, and if this was more than a family could afford, the fee was waived. Mum always made sure I went there for the next three years.

During the previous winter, Mum's health had started showing signs of failing though. After several trips to Vancouver to see a specialist, her condition was thought to be breast cancer. This was a huge setback for all the family of course, as she was still only in her late forties and had always seemed healthy and physically fit. But after major surgery and a lengthy period of recuperation and rehabilitation, she made a full recovery and was fortunate to have no further symptoms of the dreaded disease for the remainder of her long life.

Another major event that year was the first sailing of the new passenger ferry service from Q Cove across the passage to Campbell River. The service was owned and operated by Bill Hall, and the vessel used was the Victory II. Bill had purchased her from Stone Brothers at Port Alberni and she was a wonderful little vessel, serving the island until 1958, when a larger vessel replaced her. This new ferry made it possible for high school students to attend school at Campbell River. Before that, high school students from Quadra had to take their lessons by correspondence or by living off island.

At around this time, P.E. Lewis and his sons were operating two water taxis, which soon went out of business with the arrival of the scheduled passenger ferry service. The two fast vessels Alberni and Dianne had provided excellent service by being able to pick up passengers at their place of residence and delivering them quickly over to Campbell River or other destinations. I recall my Great Aunt Sarah being very impressed with them as they delivered her to our dock from Campbell River for a fare of $1.25.

With progress comes change though, and these two faithful old passage crossers were replaced by the new ferry, which had a passenger fee of 10 cents. Further progress came in 1960 when the passenger service was in turn replaced by the Highways Department car ferry the Quadra Queen.

P.E. (Jack) Lewis, if I recall correctly, was born in Ludbury, England, in 1892 and came to Canada in 1931. As a young man he had served in the British Army during World War I. Dad used to drop by to see Jack when he was still at home, and they'd talk about their wartime service, always trying to outdo each other.

Jack and his wife had three sons, all of whom went on to successful careers. Jack and his family operated a store at Q Cove, with a government maintained dock out front. This remained in operation until well into the mid-1950s, when Jack retired to Campbell River to carry on with his duties as magistrate at the local courthouse.

One of the main features of the store was the perpetual crib game that seemed to always be in progress. Men would drop by to challenge Jack as he started shuffling the cards. The games were a constant source of entertainment, with many onlookers present, and when customers needed something from the store, they were on their own to do a little self serve if a game was in progress. Jack would reluctantly leave the game for a moment to tote up a customer's bill, but even this seemed to be more a tiresome intrusion and interruption, more an annoyance to the players than a welcome bit of business.

After Homewood's summer camp was over, the Howells arrived, so the fun started all over again. Those summers of camping, fishing and being a kid were for sure the best of times. Ruth was always home at that time, and she added her wild imagination to our activities. All too soon September rolled around again though, and with the Mitchells returning home and the Howells gone for another year, this was the year Mum and the Mitchells decided I was old enough that I needed to leave home and start school.

I began in Grade 4 and started off sadly one morning to walk the two miles or so to catch the bus for my very first day of real school. It didn't turn out so badly, as I met up with Hugh, Neil and Percy at about the half way mark. Percy Beech and his family had moved from their property at the north end of the harbour to a five acre lot next to the Watson's. His father Rusty had built a small house there and settled in with Pat and their younger son Wayne. The move was made so Percy could start attending school in Grade 1 and didn't have so far to walk to catch the bus. The schools at that time were still spread out all over the Island. Hugh attended school at Heriot Bay, while Percy went to Q Cove, and Neil and I went down to Cape Mudge.

The 'school bus' was a 1946 Ford that was about half the size of a regular school bus. It did the job just fine and put on a lot of miles because of the way the schools were spread out. The roads were all gravel at that time, and very rough on the poor bus and its passengers, but it was certainly better than having to walk all the way, as my older brothers had. The bus was nicknamed 'The Peanut' for some reason, and it was owned and operated by John Blenkin, who for many years transported the Quadra Island kids safely to and from school with great care and attention. John was married to Marie Law, who was from a pioneer family who lived over at Hyacinth Bay. They had two daughters. Most tragically, in the late 1950s the entire family was wiped out in an auto accident while on summer vacation in Alberta. This was a tremendous shock to the community and later, in respect for the family, the island's main ballpark was named Blenkin Park in their memory.

I faced up to my first day of school with a certain amount of fear, and it was very much a memorable event in my young life. I had to get up early in the morning and hit the trail by no later than seven o'clock to meet the bus at the road an hour later. We picked up kids all along the way and dropped Percy and others at Q Cove. Our new teacher, Miss Sampson, also joined us along the way, and then it was on to the Cape Mudge School, adding more students all along the route. When we passed the Marcoux place, we all hung out the windows and called to Dolly the horse. She immediately recognized our voices and quickly came trotting up to the fence, chasing along after us as far as the fence would allow.

At the top of the long hill we picked up the Noble family kids, then the Richards, Alan Gray, then a huge load from Cape Mudge Village. At last we arrived at the little one room school, which housed Grades 3 and 4. We got there about 8:30 a.m., and I noticed there was already a soccer game under way in the gravel schoolyard. I only knew about half of the participants, but quickly joined the game, even though I had never played before. The girls all disappeared into the schoolhouse with Miss Sampson, and this was to be the start of a divided world; Miss Samson and the girls on one side and all the boys on the other.

Just as I was starting to get the hang of the game, two of the girls appeared on the porch, ringing a large bell. Neil told me this meant we all had to go in and get to work. I ditched my lunch bag under the steps and was the last one to enter this very scary place, with a definite feeling of doom and that this was going to be the end of any further fun for the rest of my life. It was with great sadness, fear and anxiety that I slipped into the last empty desk on the Grade 4 side of the room.

The school had about 20 kids in total and was very small and crowded. There was a small room at the back to store our coats and lunch, and there was an oil heater at the back of the classroom, but I eventually found that it was only used a few times over the winter. Danny Joyce, who lived close by, would start it up on his way to school over at Heriot Bay.

This was Miss Sampson's first assignment as a teacher and I think she was probably in her early 20's. Looking back, I can see her as a very pretty, tall blonde young woman. All the girls absolutely adored her. On the other side, we boys thought she was just an old bag and mostly treated her with subdued respect when we weren't being outright mean to her.

One thing that's 'missing' in the schools of today that I think in some ways we were fortunate to experience, was that at the old one room schools we only had 'outdoor plumbing'. At Cape Mudge we were located at least a mile from any other homes, so we were pretty much on our own, so to speak, when it came to safety and security. There was also no electricity, no telephone, no plumbing for water, or anything. During the winter, there was a gas lantern that we would light up on dark days. Water for whatever purposes came from a well and had to be drawn in a bucket attached to a rope. Toilets were two out houses located at the far end of the playground. The playground itself, which was made of gravel, had two proper goal posts at the south end and just two trees for posts at the other end.

Recess came and went and I discovered the lunch hour was a whole hour, so I rescued my lunch from under the steps for a bite to eat. Another new game for me was softball, with Miss Sampson insisting that the girls participate. That woman sure was a drag at times! After lunch, we were issued our school supplies. These consisted of an exercise book for each subject, a dipping pen with replaceable nibs, a bottle of ink, a pencil, an eraser, and a jar of white paste. We knew that the paste meant artwork or some other female nonsense, so we promptly ate the paste when teacher wasn't looking. On especially tedious days, some of us also tried drinking the ink to avoid doing our work, but this didn't work out too well as there was some difficulty in getting all the guys to participate. Such a bold venture was just too much for some of them. Over time school settled into a routine of early mornings, warm pleasant days, and then home again in time to start work on the farm. The chickens still had to be fed and the eggs collected.

One time, during our usual lunchtime soccer game, I accidentally kicked Neil in the leg. It truly was an accident, but he fell to the ground in great pain and some of the girls immediately rushed indoors to tell Miss Sampson. The result was that I had to memorize 'the Golden Rule' and write out 100 times: "I must not play roughly". I worked on those lines all weekend, which made Mum pleased I was so dedicated to my schoolwork!

One morning Miss Sampson announced we were going to have a soccer match the next week between our school and the one down the road at the village. So on the appointed morning we marched off on the two mile hike down to the other school. We were all a bit tired by the time we arrived, and so didn't do too well in the game. Albert Wilson was the referee and of course we blamed it all on him for showing favouritism towards the smaller school. Naturally this wasn't really the case, and looking back, I know he did a great job of trying to keep order among us rough and ready, unruly kids.

That was the first time I met Albert, and we were to become good friends during the ensuing years. I remember having a coffee with him nearly 30 years after that game. I asked him if he remembered the first time we had met.

"Well, I think I've known you all your life," he said. "I don't remember the first time I ever met you."

So I told him about that first time I had met him, when he was refereeing that soccer game long ago.

"Ah, yes," he said, "I remember you kids lost 2-0". Imagine him remembering the score after all that time! But that was the way Albert was.

September finally became October, with shorter days, and

I had to leave home under a darker sky. The trail from our place out to where the road started was about three quarters of a mile, and it was grown over by trees, which made it even darker; and it was just dripping wet when it rained. I was always on the lookout for cougars as they were plentiful at certain times in those days. Sometimes I took the other trail, which passed through the Walsh, McNally and Mitchell places. It was a little longer, but it gave me an extra sense of security as I walked by those other houses.

During the seven years I walked that trail, I never did once see a cougar. I had a lively imagination though and seemed to spend more time looking back behind me than looking ahead. On several occasions I recognized fresh tracks in the snow. The big cats were always a particular fear, especially in winter when I left home and returned in the dark.

With winter now approaching, a supply of wood needed to be cut and hauled to the house. We never seemed to have enough to be quite secure, and this year we set out to rectify this problem. Several large fir logs had been tied up on the beach during the summer. Mr. Sylvester, who was the founder of B.C. Airlines, arrived with his new Wasp power saw, cutting the logs into blocks with his noisy monster. This was obviously better than having to use Mum's old hand cross cut saw.

After the blocks had been cut, they needed to be split into smaller pieces and hauled home. This was where W.A. and I came into the picture. I would split the blocks with a sledgehammer and a wedge, while he used the axe to split the blocks into smaller pieces. Then we'd load it all on a wheelbarrow, with W.A. pushing and me in a harness pulling on the front; where was Dolly the horse when she was needed? Our arrangement worked quite well though, and every day after school we'd set to work. Each trip was a long pull uphill, but within a few weeks we had a sizable stack of wood stored under the house. It seemed that wood gathering never stopped though. When there was snow on the ground, we'd still get wood from above the house using a big sled to haul the wood home. This was much easier in some ways, as most of the way was downhill.

A wood burning stove in the kitchen and a heater in the living room provided the heat for the house. The heater consumed wood at a great rate, and it took most of the day just to get the house warm. Then, just about the time we were starting to warm up, it was time to go to bed. We'd all go off to our bedrooms, each with a small oil lamp for light, and crawl under the blankets, into a cold bed. If there's one outstanding memory of that old un-insulated wooden house, it was freezing in winter and boiling in summer. The water had to be kept running in cold weather otherwise the place would freeze up solid. We'd bank up the heater before bedtime, but it was always cold as ice by the time we got up early in the morning to get ready for school.

The winter of 1949-50 was frigidly cold even by our standards, and long. W.A. decided we should raise rabbits instead of cattle, as they would be easier to feed. So our barn, which was located up hill some distance from the house, was converted into a rabbit colony. We built cages for the rabbits, and they shared the barn with Queenie the cow. All winter long we'd pack hay and rabbit food up on the sled from the beach to the barn. This was a distance of about a quarter mile, all strenuously up a steep hill. Sometimes if the weather permitted, we'd haul hay up and wood down. Mum and W.A. did most of this part, as it was dark when I got home from school, but on weekends when I was able to take Mum's place, we'd work overtime to keep the animals fed and the wood hauled. The chickens were housed in a barn at Howells' place. This was about a quarter of a mile in the other direction, but at least hauling their feed was easier, as a 100 lb sack of wheat would last a month or more.

Brother Bill, Sheila and little Kathy spent some time with us that winter, as their little house down by the mill was frozen solid. I recall Mum had to spend a lot of time that winter trying to keep the water running, especially where there was an exposed section of pipe for about 50 feet, from where it left the well. Often we had to heat the pipe with a blowtorch to melt the ice and get the water flowing again. We had a thermometer on the back porch and one bone chilling morning it registered minus 20 Fahrenheit.

It was so cold that winter that W.A. said it reminded him of being on the Prairies; and I had a difficult time getting to school through the snow. We made a kind of combination ski and snow shoe from some high quality plywood left over from building the sled. We attached an old pair of large rubber boots to them that my regular boots would fit inside. This all worked very well, with me using the devices as skis down hill and snowshoes going uphill and on the level. We waxed the bottom so the snow wouldn't stick, and they even had a small keel to keep them from sliding sideways. I could move very quickly on them, and I doubt any cougar would have been able to catch me in the deep snow.

The only time we seemed to be warm that winter was on the school bus. The oil heater at school was always giving trouble and provided very little heat for the classroom.

One of the main activities that winter was practising for the Christmas concert that was to be held at the Community Hall behind the Yeatman's place. The night of the concert we decided that we would take the boat to the Yeatmans' and hike up the hill to the hall. We started off in the Mitchell's boat, with Mum and W.A. at the steering station in the stern and me, perched up in the front seat. It was a beautiful cold winter's night, with a big moon shining overhead, and the water was flat calm as we headed south past the log booms moored to Gowlland Island on our starboard side.

As we approached the south end of the harbour, I could see something white ahead. Suddenly we came to a crunching stop. The entire south end of the harbour was frozen over and we couldn't go any further. We had no choice but to push off with an oar and head back home. What a disappointment, but that was all part of living at 'the far end of civilization'.

Winter stayed on a long time that year and some of us didn't return to school until almost the end of February. Joe Clooten had a D-8 Caterpillar which he used to plough the roads during January, but as one section was ploughed out, another snowstorm would come in and fill it up again. The snow was piled so deep beside the road that the school bus could just barely be seen. Finally though, a series of south east storms blew in with rain and milder temperatures and came to our rescue, and the snow finally started to melt.

One Saturday, Neil and I set out with his dog Nipper to hike to Heriot Bay to see if we could send out the Christmas mail. By then it was already mid-February and the snow was starting to get mushy and wet. It was hard going, but we made it to the store and arranged with Bill Arnott to get the mail out on the next steamer. To sustain us for the journey home, we bought a package of cinnamon buns for 15 cents, which we shared with Nipper for his work. Everyone bought large stocks and supplies such as sugar, flour, rolled oats, wheat, canned milk and other staples to stock their homes that winter, so with the home canned goods we were never in short supply of basic food.

Even in spite of the snow, I managed to get to Sunday school most weeks that winter, as Alf was still making the rounds with the Goforth after the sea ice melted. As the weather improved, I would take the rowboat or walk.

Spring was finally in the air and we were getting ready for Easter Sunday, when I recall an elderly lady went missing in the forest near Camp Homewood. She had gone for a walk on the Saturday afternoon and failed to return later in the day. We all skipped Sunday school that week and started combing the woods. At that time, the forest was extremely dense, thick with small fir trees and low brush, but in the end we did manage to locate her, with a group of us kids led by Leo Dahlnas heading our search. She was a little shaken and quite cold from the experience, but it was heart warming she survived her ordeal of being alone and cold, stranded in the icy, thick and dark forest overnight.

We were all hailed as heroes for carrying out the rescue under such conditions, but it was really nothing to us, as we'd all had lots of experience in the woods from an early age. We knew our direction from the sun and time of day, and sometimes in the dense trees, if the sun wasn't visible, we'd be able to find north from the moss on tree trunks or the prevailing wind direction. If all else failed, we'd move down hill and/or follow a creek to the ocean.

Our next project at school that year was preparing for the Quadra Island May Day celebrations. These took place on Queen Victoria's birthday, May 24, and students from Grades 1 to 4 were expected to dance around the Maypole to honour the May Queen. Miss Sampson took on the challenge of teaching us rowdy boys how to do this May pole dancing stuff, and I must say it was better than doing schoolwork. We'd all go outside every afternoon for several weeks to practise our skills. The girls learned much more quickly than the boys as we lads had other dreams of playing baseball, not dancing. So to try to encourage us and provide a bit of incentive, Miss Sampson finally turned it into a contest, challenging us to see if we could be better than the Grades 1 and 2 from the school at Q Cove.

The great day finally arrived and we started our routine in front of Jeanne Taylor, the May Queen. We did okay the first round, but some of us boys screwed up royally on the next dance, while the Grades 1 and 2 put us to shame with their flawless performance. Miss Sampson and the girls were very angry with us, but needless to say, we survived their displeasure, and ducked out as soon as we could to start a baseball game.

One day that June an inter school sports day was held at Campbell River with all the schools in School District 72 competing. We were taken by bus to Q Cove, where we boarded the fishing vessel B.C.P (B.C. Packers) 45 owned by Capt. Harry Assu. This vessel was to become well known in later years through being portrayed on the back of the Canadian $5 bill, the only picture to be used in two separate printings of the bill.

That reminds me of a little incident Harry told me some years ago, from the days before they tightened up all the security on the airlines. Harry and his wife were on a flight to Hawaii where their family had given them a vacation as an anniversary gift. A large number of relatives had been at Vancouver International Airport to say goodbye. The flight crew noted this large crowd as they walked through to board the aircraft, so half-way through the flight the pilot thought he'd go and check out who these people were that had attracted such a large send off. He sat down with them for a few minutes for a chat, and during their conversation Harry showed him a Canadian $5 bill with the picture his fishing boat the B.C.P45 on it.

When the pilot returned to the cockpit, he announced over the public address system the story of Harry and the picture of his boat on the banknote. Harry spent the last two hours of the flight into Honolulu signing $5 bills for the other passengers. This was something he and other members of the crew were later to do for many other people when the boat later became part of the B.C. maritime history display at Expo '86 in Vancouver, prior to being donated to the B.C. Maritime Museum and eventually being returned to Campbell River's new Maritime Heritage Centre.

That June schools sports day turned out to be a great success, and our little schools from Quadra did very well against the larger schools of Campbell River. The event was held near where the Campbell River First Nation cemetery and the new boat harbour are now located, on the shore just north of the downtown area. The Ferry family home was also located near the sports field at that time, and that day was my first meeting with John and Ruebina Ferry. They later became very good friends of mine during my school years at Campbell River High School (Carihi).

After an exhausting day of fun, it was back to the dock to board the famous B.C.P45 for the trip home to Q Cove, which turned out to be the best part of the whole day. Miss Sampson let some of us boys sit on the bridge above the pilothouse. I sat beside Harry Assu, and he let me steer his vessel most of the way home, which I recall clearly to this day. There was a strong ebb tide running and he showed me how to steer safely through the tide rips off Whiskey Point, at the entrance to Q Cove.

Not long after that, the Mitchells left again for their annual trip to Banff, after getting the crops planted. It turned very hot that June and the berry crop was starting to show signs of being a real winner. Rusty and Stan Beech were logging up behind the Watson's' place and just got their last logs to the shoreline before they had to close for fire season. Ruth, Mum and I picked berries and hauled them to market. The crop did indeed turn out to be a winner due to the warm weather, and we were able to sell them at 25 cents a box.

The last day of school finally arrived and Bill Navid came home with me so I could row him over to Beeches. His mother and father were away fishing and he was to stay with Ma Beech for a few days.

This June was a big turning point for me in my sea faring career. Mum had let me go out in the rowboat as long as I followed the shoreline to my destination, but now I wanted to go off fishing by myself, out by May Island and beyond. It took a lot of whining and wheedling and cajoling on my part, but she finally gave in as I knew she would, and agreed that I could go, as long as I kept to where she could see me from the house.

That first day out I caught two nice Coho salmon using a rod and Tom Mack spoon that belonged to my brother Jim. I found a rod much easier to handle than a hand line in the rowboat, and I was so excited that on my way in I called to Mum, who came running down to the float to meet me. She apparently thought I had got into some kind of trouble, never even thinking I'd be able to catch any salmon. What a surprise when I showed her the fish! Mum wanted to can them both for us, but instead I put out our white flag to tell the fish buyer to stop in next morning. I received 20 cents a pound for them, which in total was $1.50. I went on to earn over $200 that summer, so I guess I must have caught about 1,000 pounds of salmon by the end of the season in mid-September, not a bad haul for a young amateur fisherman.

Bill, Sheila and Kathy rented the Walshes' house and moved there that year. It was much larger and about half a mile south from us. The Walsh family only used the house for a few weeks every summer, so it worked out very well for both parties. It wasn't so convenient for me though, as I had to walk or row a longer distance to visit them. Bill was still working at the sawmill and had bought a new McCulloch chain saw. It was a very heavy machine, but Bill was very muscular and strong and was able to handle it fairly easily by himself.

A big surprise for me that summer was Dad coming home, for a while at least. Alf Bayne picked him up at Campbell River in his speedboat and delivered him to Quadra. I hadn't seen him for several years and we spent some time together. On one occasion we took one of the rowboats and went visiting, stopping in to see the Walkers, as Dad wanted to investigate Homewood and the Sunday school I was attending. He was about 70 years old by this time, and he and Mr. Walker, who was about 90, got into a very heated argument when Dad mentioned that Mr. Walker was starting to look old. We also visited the Moss family who lived on one of the islands in south Gowlland Harbour. We arrived home just before dark, with Dad and me taking turns on the misery sticks (oars). Dad stayed for a couple of weeks then, left again for parts unknown. He certainly was a rolling stone. This was the last time I ever saw him.

Another day in August, Bill invited the Howells to join us for a trip on the barge to Read Island, to visit Sheila's mother and brother, Ian. Mum and Ruth decided to stay home, but the rest of us all piled aboard in a mad scramble for our places of choice. Johnny and I liked to hang over the front of the barge and watch for fish, which Mrs. Howell didn't like at all as she feared we'd fall in and be run over and carved up by the propeller. Johnny pointed out to her though that only our heads hung over, which weighed maybe about 10 pounds each, and our bodies weighed much more, which would prevent us from going overboard. Mr. Howell could see the logic in this, but still tied a rope on us just in case our heads suddenly somehow became heavier than our bodies and pulled us over the side.

As we were passing Steep Island, we met the fish packer Pine Leaf headed north. As the barge crossed the wake of the other vessel, Johnny and I received a thorough drenching from the swells when they came over the bow of the barge. Everyone got a big laugh out of this of course, as we had insisted on staying where we were, and it resulted in no more hanging over the front of the barge.

Mr. Howell brought along one of his boats on deck with some fishing gear. We set out a rod in a holder on his boat to see if we could catch a salmon. The barge was moving a little fast for really good fishing, but we were hopeful of catching our dinner. The flood tide carried us out past Cape Mudge, and suddenly we got a good strike on the fishing rod as we approached Viner Point. It was now near sundown, so we slowed down and circled back along the shoreline. We caught two very nice salmon, one of which we had for dinner. The other we kept for Mrs. McKay.

When we arrived, we anchored offshore from the Lamberts' place and spent a peaceful summer night on the barge. At daybreak we launched the small boat and all went ashore, to hike about half a mile up a steep trail to Mrs. McKay's house. We arrived just as she and Ian were getting up. They were surprised to have visitors so early in the morning, but set to with a will and cheerfully bustled about, fixing us all a good breakfast.

We spent the morning cutting wood and doing some repair work for them in return. In the afternoon, we hiked in to Rosen Lake, where we all went for a swim. After another night on the barge, we set off early the next morning for home. We had had beautiful sunny weather with calm seas, and it was a trip to remember.

June of that year brought the start of the Korean War, which of course was of great concern to the adults, as the last war was still fresh in their memories. To us boys it was great excitement as we followed the exploits of the new jet fighter planes as they took on the Russian Mig 15's. The U.S.'s General Douglas McArthur was our great hero, with his brilliant amphibian landing at Inchon.

Lots of boys used to love war stories and enact our own 'adventures' in those days, until we were old enough to look at things rationally. It was about this time that Neil suggested we be 'ground observer'. It was our duty to identify and document every aircraft that flew close enough for us to get a good look at.

It was great fun at first, but we soon found it grew monotonous and quickly gave it up for more interesting pursuits.

I attended the boys' camp at Homewood again that summer, and won the award as the 'best all around camper'. This was quite an accomplishment as I wasn't yet 10, and was competing with much older boys. The camp at Homewood had some new buildings, a log cabin and tents for sleeping quarters, and a finished cookhouse, no more sleeping on the hay in the barn, which still brings back some of my fondest memories. John Wilkinson had moved to Quadra that summer from Vancouver and attended boys' camp. We became close friends and had many adventures together over the next few years.

Summers always end too soon, even now. There were the Howells, gone again on Labour Day as usual, and this was the last time I was to see Johnny Howell. I remember helping him load up one of their boats with boxes to take home with them. I pushed him off from the beach, as their dock had been put away for safekeeping for yet another winter.

With farewells and best wishes until the following year, he was on his way to Campbell River with his friend Jack, who had been visiting for a couple of weeks. Johnny never returned, as he was employed by the Boeing aircraft company the next few summers and started a lifetime of working.

And, suddenly, it was back to school for me. September of 1950 saw the end of one room schools scattered all over the south island. We had a brand new four room school located at Q Cove, complete with gym, electric light from a generator, and central heating. This new school took students up to the end of Grade 8. From Grade 9 on, the students rode the ferry each morning across to Campbell River for high school. We also had a new and larger school bus, which was able to service the south island more easily than old 'Peanut'.

My teacher for Grade 5 that year was Mrs. Kay Noble, who had a great influence in my life, due to her dedicated approach to teaching. Mrs. Noble was the wife of Bruce Noble who, with his brother Harold, was a major landowner on Quadra. They logged and subdivided large tracks of land, and many of the present residents of Quadra now live on property that they developed. Mrs. Noble was very strict as to our studies and behaviour in class, maintaining discipline and order with a firm hand and in the process earning the respect of us wild bunch of boys. To this day I have fond memories of her persistence in teaching us 'proper' English. I would have to say that along with Mum and Margaret Bayne, Mrs. Noble was a woman of great influence in my early life.

The new school was a great source of excitement for us. The gymnasium didn't have basketball hoops for the first few months, but this didn't in any way stop us from playing basketball. We just threw the ball through the center rafter until the new hoops arrived just after Christmas.

The playing field also quickly became a sea of mud, as no turf had been installed yet. We solved this problem by instead using the front lawn, which fortunately had been planted in grass. The front of the school had large glass windows, which we immediately set out to do away with by trying to kick the soccer ball straight through them. Fortunately for the school, and us, it proved more difficult than we thought. We couldn't believe how strong these windows were. They'd bend under the impact, but stubbornly refused to break. No matter how hard we tried, we couldn't get those nice new windows to break with a soccer ball. So eventually we gave up.

About the middle of September was the official, grand opening of the school. Mr. Herbison was our principal and he had us rehearsing all our parts for the great ceremony. Many dignitaries and previous island students were invited, and a large crowd of residents attended. Thor Peterson raised the flag at the appointed time as we all sang 'God Save the King'. I recall Chief Billy Assu, from the Cape Mudge Indian Band, attended the ceremonies in colourful traditional dress. He spoke to us about his youth and the history of his people which had been passed down verbally from one generation to the next. He also related some great stories as told to him by his grandfather, who lived in the area before the first European settlement of this coast. Chief Billy was the father of Harry Assu, who became a firm life long friend of mine, and the skipper of the B.C.P45

For the first time in recent memory, all the students below Grade 9, except for residents of Granite Bay, were now attending school in the same building. This made for new friends and getting to know kids that we'd only known casually before then. As September turned to October, the older boys from Cape Mudge First Nations village came home from fishing with their fathers and joined the rest of us at school. The village's kids fished with their fathers almost from birth, and there was a large fleet of seine boats from there that regularly worked Johnstone Straits from Sunday at 6 p.m. to Thursday each week, from early June until season's end. The vessels were usually owned and then leased out to the operators by one of the major fishing companies. The companies depended on the long established fishing skills of the Cape Mudge men to operate some of these vessels. If your father was a skipper on one of these boats, you had a guaranteed summer job, like it or not.

The autumn produced a very good run of late Coho salmon near our home at Gowlland Harbour that year. Each day after school I'd head out in the rowboat to try my best to catch some. The only other boat fishing the sand bar at the mouth of the harbour at that time was Mr. Devlin from Duncan Bay, on the Vancouver Island side of the channel. The Devlin family lived in a small cottage at the head of a dock to the west of where the new Campbell River pulp and paper mill was being constructed. Youngsters Brian and Judy usually fished with their father, who was a fierce looking man with a long black beard. Judy, I recall, had the most beautiful long blond hair, and we always stared at each other as our boats passed. But I only got to meet Brian and Judy some years later when I started attending school in Campbell River.

The fishing was really good long into the autumn season in 1950. Word soon got around about our success, and many more boats arrived to help us out. One of the boats that anchored for a few days was the yacht Taconite, owned by Mr. Bill Boeing of the Boeing Aircraft Company. Mrs. Boeing would call to me as I was on my way home, to offer me a treat and find out how many fish I had caught. The days all too soon grew short again, and the salmon moved on to complete their life cycle by spawning in the local streams.

That summer was the last season that Jack Beech and his wife fished. Jack turned 70 that year and so was eligible for the old age pension of $60 per month, which was a steady enough income to convince Jack that a lifetime of hard labour was over and he could now enjoy a more relaxed way of living.

Granny Mitchell passed away at a very old age and their place was bought by Stan Beech. Eventually the Mitchell boys drifted away and settled in Loughborough Inlet along with some other old bachelors. They became known as 'the Loughborough Cowboys' to some, and The Old Goats to others, and operated a very remarkable liquor still that produced many gallons of fine firewater over the years, hidden away up one of B.C.'s many remote inlets.

This was also the last season that B.C. Packers operated a fish collecting vessel in the area. In future years we had to deliver our own catch to their plant at Q Cove. Many changes took place during 1950, and I consider that year as the end of 'the old ways' and the start of a new and changing way of life for everyone on Quadra. Regular ferry service, people clearing a right of way for electricity wires, a new school, improved roads, many new residents, and seaplane service were just a few of the myriad of changes taking place. Even fishing and logging were changing.

Extensive logging camps serviced by railroads were giving way to truck logging, with diesel engines replacing steam as a source of power. Power saws replaced the hand powered variety for falling and bucking timber. Early experimentation with powered drums for winding nets on to and off from boats was meeting with some success for the purse seine boats, while most gill netters and trollers were now landing their catch by mechanical means. Tugboats were converting from coal burning for steam power, to more modern types of propulsion. Our lives always revolved around the sea, though, for transportation, for employment and for just plain having fun. When a tragedy occurred on the ocean, it was always a great source of pain and concern to everyone.

One such tragedy which occurred was the loss of the steam tug Petrel off Cape Mudge just two days after Christmas in 1952. The vessel had left Vancouver with Captain Donald Horie in command and had steamed up through Sabine Channel. She then started across to Cape Mudge during the dark hours of a winter night, with a strong southeast gale howling up Georgia Strait. The Petrel was 86 feet in length, built sturdily of steel, and with a very low freeboard, which was typical of tugs of her vintage. Although the Petrel was never seen again and has never been located for sure, it's assumed it succumbed to a heavy tide- rip that occurs in those conditions off Wilby Shoal, just south of Cape Mudge.

The next day, Captain Mickey Ballati on the tug Nanaimo Chief located an oil slick boiling up about a mile south east of Mudge. Captain Ballati wasn't aware at the time that the Petrel was missing. He sounded the area though and found an echo that looked like the outline of a medium sized vessel. Wreckage was later discovered along the Quadra shoreline, but no other sign of the vessel or her seven man crew was ever seen again.

The tidal currents that pass southward through Discovery Passage and out past Cape Mudge into northern Georgia Strait can reach speeds of 16 knots on occasion, and 10 knots is pretty much an everyday occurrence. When this southerly bound tidal stream meets the heavy seas generated and pushed up against it by a strong wind out of the southeast, an extremely serious and dangerous condition occurs. The seas heave up in the strong contradictory current, and wave heights can reach from 20 to 30 feet. The real danger is not so much from the height of waves alone, but more from the extremely short distance between them. Vessels up to 100 feet in length can be swamped or rolled over by this very dangerous situation. It was felt that Petrel, with her high bulwarks and low freeboard, was unable to shed fast enough the water that came pouring aboard, and the sheer weight of the water on the deck is believed to have forced her under.

Many vessels have met a similar fate over the years, and I have been personally involved in a number of rescues of ships and crew caught in this dangerous maelstrom of water. There are a few other places in the world where the same violent conditions can occur to such a degree as at Cape Mudge, and experienced mariners know better than to challenge Cape Mudge when a flood tide and southeast flow occurs.

That winter passed with almost no snow and very wet and mild conditions, what a change from the previous year! School went well and our new gym was enjoyed by all as, with its help, we could continue with various sports all winter long. The long walk to catch the school bus each day was overcome by our getting not just older but also stronger. Neil and Hugh both had bikes and I would wait for them and for Percy each morning at the end of the road leading to their place. From there Neil would double me on his bike and Hugh would double Percy on his. Sitting astride his bike, Neil and I would attain great speeds down the steep hills, easily outpacing the other pair, as our combined weight exceeded that of our competition's. Hugh's bike just wasn't as fast as ours anyway! Racing downhill by bike usually means pushing up the other side though. It was all great fun, and to us was much better than walking all the way, as we'd had to do when the weather was bad.

The summer of 1951 melded into another marathon of fishing from early morning until dark, and the extra income was much appreciated by Mum and the Mitchells, as by then we were certainly no longer getting any help from Dad. During the fall of 1951 Great Aunt Sarah came to our rescue. She suggested Mum and I go down to California to spend the winter with her. This meant leaving school in late October. We'd have to take the bus to Nanaimo, Canadian Pacific Railroad ferry to Vancouver, then train to Oakland. Taking the bus to Nanaimo and the ferry there was a new experience for us, as we'd always taken a steamer when travelling to Vancouver.

Before we left, Bill came to pick us up by boat to take us

to Deepwater Bay, where he was living and working north of us on Quadra. We stayed for a week or more there and celebrated my 11th birthday with them on October 9, followed by Mum's 49th the next day.

One of the many highlights of this trip was driving from Deepwater Bay to Granite Bay to get the mail. We took an old truck from the logging camp and ground our way slowly up the steep hills to connect with the main logging road to Granite Bay. Mum, Bill, Sheila and Kathy rode in front. The family dog and I rode outside on the back deck. What a trip! Fortunately the road was in very good condition, as it was being used by the heavy logging trucks. It was general 'boat day' for delivery at Granite Bay, with people from all over the area arriving to meet the steamer, pick up their mail, buy supplies, or just sit and talk. Granite Bay, which is largely deserted now, was a sizable community at that time, with a logging camp, school, store and post office, and several residents who farmed up the valley.

When it came time to leave for home, Bill decided a nice birthday present for Mum would be to have the two of us fly home in a floatplane. You can imagine of course the strong objections that Mum quickly voiced to this, certain yet again that imminent disaster was about to befall her and her young son from this hare brained scheme. She was sure she and I were about to be smashed into a hillside or the water, and scattered in a thousand pieces over the landscape. Finally though, she was coaxed and pushed aboard a B.C. Airlines Seabee for the first, and only, flight of her entire life. Much to my surprise, once she was aboard and up in the air, she evidently enjoyed the short 10 minute flight very much, and talked about it enthusiastically for years afterwards.

Chapter 14

After a few days at home packing, Mr. Mitchell took us to Campbell River to start our journey to California. As we rode the bus through Nanaimo, it was interesting to see all the decorations to celebrate the visit of then Princess Elizabeth and Prince Philip the previous day. The class at school had travelled to Nanaimo to see the Princess, but I was unable to go with them because of our travel plans.

When we arrived in Vancouver aboard the newly built ferry Princess of Nanaimo, we also found that city all decked out with flags and other colourful ornamentation for the royal visit. The train ride from Vancouver was a great thrill for me. We made Seattle the first day, and then we boarded an overnight coach to Portland. From there we took the Shasta Daylight train for the balance of the trip to Oakland. The train from Portland south was a new and modern unit, which was very comfortable and fast. We arrived in Oakland late on Day Two after leaving Vancouver and were met at the station by Aunt Sarah and her oldest son Eddy, who had a beautiful dark blue 1950 Mercury sedan which he took great pride in keeping very well polished. He was manager of the Westinghouse Plant in San Jose and continued to live there for many years after his retirement.

Aunt Sarah's family had eight children, who were Mum's first cousins, so Sarah was my great aunt. And a great aunt she was to me in so many ways. Ed was the eldest of the offspring, followed by Florence, Alice, Rose, Philip, Dorothy, Bill and Richard, the youngest, who was about 20 years old at the time. He was in the army and was waiting to get shipped out to the Korean War. Bill was about 25 years old, still lived at home and drove a delivery truck for The San Francisco Chronicle newspaper. He got me a job selling papers each Saturday night on a corner in Berkeley in front of the Penny Saver Market, at Haste Street and Shattuck Avenue. Much to my surprise, in 1990 I took my daughter Karen to that corner to show her where I spent each Saturday night that winter, and found the market was still there and that everything looked pretty much the same as it had 40 years earlier.

The night we arrived at Aunt Sarah's I saw a television set for the first time. San Francisco had three stations at that time and I watched in fascination until they finally went off the air at midnight. The set had just been bought, a 20 inch, black and white of course. This was a large screen for that time, and we spent many hours watching Milton Berle, Groucho Marks, Red Skelton and the others. I can remember watching Joe Lewis's last fight when Rocky Marciano knocked him out. It was a live broadcast of course.

The joy of our arrival was soon over for me though, as Florence took me the next week to get enrolled at Washington School, so that I could continue with my Grade 6 studies. Washington School at that time was a village of temporary huts that were used while a new building was put up. I started in Mr. Swenson's class, where I lasted about a week. Mr. Swenson talked continually about airplanes, which for me and the other boys held a great fascination, but we didn't get much meaningful work done. The girls were all bored to death of course.

I was then transferred to Miss Dillon's class. She was an old lady of about 40 and was from somewhere in the Deep South. Each morning before classes, we'd stand and pledge allegiance to the flag of the United States, which hung at the front of the classroom. Of course we'd never done anything like that in the school back on Quadra Island, so it was quite a new experience for me.

Miss Dillon taught us to sing various Stephen Foster songs, many of which I can still remember all these many years later. She would also read to us each afternoon from the book called Little Britches. I used to really enjoy that and have read the book several times since. It was part of my inspiration to write this account of my own childhood.

During the first few weeks at the new school I made many new friends and, being a Canadian from the country, was something of a novelty among all these big city kids. As the new school was under construction, we didn't have a gym, and each classroom was a separate small building. Fortunately though, the weather was great compared to back home, so we played basketball, football and endless games of marbles outside.

In the evenings, the family would often go to Union High, a few blocks south on Grove Street, to play basketball. Angelo Marchi, who was about 15 at the time, was the oldest kid in the neighbourhood where we lived. He was our leader in all activities and turned out to be a great friend. He lived next door to us. His father and mother were old country Italian and they had a flourishing garden, and a few chickens, which seemed strange in such a big city. Mum spent a lot of time at their place because of her great love of gardening.

We kids also spent endless evenings playing touch football out on the street, followed by kick the can after it was too dark for football. I noticed all the girls joined in with us to compete in what were mostly boy's sports at the time.

On days when the weather wasn't good we'd play long games of Monopoly that sometimes lasted for several days. There was never any giving up. We all played to the death at everything.

Some nights Angelo and I would ride along with Bill as he made his rounds delivering newspapers to the various restaurants and stores in Oakland and Berkeley. This took until about 2 a.m. and we enjoyed staying out helping Bill with his deliveries.

Bill's older brother Philip showed up one day with a five ton truck full of oranges and wanted to know if we were interested in helping him sell them door to door. He said he'd give us 10 cents for each bucket full we sold, and he didn't have to ask twice. A bunch of us would pile on to the load of loose oranges, load up the buckets with the fruit and then peel off into the large housing project on Alameda Island to start knocking on doors. We sold them for 50 cents a bucket, and pretty soon we were all talking just like black people who were the main residents of this low cost housing. We really did well and in very little time had sold the whole load. We'd only go one day a week though, so as not to overload the market.

Aunt Sarah had only five grandchildren, my second cousins, at that time in spite of her large family of sons and daughters. Christine and Barbara were daughters of Jim and Rose. Jane was the only child Florence. Philip had a daughter Phyllis and a son. They were a little younger than me, but we saw a lot of them on weekends when they came home to visit Aunt Sarah. We especially had a great time at Christmas with all the family together at Aunt Sarah's large house. My sister Ruth came by train to spend the Christmas vacation with us and she was a big hit with everyone.

Bill had the most wonderful car. It was a 1948 Oldsmobile convertible, light brown in color. He'd take Angelo and me for rides along the quiet side streets, where Angelo would be allowed to practise driving. Bill would also often take us over the Bay Bridge to San Francisco to see the sights of this fascinating city.

When Ruth was visiting, we went one evening to Fisherman's Wharf. The area was still a real fishing port at that time and less of the tourist centre it is now, with fishermen selling their catch directly to the small stores where the public came to shop and buy fresh seafood.

As we strolled along, we came to a young man who had a tub full of live crab he was tossing into a pot and cooking. We watched for a few minutes, and every time some young ladies strolled by, he'd pick up one of the live crabs and chase them, and they'd run off screaming. This was too much for my sister, who could handle large crabs any time and had done so for years, and also cheeky boys as well. While he was busy on one of his chases, Ruth picked up a crab and was waiting for him when he returned. It was just like a Keystone Cops movie; Ruth chasing this poor guy and all the people watching and howling with laughter at his discomfiture. I'll never forget the look of surprise and terror on his face when Ruth chased him around the front of his store with the largest crab she could find.

Florence owned a hotel in Martinez, a small town east of Oakland on the upper San Francisco Bay. One fine autumn day Bill took Mum, Aunt Sarah and me for a drive and we stopped off to see Florence. As we walked towards her hotel, I can remember Bill reading the headlines on the newspaper stand outside. "CHURCHILL WINS". The man, who had so brilliantly led Britain through World War II but had then been kicked out, was once again Prime Minister of England.

Dorothy and her husband Elmer had a small cabin cruiser moored near Martinez, and one Saturday they took me out with them on the boat. It was a very dull and windy day and poor Dorothy wasn't having much fun, but Elmer and I both got a big kick out pounding at speed through the rough grey seas and waves in this speedy little cruiser. It was good to be back on the water again, and it gave me a certain yearning to be home.

On February 6, 1952 we saw the news on television that the King had died in his sleep. This meant that Princess Elizabeth, who had visited shortly before, was now the Queen, Queen Elizabeth II. Mum was much moved by this event, but it didn't mean a great deal to me at the time. The only changes I could see when we finally got home later that year was the new paper money which had the Queen on it , plus now we sang 'God Save the Queen' instead of 'God Save the King'.

Spring comes early to central California, and we were soon playing more baseball than any other sport at school. I bought a new glove with some of my earnings and was soon doing as well as my more experienced friends. Angelo had a bike which he seldom used, so I was able to learn to ride for the first time. I was still a little unused to the busy vehicle traffic in the city, but in time I was able to ride safely on the city streets. I did have one bad experience though, when I was almost run over by one of the electric trains that were in use at that time. It was my own fault really and was due to my inexperience with city life.

I also recall riding in the front seat of a train on my way to my paper corner one Saturday, when the train accidentally ran over a lady crossing the tracks. I felt very sorry for the engineer, who was in shock because he had been unable to stop in time to avoid hitting her. This really smartened me up, and I was much more careful with trains after these two incidents.

About 8 o'clock each Saturday night I'd leave my corner to take some papers to a hospital a few blocks away. Trustingly, I'd leave a cigar box so that they could put in their quarters for the weekend paper while I was visiting the hospital. Contrary to what one might expect today, this practice proved to be very successful and I was able to do good business as I went around to each bed to sell my papers. I always sold out, until one night I was caught by the shopkeeper who sold papers in the hospital lobby. He'd been wondering why his weekend sales had kept on dropping each week, and reported me to management. I was given the boot and told not to return, but the money was waiting for me in my cigar box when I returned to the corner.

At that time, the police in Berkeley used to use their own private vehicles as patrol cars. One cop used to visit me at least twice each night. He had a 1951 green Olds 88 with a big red light on top. We soon became pals, and it was many years later that Bill told me he'd asked him to keep an eye on me, as I was only 11 years old. I was quickly becoming quite street smart though, and when I had too much money on hand, I used to take it to one of the cashiers at the Penny Saver Market, to hold for me until Bill came by to take me home at about two o'clock in the morning.

I was earning $15 to $20 each weekend, which was very good money in those days. Regular wages were only about $100 per week at that time. I gave most of what I earned to Mum as usual, and she promised me I could buy a bike when we got home. I worked at anything I could to earn extra money, but the Saturday night newspaper was by far the best.

Chapter 15

April arrived all too quickly and it was time for us to head back north to Canada. Mum had put away almost $500, so we were able to buy our tickets with enough money left over for a brand new bike from Eaton's in Vancouver for me, as well as seeds and other supplies that would be needed at home.

We arrived in Campbell River in late April and rode home with Mr. Mitchell in his boat during yet another of the area's blinding rainstorms. It was good to be home though and to be back at school with my friends again. I had many stories to tell and Mrs. Noble gave me a big hug on my first day back. My shiny new bike arrived a few days later on the weekly boat and I soon had it assembled and was riding all the way to catch the school bus, no more walking and I could even leave about 15 minutes later and still get to the bus on time.

Baseball season was in full swing at home and everyone was surprised at how my game had improved. I had a good head start as we had been playing in California since February. School soon let out, and our friends the Mitchells stayed home that summer, rather than going to work as usual in Banff. Mum somehow managed to get a job cooking for the Ballentine family at their summer camp located on the outside of the Campbell River estuary. I went with her and we all lived in large tents, including the Ballentines.

This was my introduction to Tyee Club fishing. I had heard

about it before from my brother Jim when he was a guide at Painter's Lodge, but this was the real thing. As we still had some money left over from California and Mum had a job for a couple of months, I concentrated on catching a Tyee rather than fishing for money. Mr. Ballentine, who was to become legendary in the club over the years, gave me some of his old fishing line and someone else gave me a Gibbs #8 spoon. The Ballentines had three guides on hire all of August, one each for Mr. and Mrs. and one for a steady stream of guests and family members that came to stay. Les McDonald, who was also to become a legend in the club for his skill as a guide, rowed Mrs. B, while Joe Painter, brother of the founders of Painter's World Famous Lodge and also another name to conjure with among the club guides over the years, rowed Mr. B. Cam Crawford rowed the guests. Les showed me some of the technique used to catch these large fish, and I was on my way. Up every morning before dawn, then again during the day as tides were favourable then, out again after dinner until dark.

Tyee is another name for the large Chinook (or spring or King) salmon that inhabit the coastal waters of British Columbia. To qualify for being a Tyee they have to be 30 pounds or more and Campbell River has been a favoured location for sportsmen to catch these giants as they school in the very shallow water at the mouth of the river, waiting until the conditions are right for them to go up to spawn . These fish usually start to show up in August, and due to the shallow water and strong tidal currents it's possible to catch these fish on very light tackle. The Tyee Club of British Columbia was formed in 1924 by a group of avid sports fishermen and has been in existence ever since. The club requires that to qualify for membership the angler must catch a fish of at least 30 pounds and do it on line with a breaking strength tested at 20 pounds or less.

To become a member of this exclusive organization, a whole bunch of rules must be strictly adhered to. Tackle must be tested to make sure it meets club rules for lightness. No motors are allowed to be used during fishing and all fishing must be done by trolling (dragging a lure) from a boat or craft powered

- 114 -

only by human arms. Artificial lures with single hooks, and no longer any barbs, are required. But the main requirement is lots of patience. Some people catch one in a few minutes on one of their first tides, others take years.

One morning, at about 6 a.m., I finally got my first strike in an area known as the Potlatch Pool. I missed it because I had the tension on my reel set too light, but it gave me a great thrill to hear the line screaming off my reel for about five seconds or so, as the fish took its first big run to try to escape. No one believed me when I came ashore for some breakfast, but I knew that I had perfected my technique and it was only a matter of time before I would catch one. So after breakfast, I went back out to fish the last half of the flood tide. I rowed out to the south corner of the now well known sandbar, which is a favourite spot for the club rowers, and had another fish on within a few minutes. This one was well hooked. I pulled in my oars and settled down to business.

This fish took one very long run that took almost all the line off my reel, before it finally turned and ran towards the boat. With my old single-action reel I had considerable difficulty keeping up with this frisky fish and trying not to let any tension out of the line.

At last it broke water about 30 feet from the stern of the boat, its back coming out of the water with the dorsal fin sticking straight up. I couldn't believe how big it was. It actually scared me as I worked it closer and closer to the boat and I could see its huge size. There are few sights more breathtaking in this world than seeing a large salmon glistening in the sunlight just below the surface of the water. Each time I managed to get the fish close to the boat to try to land it, the fish would take another of its great long runs close to the surface, sending my reel screaming again.

Because of the still strong flood current, I had drifted about three miles south from where I had hooked the fish. This didn't cause me too much concern as I knew the tide would turn to ebb in about an hour and I could use its forces to help bring me home.

In the meantime, the struggle between small boy and giant fish went on for about another 45 minutes. Then a most remarkable thing happened. The fish jumped clear out of the water three times. This was to be its last bid for freedom, and sometimes I think back and wish that it had shaken the hook. But at that time I was determined not to give up, and very carefully played the fish until it was floating on its side, almost dead, at the stern of the boat. I didn't have a landing net to bring the fish aboard and it was doubtful if I could have lifted it anyway. However, I had a gaff hook aboard, which I slipped under the gills. To get the leverage on it, I stood on the back seat and heaved with all of my might, leaning back to apply my limited weight, which turned out to be about equal to that of the fish. Somehow the fish slipped over the stern and it and the gaff hook and I all landed in a pile at the bottom of the boat, with me underneath. I just lay there for a minute or so, and when I crawled out from under that fish, I was shaking so badly I had trouble rowing for the first few minutes.

My rowboat was only 10 feet long and the fish reached right across its width from one side to the other. I kept looking down at it and couldn't believe I'd done it. I felt like the central character in Hemingway's book The Old Man and the Sea, except that I had won my battle. The long row home went quickly and a large crowd gathered at the Tyee Club weigh-station to witness my unbelievable accomplishment. Bill sold the fish for me along with one that he had caught the same day to Canadian Fish at Q. Cove fo $20. I went on to catch more Tyees that summer, but that first one will live on in my memory for the rest of my life. A picture of it is now hanging on the wall of Painter's Fishing Resort in Campbell River.

September always comes too soon and after Labour Day the Ballentines returned to Vancouver, Mum and I back to Quadra. We had had a decent year financially, with the Mitchells looking after the income from our property and Mum working for July and August. In total we had about $1,000 put away. Mum noticed an ad in the local paper that Painter's Lodge was looking for kitchen help, so she phoned the resort and talked to Mr. McLean.

Thanks to a good reference from Mrs. Ballentine, Mum was hired and started work right away. This was her first steady job and at 50 years of age it took some getting used to. It was hot, difficult work, poorly paid but there was not too much choice for her at that time and Mr. and Mrs. Mclean were very good people to work for. The lodge was very busy all winter due to the new paper mill nearing completion at Duncan Bay. I stayed home with the Mitchells and started Grade 7. Mr. Baldry was our new principal and my teacher. I really liked him and it was good to have a male teacher for a change, Lots of boy talk and sports.

During September that year the new pulp and paper mill started operation, and Mrs. Mitchell suggested she would like to attend the official opening. Off we went by boat as far as Painter's and from there the three of us walked along the newly paved road to the mill site. We were taken on a tour of the mill, then to a reception held in one of the warehouses. Tom Hargraves was the first manager and, as was his way, he was a very gracious host, greeting everyone in person. After refreshments we walked back to Painter's, stopped to say "Hi" to Mum, then boarded the boat to go back to Gowlland Harbour. I can remember it being one of those rare quite autumnal evenings, with seine boats heading out for the week's fishing above Seymour Narrows and the shoreline drenched in autumn colors. Interestingly enough, when I first wrote this, I had just been invited and attended the 50th anniversary of the mill in May of 2002. Life certainly does go by quickly when one is having fun.

Bill and Sheila were living at Campbell River at the time, and during that summer their second daughter Susan was born. Some Fridays after school, I would catch the ferry to Campbell River and stay with Bill and family Friday and Saturday nights. We would pick up Mum from Painters when she was through work for the day and spend some time together. It was a good break from being by myself with the Mitchells. They were extremely kind people but so much older than I was and they weren't able to keep up with my expanding need for activity.

Mr. Baldry was a great guy and Grade 7 was probably the year of school that I liked best. It was a good combination of fun and learning. Mr. Baldry lived at Campbell River, which meant he had to commute to work on the ferry Victory II. This small vessel occasionally skipped sailings due to inclement weather conditions, which meant we had at least a part day with no teacher. One morning we went down to the dock at Q Cove, being sure the ferry would not run due to the strong winds and flood tide. As we were walking up towards the school, around the point appeared the Victory II with Capt. John Clerke at the helm and his only passenger, Mr. Baldry. It was to be the only run the ferry made that day, because of the violent winds. Mr. Baldry wasn't much of a sailor, but he had high praise for the abilities of Capt. John and the sturdy little ferry in battling the waves across Discovery Passage from Campbell River.

Even on Quadra Island, boys can find a way to cause trouble at Halloween and we were no exception. We were to have a costume party at school and Mrs. Watson made a horse costume for Neil and me. I was the head and Neil, due to his larger size, was the rear end. We tried it on at home and Mrs. Watson said we should win first prize for sure. One of the rules at Halloween was that we weren't allowed to have firecrackers anywhere near the school. That day, Neil and I decided to stay after school, rather than go all the way home and then have to come right back again for the party. This made a lot of sense since the horse costume was difficult to get into and we didn't want anyone to see who we were beforehand.

There seemed to be no one around so, to pass the time, we thought we would go out in front of the school and set off a few bombs. After a few extra loud explosions near the school, the front door burst open and out popped Mr. Baldry's head. Neil and I stood there quite dumbfounded with our hands in our pockets, trying to look innocent.

With a big grin on his face, he yelled, "Firecrackers, ah! Now you just stay right where you are. I'll be right back." We reckoned for sure he had gone to get the dreaded strap to give us our due punishment for disobeying orders, and we thought about hiding in the bush or just heading home. But then we would miss the party and get strapped the next day anyway.

We took the opportunity to discuss several other similarly weak options, and were just about to give in to our fate, when Mr. Baldry reappeared with a cigarette hanging out of his mouth and a couple of punks for us, so that we could set off our bombs more safely. Our appreciation of men in general and Mr. Baldry in particular increased dramatically in that moment, and we thanked our Creator that we weren't still students of Mrs. Noble or Miss Sampson who would have handled things very much differently.

Soon it was time to sneak into the boiler room and get into our horse costume. No one could figure out who was inside the horse and we both became very proficient at whinnying. Whenever someone tried to peek inside we would jump around and run away. We won first prize but we had to show ourselves to get our ribbons. This brought on great howls of laughter from everyone as Neil and I emerged from inside the horse. We'd had enough of this horse business, as it was very hot and uncomfortable.

After we had doffed the horse, there was a prize for the class with the most people in costumes. Our class lost because Neil and I had got undressed already and we couldn't convince the judges otherwise. Classmate Doris Lewis was quite angry with us for costing the class the prize and gave us both a good stiff lecture on how boys should behave at costume parties. It was a shock to both Neil and me that girls could be so bossy at such a tender age, but then Danny Billy showed up outside with a pocket full of large bombs, so we soon forgot our dressing down from Doris, by setting them all off before a teacher showed up to enforce the firecracker ban.

The next event on the school social calendar that year was a box social. This consisted of us all dressing up in our best clothes for an evening event at the school gym. The girls were to bring lunches in beautifully decorated boxes and we boys were expected to bid on them. We then got to sit with whichever girl's lunch we had bought as the highest bidder. John Wilkinson and I and a couple of the other more boisterous boys couldn't believe or ears! Who could possibly dream up a more obnoxious way to spend an evening when we could be doing something much more useful, like basketball or just wrestling outside in the mud?

The dreaded evening materialized before any of us brats could properly mobilize in opposition, so some of us decided we'd sneak into the gym after the boxes were set out on the tables, and when no one was looking we were going to do some switching to make the evening more interesting. Because of prior knowledge and some detective work, John and I knew Jill's mother was probably the best cook on the island. Why should we settle for less than the best that was available? We didn't care about social standing, what the box looked like, or who we had to sit with for dinner. The quality and quantity of the desserts was the most important issue.

We'd been tipped off by a family member that Jill and her mum had made fried chicken. So when we found what we were sure was her box, we switched the contents with the ugliest box we could find. In the process, we narrowly escaped being caught and had to hide, as Mr. Baldry had noticed us missing from the pre-party assembly in our classroom and came looking for us.

That crisis past, we were all lined up ready for the bidding to start. It was lively to be sure, with some of the more attractive boxes going for as high as two whole dollars. Jill's box was very pretty and quickly started to fetch an extremely high price, and John and I started to get cold feet, but we hung in there, as we knew the rewards would be worthwhile.

Finally the ugly box came up for bids and John started out at five cents and just so that the owner wouldn't be too embarrassed, I raised it to a dime. John looked at me as if I was giving away the farm, but I assured him I knew what I was doing. I was the winner of the ugly box for 10 cents, but John was forced to bid on another one, as the rule was at least one box for each boy.

Soon the auction was over and it was time to find out whom we were to sit with. Neither John nor I gave a fish's fin about our dates, as we were only out to get into the fried chicken and famous desserts. I won't say who the owner of the ugly box was to protect the innocent, and John soon ditched his 'date' in favour of sitting with me and the huge box of fried chicken. As you have probably figured out by now, there was one glaring flaw connected to our devious plan. We watched in fascination as Jill turned a very distinct shade of extremely deep red when she proudly opened her beautiful box to share with her dinner date.

John and I turned our backs, as we didn't want to be witness to anything quite so unpleasant while devouring the contents of the switched box. My dinner date had a very puzzled look on her face as we opened her ugly box and unexpectedly found huge helpings of fried chicken inside. She was about to say something to the authorities when John suggested it would be healthier for her if she just shut up and had a piece of chicken before we ate it all. Of course there were some questions as to why John abandoned his date in favour of sitting with me and the owner of the ugly box. Strangely, there wasn't much noise from Jill, as she tried to figure out how such a huge misunderstanding had all come about.

Some of the other box switchers didn't operate as smoothly as us though, and they got caught. This drew attention away from John and me and gave us some time to get busy with the task at hand, devouring the contents of the ugly box in short order and then stuffing our pockets with as much dessert as possible, before clearing out to the safety of the great outdoors. We laughed so hard we fell down in the mud and messed up our best clothes to the extent that we might as well have spent the evening wrestling.

This incident was just the first of many that resulted in a very cool and strained relationship between me and my group of friends and the girls we grew up with. It may be of some interest that much later in life when we finally found someone who would consent to marry us, they were usually ladies from far away places. The local girls, most of them having known us from birth, had seen more than enough of us to be certain we weren't ever going to be good or even acceptable husband material.

As usual, autumn gave way to winter, and at school we were having rehearsals for our annual Christmas pageant. I chose not to participate in this thespian ritual, as I'd had quite enough being Jack Be Nimble back in Grade 4. So instead of the Christmas concert, Mr. Baldry took all of us holdouts and taught us the Hokey Pokey. He could do the best Hokey Pokey I've ever seen, and even now just thinking about him and his crazy gyrations can make me burst out laughing.

By now my $49 bicycle from Eaton's had become my primary mode of transportation. The rowboat was much slower and was not nearly as convenient. But the bike was beginning to show signs of wear and tear already, as the rough country roads and trails took their toll and were much rougher on my trusty steed compared with the paved roads of Campbell River. Mum hadn't consented to my using her 14 foot Turner boat with its 2 h.p. Briggs and Stratton engine, so when I attended Sunday school at Homewood each Sunday, I found my bike much better than rowing all that distance, especially during the frigid winter months.

When the time finally came for our annual Christmas concert though, Mr. Mitchell wouldn't allow me to ride my bike at night. I stopped on my way home from school to see if Stan and Joan Beech were planning to attend. They said that they would be going by boat and that I was welcome to come along with them. Stan had purchased Cecil Mitchell's former Japanese owned fishing vessel named Peachland. It was a cod boat similar to Rusty's, about 30 feet long and powered by a four cylinder Ford Model A car engine. There were many similar boats in use at that time as they had been sold off by the Canadian government after being seized from their rightful Japanese Canadian owners at the outbreak of World War II.

There was still a government wharf in front of Stan's place at that time, so I hiked down over the trail to their place and we set off for Q Cove. We tied up at the B.C. Packer dock and walked the short distance up to the school.

The main part of the Christmas program consisted of all four classes putting on 'A Christmas Carol' by Charles Dickens. Malcolm Ferguson was Scrooge and brought the house down with his excellent acting. The whole play was a great success and although I felt a little left out by not being a part of it, I sure enjoyed being in the audience. Besides, I had learned to do the Hokey Pokey while the cast was busy rehearsing.

After the play Stan, Joan and I boarded Peachland for a wonderful moonlight cruise back to Gowlland Harbour, reviewing the enjoyable evening all the way home. From there I hiked home by moonlight over the trail, getting home about midnight. The Mitchells had apparently been a little worried about me being out after dark and hiking through the woods in the darkness, but to me it was a normal part of living in the wilderness.

Mum got some time off from her job for Christmas and came home for a few days. Our family was never big on the department store driven aspect of this holiday and concentrated more on its real meaning as an important time to remember our Christian faith. This was not always popular with me during my growing up years, but I can certainly see now that the whole thing has turned into a three ring commercial circus in which I don't usually participate.

That Christmas I went hunting for the very best tree that I could find. There were lots to choose from on our 100 plus acres of wooded property. I found a perfectly shaped balsam fir, very dark green and just the right size. Mr. Mitchell helped me build a stand and we set it up in the living room. Mum didn't fully approve, as I wouldn't today, but I decorated it with whatever I could find and it had a wonderful balsam smell that invaded the whole house. As we had no electricity, the tree was without lights. I tried to convince the adults that we should put some candles on the tree, but this not too brilliant idea was quickly and rightly shot down 'in flames' for good safety reasons.

Christmas Day was spent feasting and being thankful to our Creator for his wonderful gift of life and unfailing love. We tuned in the old radio to hear the Queen give her first annual Christmas message to the Commonwealth. For reasons that somewhat escape me today, this Royal Yuletide message by the monarch has always had special meaning to us, in the family. Perhaps it helped with the loneliness that people isolated from the world find especially strong at Christmas time. The previous Christmas we were in California and Mum tried to find the King's seasonal radio message, but it wasn't broadcast anywhere in that great independent republic. Of course it was the last that he gave.

Sunday school at Homewood will always be remembered by me as a time of learning and strengthening of our faith at Christmas. Margaret was unfailing in her dedication to us, and I think she took special interest in us boys because of our naturally wild and unpolished ways. We must have seemed hopeless to her at times, but I am truly thankful today for her steadfast and unwavering resolve to see her job done regardless of our protests and bad manners.

After Christmas came New Years and then it was back to school yet again. I spent New Year's Day 1953 listening to a couple of college football games I found on the weak radio signal from KGO Seattle. This brought back memories of the previous year when I had watched the Rose Bowl game on Aunt Sarah's television. After that game, every house on 61st Street emptied onto the street and we all replayed the whole game for hours afterwards, until darkness drove us home.

It's interesting to look back on 1952 now and see all the great changes that had taken place over the last year. Little did I know that this was only the beginning, and that the next three years would see my life change drastically.

Bill, Sheila and the two girls moved from Campbell River to Granite Bay on Quadra Island that spring. Bill had a job falling timber for Les Bestwick, who owned Coal Creek Logging, a sizable logging camp that employed about 20 men. There was no road from the southern end of Quadra to join up with the logging roads that ran from the north. So Comox Logging, owned by the Filberg family, started building road from the north end of Gowlland Harbour to reach their timber holdings of old growth fir located in the central part of the island. They constructed a log dump and booming ground at the head of the bay, which until recently ruined our swimming beach and crab catching location. Their road came to within about a mile from joining up with the logging road running south from Granite Bay. But until these roads joined up in 1955, one had to walk through a trail to get from Granite Bay to the southern part of the island.

Meanwhile, my oldest brother Jim had graduated from the University of Toronto and was offered a post with the University of California at Berkeley. He was going to be home by the end of April for the entire summer before taking up his new post and intended to go guiding at Painter's Lodge again. This was great news for me, as I was still living with the Mitchells mostly by myself. With Bill and family at Granite Bay, Ruth in Victoria and Mum working, life at home was a little dull to say the least. Nice and kind people though they were and they greatly cared about me, they were, after all, approaching 70 years of age. While Mr. Mitchell taught me a lot of things that were to be very useful in the future, I missed my family and was looking forward to Jim being home for the summer.

Spring that year was in full bloom on Quadra with the usual May Day celebrations that were the highlight of our island social calendar. Baseball, track and field and other sports took up much of our time. My trusty bike certainly got great use and opened up new friendships farther from home. Heriot Bay was now less than an hour's ride from home. David Lund and Leo Dahlnes became close companions. We would sit and talk for hours about our ambitions and dreams. They most always included getting away from Quadra some day to find our place in 'the real world', but that wasn't until much later. This ambitious adventurousness was amply fuelled by my stories of California and travels to the east. Little did we know at the time just how well off we really were right there in rural Quadra.

David had been as far away as Courtenay, but Leo had seldom even left the island. I remember him standing beside me on the dock at Campbell River one day after having met him getting off the ferry. A white van drove by and Leo pointed and shouted out with surprise. What in hell is that? Apparently, he had never seen a van before and thought it must be a large home freezer that someone had motorized and put wheels under. We all laughed at him with our superior knowledge of worldly things, but it showed just how isolated we were from the outside world.

Jim finally arrived home in May at just about the same time the Mitchells left for Banff. They had put in the garden for the year and the strawberries were in bloom. They hadn't gone to Banff the previous summer but this time, under persuasion from their employer, they agreed to go back again in 1953. It was still too early for Jim to start guiding at Painter's, so we took Mum's boat and started fishing. Jim needed all the extra money he could get so he could get moved to California by mid-September.

With the Mitchells gone and Jim and I alone at the Quadra home, Mum expected us to look after the place and make sure the garden was properly tended and the strawberry plants kept free of weeds. Jim disliked this kind of work almost as much as I did, so we just fished as much as we could and left the garden to chance. I have to say in our defence, we did do some work, but we weren't about to put in any full days in the garden when there were lots of blue backs to catch and money to be made. I was still in school until the end of June, so my fishing time with Jim was limited. In between, we tried our best to look after things at home and set out little rewards for ourselves for projects completed.

One weekend we worked on next winter's wood supply and decided that our reward would be a trip in Jim's green 1949 Austin up to Kelsey Bay, some 80 kms up the coast past Seymour Narrows. Neither one of us had ever been there, so we thought it would be an interesting trip for us. We set out early one morning in Mum's boat for Painter's, where Jim had left his car. After we passed the mill at Duncan Bay, the pavement ended and from there on the next 50 miles was nothing but mud and potholes, potholes and mud. We managed to get as far as Menzies Bay before we gave up. That poor little Austin just couldn't handle that kind of rough treatment. So we turned back to what we knew best for the remainder of the day, fishing.

With Mum gone of course we cooked for ourselves, as one of the first things an up coast boy learns is how to look after himself in all aspects. Some of our meal creations were quite interesting, to use a euphemism. Jim had a Master's Degree in engineering, and along with this achievement he had also naturally acquired an inquisitive and inventive mind. This carried over into our cooking and he always had some bright idea of how to do things differently from the norm. I was always a willing participant in these experiments, but in my case it was just pure laziness when it came to housework and cooking

Jim's wife Rosemary, along with their two children Heather and Michael, had stayed in Victoria for a visit with her parents, Mr. and Mrs. Darville. Soon they arrived at about the same time Jim was called to start guiding at Painter's, so they took up residence in one of the small beach front cabins at the Tyee Fishing Camp. We stayed there for a few weeks and Mum would walk down to be with us each day when she was finished work.

Michael was about two years old at the time and what a handful he was! Rose had to tie him up with a rope to prevent him from running into the ocean when nobody was keeping a close watch on him. One of my duties was to baby sit him on the beach each day while Rose tended to household duties. One day as I was watching him, he started chewing on the braided cotton line that Rose had secured him with. I watched with fascination as he patiently chewed away with his sharp little teeth.

Finally he parted the line and ran towards the ocean, with me in hot pursuit. He was still running after his head was well under water with bubbles pouring out of his mouth. I managed to grab him and pull him blubbering from the water. I set him down on the beach and had called out to Rose for help when he took off for the water once again, laughing and squealing with delight at this new found way of having fun.

It was about this time that I met Doug Thornton and his family. Doug and Dorothy had two daughters, Pat and Barbara. Doug was building boats and was head guide at the Dolphins Resort. He wanted me do some guiding as well, but it was decided by others that I was still too young. I certainly didn't think so, as I was almost 13 and could catch as many fish as some of the old time career guides. I wasn't to know of course, but this was to be my last completely carefree summer as a kid, and I'm happy that I was able to spend it with my brother Jim, who up until that time was almost a complete stranger to me.

Mrs. Darville arrived for a short visit with us while we were still at the Tyee Camp. One day when a strong south east wind had blown up and an in harbour no sailings day was declared, Jim decided it would be a good day for him to drive her back home to Sydney.

We started off early in the little Austin car with Mrs. Darville lodged in the front passenger seat and me in the back. They talked incessantly about the apparently strained relationship between Jim and Rose and where it would possibly end up. I suppose Jim's being in university for about six years and having to live away from home, and the family in poverty hadn't helped their marriage a great deal. Intimate relationships between people have never been my strong point and at the ripe age of 12 it was of no interest to me whatsoever.

We delivered Mrs. D and started back for home, a long trip for a little car, especially with the Island Highway at that time being just a narrow track along the coast. Jim had driven that little car all the way from Toronto and was to take it to California with him at summer's end, and it was quite surprising how much speed he could get from its listless little motor. We'd pass a group of cars and sped along for a mile or so, only to come upon another group of idiots driving at the speed limit.

At the proper time, with horrifying grinding of gears and white knuckles hanging on for grim death, we'd pass the bunched up cars with Jim complaining about how slow everyone drove out here on the coast.

Soon after, the cabin at the Tyee Camp was needed for guests, so Rose and the children left for Sydney also. Jim and I moved into what was and still is known as the Frenchman's Shack. It now forms the garage of a beautiful waterfront home where long time area resident Thor Peterson lives on the northern side of the Campbell River estuary. In 1953 it was just a shack with a sloping floor, no electricity or plumbing. It had an old wood stove, which we seldom used, favouring instead a gasoline camp stove. I can't remember where we got our water, but I think it had a well with a hand pump on the property somewhere. A short trail connected us to the Tyee Camp then, ran on to Painter's main lodge building. I tied my rowboat up to the float at the Tyee Camp, but as I had my bike with me, I did more exploring than fishing.

Once again we were cooking for ourselves. Mum used to come down once in a while, but was generally disgusted with our living conditions. We thought it was just great, and Jim's inventive mind once again kicked into full gear. We both came to the conclusion on the same day that this business of having to wash dishes once in a while was not accomplishing anything worthwhile, as they just needed washing again almost right away. The solution was so obvious; we even had dreams of patenting our ingenious idea so that we could eliminate this drudgery worldwide. A throwaway cover for the dishes had to be the answer. After each meal, the used cover could be removed from the plates, bowls and cups then simply discarded in the garbage can, leaving the dishes clean for the next meal.

We couldn't wait to try out our world changing invention. We were somewhat at a loss as to what material to use to try out our experiment, until we noticed that we had several rolls of wax paper. This would be perfect; we covered our plates prior to our evening meal of boiling hot stew that Mum had made for us the day before. What a horrible mess, the hot stew of course melted the wax from the plate coverings, and it stuck to the plates as if it had been embossed at a factory under millions of pounds of pressure. We scraped wax from those plates and picked it out from our teeth for the rest of the summer. Mum very forbearingly laughed and felt sorry for us and tactfully made no mention of ever helping us to get our dishes clean again. However, this failure didn't stop Jim. He was soon talking about chocolate bars that could be eaten wrapper and all.

As I did most of the dish washing on the few occasions when we felt it was absolutely necessary, I thought it would be a good idea if Jim went back to engineering school for a few more years before he came up with any more newfangled inventions.

What a great summer that was! I did some fishing, but mostly just goofed off. I spent a lot of time at the Painter's dock getting to know the guides and their guests. Jack Anderson was the wharfinger and he took a great liking to me. I helped him out with his job by washing out boats and filling up gas cans. Jack had two sons Wes and Stan, who were about my age, and they had two younger sisters. Stan became a well known real estate executive on the Sunshine Coast, but I haven't heard from Wes for a long time. Jack had the very first fibreglass boat that I had ever seen. It was a Davidson, built in Vancouver. He had a 15 h.p. Evinrude on it and we marvelled that we could see the movement of the water right through the hull.

I wanted to make a good impression on everyone around the docks, as I was hopeful that Mr. McLean would let me start as a guide the following summer. I met Richard Tharpe, his wife Marg and their daughter Sue that summer. They lived near San Francisco where Dick was a senior vice-president of the Firemen's Fund group of insurance companies. They started coming to Campbell River each summer in 1952 and spent their last summer on Quadra more than 35 years later, in 1988. We all became very close friends and in 1969 Mum sold them a piece of our property on Quadra, where they built a summer home.

Dick was in the army during the Second World War as an officer under General McArthur. After the war he was made up to a full Colonel and served on the General's U.S. occupation staff in Japan for two years. I asked him how he got along working in the same office with the General, who was well known for being something of an eccentric. Dick said that in all the years he served under him, two of which were in the same building, never once did he meet the General. I believe that answered my question.

Jim guided Dr. Campbell from Los Angeles again that August Tyee season. Jim had rowed him previously in 1948, and my brother Bill had been his guide in 1952. He was getting on in years in '53 but was still an avid fisherman. He never fished on Sundays, which meant that Jim and I could spend the day together. This usually meant fishing and we caught several Tyees together that August. Jim had a fish knife with a wooden handle and each time he guided Dr. Campbell to a fish in excess of 30 lbs. he would carve a notch in the handle. He ended the season with 32 notches, one less than Bob Groulx who guided for 33 that year.

Dr. Campbell didn't like to fish for Tyees all the time, so instead they would try for Coho on some tides. One day they were fishing the Frenchman's Pool, which was right in front of our shack, when Jim saw a Tyee roll on the tide change. They quickly switched over from Coho gear and got a strike right away, landing a beautiful bright fish fresh in from the ocean. Dr. Campbell wanted to go in as it was lunchtime, but Jim persuaded him to drop his line in for just a few more minutes to catch the end of the tide change. Once again they had another fish right away. All this was within sight of Painter's dock, and when they finally came in for lunch, everyone was waiting to see their catch. The fish were exact twins of 42 lbs each, one male, one female and as bright as new silver dollars.

The sadness of another summer ending was all too soon upon me. The Mitchells weren't home from Banff yet, but Mum said that it'd be all right for me to stay at home on Quadra by myself for a couple of weeks until they got back. Jim brought me home in Painter's boat #32, towing my little rowboat behind. He dropped me off and we said our good byes as he was leaving for California the next day. He was to live there for the next 10 years. I don't think he ever looked back that evening, but perhaps I had some premonition it was going to be a long time before I saw him again, as I watched with tears rolling down my face until his boat disappeared through the gap between Steep and Gowlland Island. I have to admit I bawled like a baby for the next hour or so, until I could finally get a grip on myself and start getting things in order for school to start the next day and start yet another new chapter in my life.

Grade eight started off with some major changes. Mr Baldry was now principle of a new elementary school located in Campbelton, a northern section of Campbell River. Mr. Wright was our new principle and grade eight teacher on Quadra. Mr Wright made sure every boy in class got the strap at least once and even some of the girls didn't escape his eagerness to strap us into obedience. If one so much as dropped a pencil in class, it was out into the hall for a whipping. I wasn't very big for my age but was tough as nails and strong. Some of the bigger boys like John and Leo thought that we should gang up on him after school and teach him a lesson. He somehow found out about this plan and strapped every boy in class.

Some of the parents started to complain that he was taking this discipline too far and our learning was starting to suffer. Mum asked Mr. McLean if it would be all right for me to come to live with her at Painters and he readily agreed. We were given one of the summer cabins to live in so I transferred to Campbell River High that taught grades seven to twelve. All students from Quadra after grade eight had to take the ferry daily and attend Carihi anyway, so I was just starting a year early.

My Last day on Quadra as a student was a Saturday and I stalled around Q Cove until the last ferry left for Campbell River. It felt to me that I was leaving my whole life behind, which upon reflection certainly was not the case. I sold my bike to Neil for $25.00. Gary Taylor wanted to buy it, but I thought Neil needed it more as Gary lived within walking distance of the school. The three of us had a great time that last day and I was nervous about leaving on the last ferry to start a new adventure.

Gary moved to Vancouver shortly after and years later went on to become a well known night club owner during the 1970's and 80's. Neil, after a career at sea, owns a sizable tug and barge fleet that operates out of Campbell River.

This move to Painter's brought me into close contact with Mr. and Mrs. McLean's daughter Georgia who was my age and in grade eight also. Georgia was an only child and very studious, just the opposite of myself at that time. We walked together to catch the school bus each morning meeting up with Joey, Barbara, JoJo Painter and Arlene McDonald along the road to the highway. My first day at the new school went smoothly and I was assigned to grade 8A with Mr. Hughes as our homeroom teacher.

I don't know how to accurately describe Mr. Hughes. He must have been in his late 20's at that time and was almost completely bald. Of course most of us boys referred to him as old skinhead when he wasn't listening and Sir when he was. He was probably the most humorous and fun loving person that one could expect a teacher to be. While we did learn some very important lessons from him, most every English class that year was spent either on the baseball field or at some other sport if the weather was not suitable to be outside. This was just great but I think we suffered for it in the end as none of us turned out to be professional baseball players. I met up with old skinhead in 1987 at a class reunion which he attended. He was retired and had ended his career as principle of a high school at Squamish, B.C. Jack Cooley, one of my grade eight classmates, was one of his teaching staff.

There were about 100 students attending Carihi in 1953 from grade seven to grade twelve. Not a very big school by today's standards and small enough that one got to know just about everyone in attendance. The school was new, having been built in 1952 and had all the modern facilities such as shops, sewing rooms and a large gym with bleachers. Mr. Orm was principle with Mr. Tweed as vice. The school had a public address system, telephones, electricity and indoor plumbing which was a huge change from my first year at Cape Mudge

School. The bus stopped on it's way into town at the Campbelton School to let off the elementary students. On my first day riding the bus, Mr. Baldry was surprised to see me and we talked together often as he was one of my favorite teachers.

Most days after school I would go over to Ed Painter's boat building shop to help him with the construction of his famous rowboats. His shop was located next to the lodge and we had some great times together. At one point he was building a boat for speed, rather than rowing, that would take up to a 25 h.p motor. It was a beautiful little craft, 16 feet long and modeled after the Peterborough boats. I wish now that I had been older or had paid more attention to learning Ed's considerable skills. His boats are a work of art, as useful as they were pretty to look at. Mr. McLean let me keep our boat in a boathouse that belonged to a friend of his. This kept the boat in good condition over the winter while Ernie Latta helped me do some of the much needed repair work on the old engine. I fished on some weekends and Mr. McLean was surprised at how many salmon I caught over the winter, He still wouldn't budge on me being sixteen years old before I could be a guide at Painters Lodge.

In January, Carihi had what was at that time an annual event. A formal evening with the girls dressing up in Gowns and the boys in their best suits, with polished shoes and even a tie. This was called the Snowball Frolic and was much anticipated by the older students but not by fourteen year old boys. It surprises me even to this day how much people can punish themselves in the name of having fun. It was agreed between Mum, Mrs. McLean and Georgia that I would be her escort on this night of nights. I was not consulted of course, but overheard all the preparations as to what Georgia was going to wear and Mum showed up one day with a new suite, white shirt, new shoes and tie for me. As a male drone in this carefully planned female affair my only duty was to ask Georgia if I could please have the pleasure of escorting her on this magnificent evening. Of course this was the last thing I wanted to do and Mum nagged me every day as to when I was going to get off my but and be civilized for a change. It wasn't that I had anything against Georgia, in fact

I liked her very much. We walked together to catch the school bus each morning and home again after school. Also we saw a lot of each other because we were both living at the lodge. I was just a wild kid that wasn't ready for the so called finer things of life. Finally on the Friday afternoon of the frolic, we were walking home from the bus and I thought I may as well get over with, and asked Georgia if she would like to attend the Snowball Frolic with me that evening. I have seen ladies in various stages of outrage over the years and at the age of fourteen had even overheard stories of how angry they can get with men over nothing. But this information had not prepared me for the deep red colour of Georgia's otherwise pleasant face or the angry way she declared that she wouldn't want to be seen with me at a dog show let alone the social event of the year. Joey Painter shrugged and walked on very quickly leaving me by myself with this angry woman who stormed off towards home. It had worked out all right as far as I was concerned as I wasn't keen on going to this party dressed up like a mannequin anyway. But I couldn't quite understand why Georgia wouldn't walk with me the rest of the way home.

Latter Mum said it was getting late and I had better have a bath and start getting ready for the evening ahead. I explained to Mum that Georgia had changed her mind or something and didn't want to go to the frolic. Mum said, "Don't be silly" because Georgia was already dressed and waiting in the lodge lobby. Do they do these things on purpose to confuse men or is it normal for ladies to say the opposite of what they really mean? Sure enough after much strangulation from the necktie I arrived at the lodge to find Georgia looking as pretty as a picture sitting beside her proud mother waiting for me.

Chapter 16

In the spring of 1954, the Nason Family moved in next door on Quadra, half a mile away in island terms, and lived in Bill Walsh's house for a couple of years.

They had moved to the coast from Alberta. The best way I can describe them would be to say that they would have been right at home as Kentucky hillbillies feuding with the McCoys and Hatfields. And there were lots of them; Herb and Ruby were the parents, Frank, Eddy, Leola, Wilfred, Jim, Brenda, and Ann the children. Frank and his dad worked at Coal Creek Logging at Granite Bay. The Nasons were truly beyond understandable description, from my knowledge of the English language anyway, and were certainly unlike any family I had ever known. Fortunately, I seemed to fit in with them pretty well and managed to talk Mum into letting me stay at home by myself on the island when Ruth left for Victoria after spring break. My plan was to commute to school in the family's new boat, and this worked out all right for the remainder of the school year.

Frank Nason was the oldest of the family at 22, and although I was only 13, we became the very best of friends. I think I could write a whole book about our adventures together over the next few years, one that would scare any mother into never ever letting her children out of sight again, but I guess this account will have to do.

None of us ever called him Frank; he was Trapper to everyone. I won't explain how he acquired the nickname since some might be offended, but very few of his many real friends called him anything but Trapper.

Trapper was larger than the rest of the boys in the family, who tended to be undersized. He was also of above average intelligence, but had absolutely no common sense about everyday life. He was very impulsive, prepared to do anything on a dare, fun loving in the extreme, and a complete non-conformist, as I was obviously becoming myself. All the girls loved him as a brother, but I think they were also rather scared of him at the same time. Looking back at some of our capers and pranks together, I can see that perhaps we were also a little admired for our craziness. A few others would want to be the same, but they didn't have the nerve or our reckless free sprit. Trapper never had what could be referred to as a girlfriend, even though some of us tried our best to convince our older sisters he would be an exciting adventure for sure. Ruth met him while still at home during her spring break from nursing school that year. If anyone could have been a match for Trapper, it would have been her, but even Ruth backed off after a couple of brief encounters, and his relationship with the girls we knew never got beyond a brother sister arrangement. Trapper knew by age 22 that his destiny was to be solitary as far as female companionship was concerned. He didn't seem to mind, and over the years he planned his life accordingly.

Trapper brought a car with him when he moved to Quadra that year. I think it was a 1928 (or thereabouts) Model A Ford sedan, black of course. It was a perfect island car, tough, noisy and reliable, and we roared around the rough dirt roads with no consideration for others, always loaded to overflowing with our friends. I don't think it even had a license, as no one cared. The police only showed their faces when there was a dance in progress at the community hall, to keep liquor under control. They usually failed miserably at their task and sometimes even joined the folks drinking beer in the bush out behind the hall.

In spite of the general disdain in which the girls of Quadra held us boys, some of us did have girl friends. The cream always does float to the top I suppose, and some of these island girls were just a little tougher than others. So at the ripe old age of 13 (soon to be14), I sort of had a girlfriend. It was nothing more than a girl that I liked slightly better than most of the others, and she the same with me. One shouldn't read too much into this, as we rascally boys all still pretty much distrusted girls in general. All our school lives they had been bigger, tougher and meaner than us, and even though this was now slowly changing, some of the older girls could, and still did, beat us up if necessary.

One Saturday I told Trapper I needed to take my boat to Q Cove to fuel up and change oil. He said he'd meet me there with the car and we'd find some of our friends and roar over to Heriot Bay to get some beer. After fuelling up at Grouse Island, I moved the boat over in front of Judge Lewis's store at Q Cove, so that Trapper could find me easily. After I tied the boat up securely a problem arose. I had dressed that day in some of my good school clothes, rather than my usual boat and fishing attire. Mum was extremely weary of me ruining my clothes with fish slime, oil, battery acid and just about any other kind of filth I usually acquired around the docks. Trapper arrived and urged me to get busy, as we were wasting valuable goofing off time. He wasn't about to help me change oil, as he had on clean clothes also. As usual, Trapper came up with a simple solution to the problem. Someone, either on purpose or otherwise, had left a perfectly good dress on the float along with some other assorted old clothes and garbage. Trapper suggested that as there was no one around to see me, why not just take off my good clothes and put on the dress. It was the kind of solution which was typical of him, simple, but with unforeseen consequences. After the oil change I could change back into my good clothes, he said, throw away the dress and get on with going to Heriot Bay with our friends. What a great idea! If I used my head more, Mum wouldn't be so angry about the disgusting state of my wardrobe. So I quickly climbed out of the boat, doffed my clothes and put on the dress. It was a bit big for me, but this was good, as it covered me all the way down to my ankles. Trapper said I looked stunning and chuckled a little as I began to get to work. I got down under the engine to start the job of draining the old oil out of the crankcase, and all was going well, and it sure was a good thing that I hadn't tried to do this in my good clothes, as the dress was already starting to look like a mechanic's coveralls.

As I was lying down in the bottom of the boat replacing the oil plug so I could fill the engine back up with fresh oil, Trapper burst out laughing again. I didn't have time to see what this was all about and continued working away, when suddenly I heard a girl's voice ask Trapper if he'd seen me around anywhere. I couldn't believe my ears, it was my girlfriend. There was no escape, so I thought that I may as well stand up and be counted. But in many a disaster, things sometimes go bad a little at a time, getting progressively worse, until finally everything comes crashing down around you. As I popped up and stood there in my oil covered dress with a crescent wrench in one hand, not only was my girlfriend staring at me with wide eyed disbelief but so was her mother.

It took me a long time to fully understand why Trapper laughed so hard, the tears rolled down his cheeks. Every time afterwards that he told the story, he would bust up and loose his breath before he could get finished. He said he was never quite sure exactly what triggered this hysterical behavior, me standing there in the dress, the look on the mother's face, or just the stunned silence emitting from all three of us. We all just stood there for what seemed to me to be at least six hours, staring at each other, the silence only broken by Trapper's mirth. Never mind, the oil got changed, I got dressed again in clean clothes, and we picked up our friends at the B.C. Packers store and headed off to Heriot Bay. To save myself embarrassment, I begged Trapper not to tell anyone, and as a measure of our true friendship he didn't say a word about the dress caper, until at least a year after the incident.

The history of the Heriot Bay Inn is the history of Quadra Island itself. A couple of years later, we renamed it the Heartbreak Hotel after the famous song by Elvis that really described its existence better than just spoken or written words. A few years ago I was sitting in the hotel with some friends from Calgary looking at all the great pictures on the walls. The waiter asked me if I had ever been there before.

"Well, yes, I've been a few times over the years," I said. "I first became a customer when I was 13 years old, back in '54. " I could tell from the smirk on his face that he had better things to do than listen to my BS, and I could see him shaking his head and laughing as he nodded his head in our direction and whispered something to the lady behind the bar. It was quite common for people to bring their whole family to the bar in those long ago days. What else could you do with them? At least they were kept under some sort of surveillance. Being served beer at the age of 13 wasn't all that unusual in 1954.

The Heriot Bay Inn first opened in the 1890's and was owned by Hosea Bull. The original hotel was destroyed by fire and rebuilt to look somewhat as it did in 1954. In the 50's people were acquiring light plywood boats with 25 horsepower outboards, which made them travel much faster if not more safely. The big draw at the hotel was the beer parlour. People from as far away as Stuart Island could travel to Heriot Bay in less than an hour in their new fast boats. Church House Indians were frequent customers, along with employees of the numerous logging camps established in what was the heyday of the 'gypo logger' on the coast.

Before the road was connected to Granite Bay, the loggers used to drive to the end of their logging road, hike the trail, take whatever available car was parked there, and drive through to Heriot Bay. This happened every Wednesday night, with the return trip being always done in complete darkness. This Wednesday night assembly became a regular tradition, and was soon joined by speedboats full of loggers from the nearby logging camps. The next day was known as Thirsty Thursday, as the men struggled back to work after a mostly sleepless night of drinking and travel. The social life at the hotel was a breeding ground of discontent for some, resulting in wives and husbands changing places of residence with unpredictable regularity. Fights were as common as Wednesday night, and although it seemed a normal part of life, the whole scene would have made a terrific Wild West movie.

Quathiaski Cove was dull and lifeless compared to Heriot Bay of the 1950's, so that is where we always ended up when a bunch of us got together. Beer was $2.50 a dozen, with 20 cents' refund for the empties. I've never really liked beer myself and even today very rarely have one, but I couldn't say the same for most of my friends. Some of our wildest adventures were the result of meeting someone along the road and stopping to share a beer with them. Almost everyone who had a car could be counted on to have a case or two stashed in the back seat.

One day Trapper told me that he'd bought a newer car from my brother Bill. He intended to keep this car at Campbell River, so that we would have a good set of wheels for the city and the old Model A for the island. We were eager to try out this new little '51 Ford, so I picked up Neil in the boat and met Trapper at Quathiaski to catch the ferry to Campbell River. Mum needed some farm supplies that were only available in Courtenay, so this was our excuse for heading south. We loaded up with chicken feed at Buckerfields and spent the rest of the day just cruising in the new car. We packed the chicken feed on to the last ferry home, then we loaded up the boat and I dropped Neil off at his place. It was a great day with just the three of us, just being boys, and we felt on top of the world.

Trapper had a younger sister named Leola, who was about 19 or 20 and a very attractive redhead, which triggered a lively competition between Teddy Mitchell and young Pete Craddock. Young Pete, as one might guess, was the eldest son of old Pete, who was another of the true characters of that era. He was born on a sailing ship taking on cargo in Sydney, Australia, and spent the early part of his life in Australia before going to sea on merchant vessels at a young age. He reportedly jumped ship in Vancouver after spending some time in Costa Rica, and was to enjoy the rest of his illustrious life on the B.C. coast, moving to the Campbell River area in the late 1920's and landing a job with Lamb's logging company at Menzies Bay. Daddy Lamb was one of the great timber barons of the early part of the century and I had the pleasure of meeting him in his old age when he lived next door to friends of mine on Hosmer Avenue in Vancouver.

Old Pete finally ended up on Quadra at a time when many of the area's pioneers and original settlers were still around. He was a great storyteller and it was always interesting to listen to him talk about how life was in the early days.

Old Pete, or Ghandi as he was known by some, logged mostly by himself at Viner Point on Read Island for as long back as I can remember. He had some of the most run down equipment one could imagine, perhaps only outdone by Martin Germyn, who logged the Comsak Creek valley at the head of Bute Inlet. Old Pete was a real marvel at keeping his and other people's equipment in working condition regardless of age and the magnitude of the problem. We could always get a good laugh by just looking at some of the gerry-rigged repair jobs he had done. But through it all he kept right on logging and we all learned some of his fine art, which was so necessary to our way of life.

Young Pete was the eldest of three children born to Old Pete and his wife Dorothy Rose. Teddy Mitchell was the only son of George Mitchell, not to be confused with the Mitchell's who lived with us for six years. Teddy lived next door to the Nason's, just a five minute walk away and this gave Teddy a distinct advantage over young Pete in their struggle for Leola's attentions.

As mentioned earlier, May Day on Quadra was and still is one of the major social highlights of the year, with picnics and Maypole dancing at what is now Rebecca Spit Park, on the east coast of the island, looking down over a broad reach of the northern part of Georgia Strait to the islands and Mainland to the southwest. 1954 was no exception for the celebrations. Trapper was unfortunately away at a logging camp and not around for the festivities, but this was only a small inconvenience, as we would have to operate without wheels. The usual good times were had at Drew Harbour next to Rebecca Spit, with the crowning of the May Queen, sports, lots of food and companionship. Leo, David Lund and a couple of other young ruffians like me decided we should all go to the dance to be held that night at the community hall. As outlined before, we had no interest in dancing but that didn't stop us coming up with a scheme to make some fast money from the event. We knew a considerable amount of alcohol was present at these affairs, usually in the form of beer hidden in the bushes outside the hall just in case the cops showed up. Why not follow the drinkers discretely to their hideout and afterwards move the cases to our own hiding place, where we would leave a guard on duty. We could then sell this beer to anyone who either didn't have any, or maybe, if we were shrewd enough, sell it back to the poor deprived original owners. Naturally this was a venture overflowing with risk, but we planned ahead and reckoned life itself was risky enough as it was, so why not give it a shot?

After a quick trip home from the May Day Picnic to change into some warm clothes, I started off on the long walk to the Community Hall. On my way past the Mitchells' place, who did I come upon but Teddy and Leola necking in the back seat of their car. They were sure surprised to see me and by the look on their faces not at all happy to have been caught in what they thought was a deserted paradise. I quickly moved on, since they wouldn't give me a ride as punishment for my indiscretion. I met Leo at the end of the Gowlland Harbour Road and we walked together from there to the hall, fine tuning our bootlegging plans and making ready for an evening of excitement. Our partners from Quathiaski were waiting for us at the hall when we got there and we had another 'board meeting' of the schemers to pass the time. One small problem was that there was a substantial admission charge to get into the dance. We tried to overcome this by saying we were just little kids and didn't plan on doing any dancing anyway, but this didn't work, so Johnny explained that being so young we needed to be watched by our parents so as to not get into any trouble outside, which was where all this drinking was going on. Some people are just impossible to deal with, I suppose, and the old bag selling tickets at the door wasn't buying any of these specious arguments we were trying to put forward. So in the end, we partially solved the problem by pooling all our resources for one ticket. Dave was chosen to be the spotter inside, and we were soon in business.

The plan was simplicity itself. Dave would wait around inside with his ears and eyes on alert and give us any information he thought might be useful to us bootleggers outside. It wasn't long before Elmer Krook and his wife invited some friends outside for a spot of beer between dance sets. This was going to be a risky business for us, as it wasn't dark yet and that early in the dance no one had been drinking enough to not notice our presence in the vicinity of the beer stash. Leo said though that Elmer was a good friend and a neighbour of his, and he assured us he could tag along with the drinkers. He even got offered a beer and had to use his best business like control to refuse it.

Soon the band started up again and the drinkers returned to the hall. We had a quick meeting and decided that to snitch all Elmer's beer at one time wouldn't be wise, as this would alert others at the dance that thieves were on the prowl. As it was now starting to get dark, we decided instead that one full case wouldn't be missed until later, so we went ahead with the raid as now planned. In the meantime, others had begun wandering outside between sets to partake of their own particular little caches of beer, and their locations were easily recorded in our young, brilliant minds, which hadn't stretched far enough to think about someone bringing a flashlight.

Despite the handicap, we quickly acquired quite a sizable amount of beer, but then trouble started to rear its ugly head, so much trouble in fact that to try to sell any of this stolen beer to anyone would have resulted in severe beatings by the enraged adults. We did the only sensible thing that came to mind. To squirrel it away for later, we moved it a fair distance up Bryant's Road and hid it in an old hollow stump. But that left us with the problem of still having to get rid of it somehow, and the only logical solution to having too much inventory that came to mind was to start drinking it.

As I said earlier, I've never really developed a taste for beer. At the age of 13, I had no taste for it at all. However, I did struggle through one bottle while the rest of the boys demolished more than what could have been considered as social drinking. We were licking our wounds as we hadn't made any cash and we were well aware we'd caused a good deal of squabbling among our elders while they tried to figure where all their booze could have gone to so quickly. By now, daylight would be upon us shortly, so we decided to head for home, leaving our hoard nicely hidden and covered with last year's dry leaves. I suggested to Leo that I could always make money fishing, and if we made tracks for home, we could spend the day fishing for blue backs around May Island. We stuffed our pockets with beer, as we thought we may yet be able to do some trading, and started trudging off up the road, somewhat weary having not slept for 24 hours. We hadn't gone far when who should come along but Teddy and Leola. They were in a more benevolent and helpful mood now, particularly when Leo and I gave them no choice but to stop, by sitting down in the middle of the road. (This was a trick also successfully used by my daughter Jennifer to extract $50 from me in later years. I wonder where she learned that from!) We then offered them a beer each in exchange for driving us home. Having been an unusually dry night for beer, they eagerly made the deal. But then they wrestled us both to the ground and took all the beer we had, which was about six bottles. After that they were going to make us walk home anyway, but we satisfied their greed by offering them more beer at a later time. They fell for our trickery and we got a ride as far as the Mitchell place.

By this time it was full daylight as we wearily trudged along the trail to home. We were so tired that when a deer jumped out of the bush in front of us, we jumped with fright almost as high as the deer. We arrived home and went down to the dock right away to get out fishing. Leo enjoyed the day very much, as he had never fished the West Coast shoreline of

Quadra before. After we had caught a few fish, we headed for home, as our inability to stay awake was overtaking our ability to navigate the boat properly. When we arrived at the dock, Ernie and Jenny Latta were waiting for us. Jenny was head chef at Painter's Lodge and was mum's boss. As she had the day off and was going fishing with Ernie, Mum had asked her to look in on me to see how I was doing living by myself. She couldn't have come on a worse day. Dog tired, somewhat still hung over from my one beer and with my friend Leo still much worse in the hung over department. She asked us if we had eaten lately, and we had to admit that we hadn't. We probably couldn't have eaten anyway, as I was starting to feel quite ill from the effects of the previous night. Ernie kind of winked at me when Jenny wasn't looking, as if to say he would handle Jenny so Mum didn't get too bad a report. So off we went to the house for an extended sleep, as The Great May Day Beer Caper came to a close. When Trapper came home, we picked up the rest of the hidden beer, and he told us that for weeks afterwards the adults from the dance were still accusing each other of being thieves.

Meanwhile, school was still in session and my daily commute was interrupted by my playing hooky whenever the blue backs showed up in good numbers. The last major school event that year was to be a music festival to be held in Courtenay, about 30 miles down the coast from Campbell River on Vancouver Island.

Mrs. Grey, our music teacher, had us practicing daily for this event, which would have all the schools in the district in attendance. We rode to Courtenay on one of the school buses, and I sat both ways with Isabel Parkin, the only girl in my class at that time that I had any time for, among what I considered to be a bunch of snobs. This so called snobbery or standoffishness of course wasn't really their fault; it was mostly due to the daily outrageous behaviour of my friends and me. Isabel and I talked a lot on that trip about our future as adults and what our dreams and ambitions were. The music festival was a success, and for once we boys behaved ourselves and our teachers said they were proud of our accomplishments. Because of Isabel and her gentle ways, I was starting to have a little more respect for the young female population in general. Even all these years later, we remained friends, and at the time of writing I still see her once in a while.

Soon school was out and Doug Thornton asked me if I would like a job as a fishing guide for guests at the Dolphins Resort. Would I ever! He took me fishing with him a few times where I was supposedly the guide and he was the guest, so that I could learn the ropes. This seemed to work all right, and he said there'd be business for me after the July 1st holiday. I brought my boat across to the Dolphins dock, as I would be using it for taking out guests.

Dolphins was built, and owned at that time, by an older lady by the name of Miss Lucy Russell. She had previously owned the Dolphins Teahouse near English Bay in Vancouver. The Dolphins Resort was just a small operation in 1954, but very exclusive, just as it is today. Miss Russell was very knowledgeable when it came to the hospitality business and put her knowledge to good use at the resort.

I was very excited about this job, and as it turned out, it paid very well. We guides received $14 per day for guiding one person and $16 per day for two or more, which was big money in those days. In addition, I received $10 per day for the use of my boat, and quite often was given most of the catch. At that time, we could sell the catch given us to one of the fish buyers at Quathiaski. If we were well liked and successful at fishing, we also quite often received some very generous tips. This all added up to much more money than I could ever have made just fishing.

I wasn't overly busy that first year with people to guide, so in my spare time I continued to fish by myself, which brought in even more income and also honed my skills for future guiding.

During August, the Ripley family arrived at the Dolphins for two weeks of vacation and fishing. They were from Santa Barbara, California, and consisted of Mrs. Ripley and her three

LAWRENCE FOORT

children, Sue, Polly and Bob, who were all about my age, with
Sue the oldest at 16. Mrs. Ripley adopted me as well, and always
invited me to stay at mealtime every day, which was also a big
help financially and nutritionally. She was a great mother and I
can still remember the wonderful food she produced. We caught
lots of fish together and the family enjoyed their vacation at the
Dolphins very much, returning each summer for several years,
until Mrs. Ripley remarried. I met her new husband one time
when I visited years later in Santa Barbara, and it seemed he
just didn't like fishing.

One day we were fishing off May Island, when I happened
to mention that we were right in front of our home. Mrs. Ripley
asked me to take them in for a visit. They immediately fell in
love with the place, and we had a picnic in the front yard. The
next day Mrs. Ripley went over to Painter's to see if Mum would
sell her a small part of our land on which to build a summer
home. Mum didn't want to sell at that time, but in her usual
way said they were welcome to come to camp there any time
they wanted.

After the Ripleys left promising to return next year, which
they did, I guided Dr. Zilliach and his wife, who were from
northern Michigan. After they left, a retired army General from
San Francisco came for a week At the end of August, Doug
paid me, and I said my goodbyes to Miss Russell and headed
for home, after going over to Painter's to give Mum my summer
savings, almost $1,000! This was much more money than Mum
had been able to earn at $1 an hour working at Painter's for
most of the year!

I crossed the channel for home on a flat calm evening,
with summer once again in full retreat. I stopped off at the
Nasons' and stayed a couple of days with them, then went home
to get ready to start high school. I was going to stay at home
by myself and go to school at Carihi in Campbell River. I was
starting grade nine and the Quadra School only went as far as
Grade 8. There were only six high school students from the
island at that time that didn't live at or near Quathiaski, so to
save room on the school bus we were picked up each morning

by Frank Brasseux in his taxi. He had a contract with the school board and he always came about half way in on the Gowlland Harbour road to pick me up or drop me off after school. This meant I only had about half the distance to walk to get my ride to school. This was a big help when the days of winter were upon us with shorter times of daylight.

There were four girls from Heriot Bay and I that rode in Frank's taxi each morning and afternoon. The girls all sat in the back seat and continually talked about their current boyfriends while I rode in front with Frank. We both used to roll our eyes in disbelief at some of their incessant gossip and chatter, and often Frank would tell them to shut up and be quiet for a while, but this would only last for about a minute before they would start up again.

When we arrived at Q Cove, we boarded the 8 a.m. sailing of the Victory II for the 15 minute voyage to Campbell River. All the girls rode in the forward passenger cabin, while we boys rode on the back deck in good weather or the engine room if the weather was foul. From the ferry landing, we'd all walk up a steep trail behind the Seaview Café, then up the road to school. We usually arrived a few minutes before 9 a.m., but sometimes were delayed by bad weather on the crossing. On days when tide and winds were too strong, the ferry wouldn't sail and we'd miss a day of school. This didn't happen nearly often enough, but when it did, we'd just hung around the cove for the day, getting into as much mischief as possible, as usual.

It was a little lonely living by myself on Quadra, but I much preferred it to being at Painter's Lodge in Campbell River. Every day after school, I'd stop off at the Nasons' on my way home and stay until bedtime. I always went home to sleep, as there wasn't room at their house. This meant hiking home in the dark along the old trail that ran from their house to ours. The Nason's had a dog, which was just about as wild as they were. One time Ed suggested that I take it home to live with me for company on those lonely nights, but this wasn't a good move for either the dog or me. I still, after seven years, missed my dog Pete and this animal wasn't a good replacement. It had never been trained and I was having a very difficult time looking after it properly. Finally, after a few months, I took it out in the woods and shot it with my rifle. It was not easy to do and I still feel bad about it to this day. If I'd been older and more responsible, I might have had more success in training him properly.

Bill and family had moved that year from Granite Bay to what was to be their permanent home for many years. They had purchased 160 acres at the head of Hyacinthe Bay, on the other side of the island, from William Law and family for $5,000. The Law's were originally from New Zealand and had raised sheep on the property since the early part of the century. Bill set up his faithful sawmill at the mouth of the small river that flowed into the bay. He cut lumber and had a house under way in traditional coastal fashion before winter set in.

The Comox Logging Company had built a road from the north end of Gowlland Harbour a few years previously, and this meant that I could walk along the trail from our place for about half a mile, then along the logging road to Hyacinthe Bay. This was a total distance of about three miles as compared to about 10 by going by road via Heriot Bay.I sometimes walked over to Bill's to spend the weekend with them. One time I actually walked from there to home, changed into my school clothes, and then on to meet Frank with the taxi to take me to the ferry and school with the babbling girls. This was a bit too much of a trip for me and I ended up falling asleep in class that afternoon.

It was near Bill's place that I saw my first cougar. Those of us that live in the wilderness are always alert for danger of any kind, and cougars fit right into this category. They're normally a timid animal but they're not to be trusted when it comes to children, or sometimes even lone adults. Cougar attacks against humans are still more common on the islands than anywhere else in North America. Some scientists feel that they are a sub-species of the mainland cats. Even so, these attacks are usually by old animals which are often sick and starving, or by the very young that haven't learned yet to hunt properly.

I should mention just as a tip in passing, that they can usually be forced to back down by acting aggressively and waving a stick or something and shouting at them, but you should never turn your back on them or try to run. Make as much noise as possible, make yourself look bigger by extending your arms and clothing, and steadily advance towards them. Bears are much more dangerous as an animal, and we were fortunate at that time not to have had any on the south island.

This is the only picture I have of my two uncles shown with my Grandfather and Aunt Bahia. The two boys were sent away from Lebanon by Granddad due to the trials of the First World War. Uncle Mofed, on the left was sent to a relative living in Argentina. Uncle Toffe(Ted) was sent to Canada along with other members of the family. Ted settled in Detroit Michigan and he served in the U.S. Army during the Second World War. This picture was taken on the day of their departure from Lebanon. The boys were never seen again by their parents.

Passport picture of my mother when she came to Canada
1920 at age 19.

My father, Major Fredrick Foort, about the time of the First
World War

The house on Quadra Island where I was born.

View from the living room of the house on Quadra Island.

C.P.R. ferry from Victoria to Vancouver, B.C.

The barge built by my brother Bill & Buford Haines
used to haul lumber from his sawmill

Tug Le Roi moored at the south end of Gowlland Harbour.

Brother Bill hard at work sawing a log in the water with a hand saw.

Freight shed at Government Dock,
south end of Gowlland Harbour.

Syd and Rita Moss. Syd was lost
at sea while Captain of the tug
Escort ll.

Mum and me at an
early age.

Mrs. Marshall (nee Beech) walking with me in
downtown Vancouver.

My Uncle Ted and wife Josephine   Brother Bill as a teenager.
with daughter Bonnie Detroit
Michigan 1947.

Brother Bill holding
me as a baby.

My brother Jim wearing his
Canadian Air Force uniform 1945.

My sister Ruth with me in the pram

The historic ship S.S. Empress of Russia.

Tug B.C. Boy with Captain Micky Ballatti and crew. This was the vessel that had attempted to bring the doctor from Campbell River to attend my birth.

Tug Morsby at mid channel between Quadra Island and Campbell River.

Lawrence at 11 years of age With his first tyee in august of 1952. The fish weighed 42 ½ pounds

Below:
With W.A. Mitchell, checking on our boats moored to the float in front of our home. This was the unusual snowfall and cold winter of 1949/50. When this picture was taken there was six feet of snow on the ground.

NEXT PAGE:The final destruction of Ripple Rock April 5, 1958 by the worlds largest non-nuclear explosion up until that date.

Mother and me at Great Aunt Sarah's home Oakland
California 1952.

Mother and me downtown Vancouver 1960.

Wedding picture of my brother Bill & Sheila MacKay 1947. from left: Bill, Sheila, Sheila's Aunt Jean, Ian McKay Mum, Lawrence, Mrs McKay and Ruth.

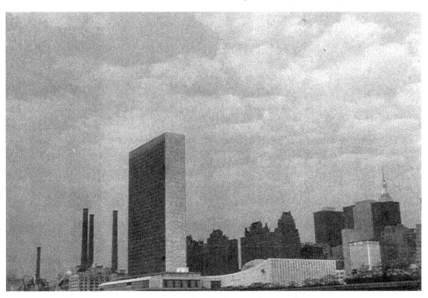

The United Nations building as we sailed up the East River to City Island.

Mooring the Yacht Hildur near the Eaton family summer
home, Georgian Bay Lake Huron on July 1, 1963.

Capt Joe and Capt Ed taking sextant shots to locate Great
Inagua Island.

Art White, Joe Turcott and Capt. Joe Prosser trimming the main sail on yacht Hildur.

Memorial to Princess Pocahontas near Jamestown Virginia. My wife Betsy is a ninth generation descendent of Pocahontas.

Lightship near where the liner Andrea Doria sank in the summer of 1956

S.S. Constitution outbound from New York passing under the partially constructed Verrazano Narrows Bridge.

Yacht Hildur at rest, Miami Florida.

The author working on the rigging up the main mast.

Skyline of Manhattan as we entered New York Harbour May, 1963.

Sea Queen in northern waters.

Norango off Icy Bay Alaska summer of 1964.

Cape St. Elias, Alaska. A desolate landfall to be sure. Note the lighthouse at the foot of the fog shrouded mountain just visible at the left of the photo.

Chief officer Vic Fry, (right) of Norango flying in to Yakatat Alaska. Vic was later to become Superintendent of Marine Pilots on the B.C. Coast.

The launch we picked up off Guadaloupe with the President of Air France and guests on board

Lawrence as owner of the tug Monarch II 1966.

These kids and their dog always came to meet us when we docked at Yakatat Alaska.

From a tropical beach at
Christmas....

....to an ice covered bay in June.

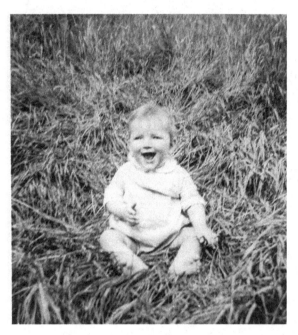

The author........what a difference a few years can make!

Chapter 17

By Christmas time 1954 Mum had run out of patience with her unruly teenager living by himself back on the island, so it was back to Painter's Lodge for me again, and I must say that this did make life easier for me; school each weekday, Ed Painter's boat shop in the afternoons, and fishing on weekends.

I was still in the process of proving winter fishing was worthwhile, and Mr. McLean was giving some second thought to maybe letting me guide during the next summer after all. Ernie Latta became a good friend and helped me out with some off season repairs to the new boat, which was once again stored in the covered boathouse.

I had grown up very quickly after the Mitchells left. I now settled back somewhat to do some fun things as a kid. We went skating some nights at nearby Hudson's farm with friends from school. I still have a scar on my chin from being on the end of a 'crack the whip' manoeuvre, when Diane Hudson couldn't hold on to me any longer and we both ended up in a pile on the ice. I spent a lot of time with John Ferry and his sister Reubina. Her dad had a 1953 Chrysler that Reubina sometimes brought to school. Some of us would play hooky, pool our money for gas, and go cruising to Courtenay. She was a great friend, but I have never seen her since those long ago schooldays. John married a classmate of mine from Quadra but died at a young age. I used to stay at their place on the Indian reservation quite often, and John introduced me to eulachon oil, which is a traditional delicacy greatly cherished and enjoyed by native people. Eulachon are a small and very oily fish somewhat like a smelt, which are gathered near spawning time at the head of some of the long inlets that invade the B.C. Mainland coast. Knight Inlet certainly used to be a favoured location for harvesting the fish, which are definitely an acquired taste. The fish are caught in nets and left to rot in large wooden pens. Then, after curing for a time, the resulting mess is transferred into huge pots placed over open fires and cooked. The oil rises to the top where it is skimmed off and put in containers. I didn't like it at first, but I eventually learned to, and it is quite nice spread on toast.

The winter and spring of 1955 were probably the most carefree time of all of my time at school. We were a close knit school at Carihi, and living at the lodge was a luxury compared to being alone on Quadra. Mr. Mclean still wouldn't give me a job guiding, but he did employ me to help Einer Anderson to paint and repair the rowboats for the coming season. I also cut grass and generally helped Madge Painter, who was manager at the Tyee Fishing Camp.

My sister Ruth was also in the process of graduating as a nurse from the Royal Jubilee Hospital in Victoria. Mum travelled down to Victoria ahead of me and I took the bus from Campbell River to arrive in time for the ceremony. I had never travelled so far by myself before. Mac, who had been driving the bus to Nanaimo for years, said he would make sure I got on the right coach for Victoria when we arrived in Nanaimo. Mum met me at the bus terminal in Victoria, and we stayed with Percy Mills and his wife, who were long time friends. Mum was really thrilled to see her daughter established as a fully qualified Registered Nurse, and the profession was to serve Ruth well for many years.

Back home again, the guides were starting to show up in late May and early June, as guests began to arrive for the early fishing. Madge was short a guide one evening and asked Mr. McLean if it'd be all right for me to take out two men fishing, just this once. He said that would be fine, as they had no one else available.

I recall it was a rainy evening with a bit of a southeast wind blowing in, which is always the most difficult wind in Campbell River and Discovery Passage, but I was determined to get across the channel to where I knew I could get fish on the flood tide. I scared those guests plenty during that bumpy crossing, but we had our limit of eight big spring salmon in the boat by the time the tide changed, and they were so excited they didn't even notice the fairly rough ride home. Madge was amazed and Mr. McLean just rolled his eyes. I still had to wait until I was 16 before I became a regular guide.

June quite often can be a stormy and wet month on the coast, and that year was no exception, in fact more so than usual, and the fishing turned out to be as unreliable as the weather. One of the new guides that year was Andy Anderson, who was Danish and a bit of a drinker and had sailed on deep sea ships all over the world. He even had an ocean going mate's certificate to prove it. Andy was assigned to guide a young couple who were engaged to be married soon. The father, mother and younger sister of the bride to be were also along for the trip. The father was a tough old commercial fisherman who owned a couple of large seine boats and wanted to take the family on this vacation before he had to leave for the summer to the fishing grounds.

As I recall, the daughters were both very pretty and the story is that Andy was out to show off his seafaring and other qualities to the young lady who was engaged. Andy was a big blond, handsome guy in his late 20's, who had somehow charmed this future bride to an extent beyond belief. He even managed to take her out fishing one evening without her beau. It was an extra stormy night, but Andy had been catching fish for this young lady at a rate no one thought possible, so off they went, just the two of them, when no one was watching. Unfortunately, a northwest wind increased to a quite alarming speed that evening, and there was also a strong ebb tide, just to make conditions worse. By well after dark, the twosome still hadn't come back to the dock. Mr. McLean was starting to get frantic, as was the future bridegroom, who was starting to reckon on becoming a widower before getting to the altar, while the father of the bride remained as calm as could be. As an experienced fisherman, he knew and trusted Andy's seafaring qualities. Finally, a search party was sent out. Andy had hid out well though, and we returned to the dock empty handed. I must say that by this time I think we were all beginning to wonder what was going to happen next. It was at least an hour after dark and very rough indeed out on the water when at last we heard a motor sputtering towards the dock. Andy and the young lady arrived with a flourish, and even had two small spring salmon to show to try to prove that at least some fishing had been conducted. Mr. McLean was furious and demanded what Andy had to say for himself being out in such terrible weather with a guest. Andy's reply was a classic.

"Vel," he said with his thick Scandinavian accent, "it vas yust like deep sea." With that the pair of them lurched out of the boat and strolled up the dock arm in arm. Jack Anderson, the wharfinger, made sure no one saw the half empty rum bottle that was rolling around in the bottom of the boat. He held up the two scrawny springs for all to see, to divert attention away from the bottle.

"Now there's a lovely pair of fish!" he said. Everything seemed to return to normal fairly instantaneously, as the guests were leaving the next morning for the trip home to Vancouver, but to me the future son in law seemed quieter than usual. He was a city boy and it was apparent his fisherman father in law to be, who was the rough and ready type, didn't think too much of him. Mr. McLean handled it all fairly coolly and Andy was soon guiding again after a good talking to by Mr. McLean. I've often wondered whether those two conspirators really caught those fish that evening, or whether they somehow smuggled them aboard before leaving the dock to provide themselves with an alibi. Never mind, life goes on and after a while all was forgotten.

Once again it was May Day on Quadra. We all always

seemed to go a little crazy on this happy day and 1955 proved to be a classic. A mob of us, both boys and girls, from school decided we would go to Quadra for the day, stay overnight, attend the dance, then come back to Campbell River on Sunday. We all caught an early sailing to Quadra on the Victory II, arriving at Q Cove at about 9 a.m. David met us there and we hung around the store trying to decide how to get to the picnic at Drew Harbour.

The solution to our transportation problem was simple. As usual, David and I simply borrowed someone's car from the ferry parking lot. There were plenty parked there for the ferry, most of them were just old wrecks anyway as no one kept their good car on Quadra. We wired up an old heap, but the starter wouldn't work. No problem, we just got a couple of the girls to give it a push and off we roared to the store, where we picked up the rest of our gang for the day. Jim Hunt lived at Quathiaski and was a good friend of mine. His girlfriend climbed in with us, as Jim hadn't shown up yet. I was a little nervous about this and asked her when Jim was going to show.

"Oh, him!" she said. "I hope I never see him again!" It turned out that my friend Jim had been seen the evening before driving around Campbell River with another young lady, Marvelle Green, the very attractive daughter of the new assistant manager of Painter's Lodge. I couldn't believe how things could have changed so quickly between Jim and his girlfriend, but off we all went at high speed to the picnic in our stolen auto.

The evening affair was far different than the previous year, which had been the start and end of our bootlegging career. This time the boys actually attended the dance and delivered the girls to their respective homes at a decent hour. Jim asked me to stay over at his place for the night, so after Dave and I delivered our stolen auto back to the parking lot, I walked the short distance up to his house. Next day Jim said he felt like going for a long walk. We started off quite early and walked almost to Heriot Bay and back, a pretty fair stroll. We met some kids we knew at various places along the way and we stopped to chat, but Jim didn't seem to want to talk about what was on his mind and I didn't think I should ask. It was a very hot day and after arriving back at Q Cove, he saw me off on the ferry back to Campbell River.

Soon it was graduation time for the Grade 12 students at Carihi. Jim was in that year's graduating class, and we teamed up together after the ceremony. Jim had brought the lovely Marvelle along as his date and I was by myself. Most people headed south to the Blue Grouse, which was a late night diner several miles south of town at Oyster Bay. I rode along with Jim, Marvelle and some other kids, and we had a great time together until well after daylight. But on the way home, Jim suddenly stopped the car and asked me to get out. I thought this was a little strange as we were at least 10 miles out of town, but he was quite insistent, so rather than making a big fuss, I got out and watched them all drive off and leave me. Something was really bothering Jim, and I had sensed it on our long Quadra walk the previous week. I had only walked a short distance when Skip McDonald stopped and picked me up in his nice new Pontiac. He drove me right out to the lodge and I was just in time to start work for the day. Skip went on to become owner of the Beehive Cafe located on the waterfront at the head of the old government dock, and served as mayor during the early boom days of Campbell River. He remained in town for many years afterwards and was still living up on Ash Street at the time of writing, still keeping a firm finger on the pulse of the community and its many issues well past the turn of the century. Jim Hunt went on to study electrical engineering and worked for Boeing Aircraft down in Everett, Washington. I never did find out why he had decided to strand me out on the road that night.

That was the summer I was fired by Mr. McLean. I really didn't like mowing lawns and cleaning cabins when I thought I was capable of guiding, and this dislike for my work resulted in me getting myself fired, which was entirely my own fault. I was certain I'd never get to be a guide at Painter's now, and called Doug Thornton right away. He said he was counting on me to be at the Dolphins as soon as school was out, which was good news for sure. I took my boat out from its winter moorage and headed for Quadra. After a few days at home and with the Nasons, I packed up and headed back over to Dolphins. As I couldn't live at the lodge during the summer season, I brought along my pup tent. I set up camp in a small clearing across the road from the resort and settled in for a great summer. One small problem though, I wasn't allowed to use my boat that year. Doug had built some new boats over the winter, and I was required to use his boats for taking guests fishing. His boats were certainly better than mine, but it meant less income. Doug assured me that this would be more than compensated for by the continuous bookings he had for that summer. Luckily this turned out to be ture and by September I had given Mum another $1,000 from my earnings.

That was the summer John Wilkinson got a job as a crewmember on the seiner Adriatic Sea. Doug Burnett was the skipper and we all felt John was very fortunate to have been hired on. They would come home on weekends and John would tell great stories of their adventures while fishing in Johnstone Strait north of Campbell River on the inside passage. We'd hang out on the boat every chance we could get, and John proudly showed me the new engine that had just been installed. She was a good little ship for her day, sporting a 6-110 G.M. diesel, but at that time the large nets were still pulled by hand. John showed me another boat, the Rose N that had a power block on the back used for pulling in the net.

As far as I know, this was probably the first boat to have a power block as a means of retrieving the net. We all marvelled at this new device and system and by 1958 almost every seine boat on the coast had one of these great labour saving inventions.

During that summer, I had time between guiding jobs to hang out with some of my friends. One Saturday, I was in town to get some new fishing gear at Smoothy Marshall's tackle shop and met up with Buster Saville, an native friend of mine from Squirrel Cove on Cortes Island. He was crewing on a seine boat that summer and he had the weekend off, as fishing was closed until Sunday night. Buster asked me if I was going to the dance at the community hall that evening, which I think was July 1, known then as Dominion Day. There was always a parade, with lots of activities concluding with a dance to celebrate the founding of Canada in 1867. I met up with some other friends who were going to meet at the community hall later that evening, and they asked me to join them.

I had never been to such an event before, except on Quadra, which was small time compared to this. Buster showed up with a couple of bottles of lemon gin, which we all sipped on out behind the hall during the course of the event. Some sipped more than others, and after we had made a sizable dent in Buster's supply of gin, Dave Danis decided that he'd taken on board enough fuel to start flying. He went roaring off back to the dance with his arms outstretched, declaring that he was a jet plane. After a few circuits around the hall, Jack the Dutchman and I were able to shoot him down and load him into a car. We drove him to where he lived with his mother and quickly deposited him at the front door before making a fast getaway.

I guess Dave's mother wasn't home and the fresh air must have brought him back to life, because he soon showed up again back at the gin bottle out behind the dance hall. He spent the rest of the night roaring around town with outstretched arms shouting aloud that he was a CF-100 to anyone who would listen. He finally had a crash landing about 3 a.m., when the Dutchman, who was a huge muscular young man, picked him up and lugged him home in the light of the approaching dawn. I hitched a ride back home to my tent and arrived well after sunrise. Happily I didn't have to be back on the job until that evening.

Dave's raucous imitation of an aircraft reminds me that a few years ago I was flying, with the aid of an aircraft and no gin, from Sandspit in the Queen Charlotte Islands to Vancouver. I found myself sitting beside Jack the Dutchman, whom I hadn't seen for a few years. We started talking and laughing about some of our early life capers, and he asked me if I remembered the night Dave thought he was a jet plane. We laughed so hard about this and other times we'd had together during our youth that we both had tears streaming down our faces.

The highlight of that summer was the return of Mrs. Ripley, her family and their friend Susan. I guided Polly and Susan, and Doug took out Mrs. Ripley, Bob and Sue in his larger boat. We caught fish everywhere we went that year, big springs, Coho salmon and even pinks. We all started to get a little tired of all the fish, and Mrs. Ripley asked if it would be possible to just go for a day of cruising and sightseeing. We all agreed this would be a welcome change, and it was decided we would go to Shoal Bay and Phillips Arm, over on the Mainland.

We started off early in the morning to catch the high water slack tide at Seymour Narrows. There was a light westerly wind blowing, which made it a little bouncy until we reached Howe Island and turned into Nodales Channel round the northern end of Sonora Island. From there the water was like glass, and we were soon at Shoal Bay. We took on fuel for the trip up Phillips Arm, which lay straight ahead of us. It was one of those perfect days you can get in the area, when a summer high pressure system rests over the south coast. It looked to me as though one could reach out and touch the head of the inlet. In fact, it was more than 12 miles distant, but the high mountains and glassy calm water made it look deceivingly close.

We landed at the head of the inlet and travelled up the river as far as we were able. The Elingson family were logging the valley and used a flume to send the logs down to the salt water. The oldest son was in charge of the operation, and he told Doug his father had just passed away the previous winter. Doug had known the father from previous trips and was saddened to hear of the passing of his old friend. We were asked to be very careful when starting a fire on the shore, as the weather was very hot and the wood very dry, but we were welcome to stay down by the river to have our picnic lunch.

After lunch, we had a quick swim in the cool, glacier fed river then started off on a hike inland. We sighted a Grizzly bear fishing for salmon upstream from us, so we abruptly cancelled our hiking plans. Luckily, the wind was carrying our scent away from the bear, so it didn't sense our approach. This was the first grizzly I'd ever seen. Doug suggested that we shouldn't go any further, as there could be more bears in the area due to the abundance of pink salmon migrating upstream. We hiked back to our boats and did some fishing as we travelled down the inlet. We didn't catch anything, as we weren't familiar with the waters, but it was such a perfect day that fishing didn't matter to any of us.

We got back to Shoal Bay, topped up with fuel and started to make our way home. The trip back would have been uneventful except for one small incident. My boat was a little faster than Doug's, due to the extra weight he was carrying, so I arrived at the narrows about an hour after the start of the ebb tide and waited for the other boat in Verde's cove. Somehow Doug had slipped by without us seeing each other. We waited another hour before I decided we had to make a move. I told the girls to hang on as we were going to buck the tide back through the Narrows, with its notorious Ripple Rock, dangerous whirlpools, eddies and strong currents. I knew how to do this, but had never actually done it by myself. We made it past Maud Island Light with its overfall rapids along the shoreline, and then shot across in front of Ripple Rock to Wilfred Point. By then we were through the worst of the danger, and made Race Point with ease, keeping close to shore down the Vancouver Island side past Duncan Bay and home to Dolphins. When we arrived, Doug was just getting ready to come back to look for us.

We were all tired but happy to be home after one of the best days cruising I can ever remember. Mrs. Ripley said we could have the following day off to rest up, and I left for the short trip over to Quadra and stayed at the Nasons' place for the night, which was a nice change from the tent. While there, I was surprised to hear that young Pete had won out in the long struggle for the lovely Leola with Teddy Mitchell. Pete and Leola had run away and were now a happily married couple residing at Old Pete's place.

The day before the Ripley family left for home, we had an evening beach party with a huge fire and a full moon rising over Quadra Island. It was sad to say our goodbyes for another year. The past two weeks had to be some of the best of my life up until that time, and I think everyone else felt the same way that night.

The rest of the summer was dull in comparison, except for one of my friends getting into trouble, bigtime. Bill Mould and his brother Jack were descendants of the Mould family, who were friends of my parents when they lived at Surge Narrows during the late 1920s. Mould Bay, located inside the Breton Islands, is named after the family, as their homestead was located at this secluded location. Bill is a few years older than I am, but this wasn't a deterrent to our friendship and family connection. Bill, not unlike most of us lads who were still young during those years, had a wild side to him. Except that somehow it managed to exceed even the rest of us.

Bill and Bob Johnson found themselves at Blind Channel with a speedboat one day that summer, having just left a logging camp where they had been working. They had their paycheques with them from the time spent in camp, but decided that this wasn't enough for the hoped for trip into town. I'm not sure who got the bright idea first, but they decided that robbing the store could be of some monetary benefit to them. They were both as tough as nails, and then some, and upon sticking a rifle in the face of the owner, they soon made their escape by boat heading for Campbell River. Being somewhat inexperienced at armed robbery though, they neglected to disable the radio telephone at the store, and sure enough, the police were waiting for them when they arrived at their destination. They did some time as residents of the 'crowbar hotel', but were apparently fortunate enough to be given fairly light sentences due to their young age. This was a definite learning experience for Bill and one that he evidently learned well. He went on to be a reasonably accomplished bank robber in Vancouver and ended up years later doing a longer term in the pen as a result. He was convicted on one count of armed robbery, but in fact had allegedly been involved in about 20. Upon release, he gave up robbing banks since he said there wasn't any real money to be had from banks. The most he ever got at any one time was about $3,500, as banks were then keeping very little cash outside their main vaults. This of course didn't discourage Bill, who was a genius at dreaming up safer and more profitable ways of supporting his high lifestyle throughout his illustrious life.

All too soon I was back living by myself on Quadra and back in school. Yet again, I had saved well over $1,200 that summer that I was able to hand over to Mum to put in her bank account. She came home after the first week of school to harvest our apples, and this year there was a huge crop, so much so that there was more than we could handle by ourselves. Mum called Bill and Sheila to help us out. They drove from their place to the north end of Gowlland, where I met my brother and his family in our boat for the short ride home. The harvesting went quickly with this added help and we spent a fun filled time together that weekend.

With both Mum and me earning and the extra revenue from the fruit trees, we were just starting to get ahead financially when disaster struck. I received a phone call from Mr. McLean to say that Mum had suffered a serious stroke and was in hospital. Obviously this was a blow, and even though she lived for another 32 years, she was never the same again. She wasn't able to go back to work at Painter's Lodge and it took several months for her to recover. After her release from hospital, she stayed with a friend in Campbell River, where medical attention was closer than on Quadra. I continued to live by myself and hiked off to school every day. It was a long day, leaving home at 7 a.m. to catch my ride to the 8 o'clock ferry over to Campbell River. We rode the 3:30 p.m. ferry back to Q Cove after school, and I'd arrive at the Nasons' about 5p.m. and then hang out there until late before setting out on the long walk home along the trail in the dark.

Meanwhile, Mum was improving in her health. I recall I was never able to get enough sleep with these long days travelling to and from school. Not surprisingly, part of this was my own fault for hanging out at the Nasons' too late, instead of going straight home, so I thought about it and decided that being with friends was preferable to being by myself at home. With the days getting shorter, I knew I'd soon be spending long evenings by myself and I felt I could catch up on my sleep on weekends. Birthday Number 15 on October 9, 1955 was a memorable event. Some of my friends asked me if I could stay in Campbell River on the Friday night instead of going home. I went home as usual to change my clothes, and then headed back to Campbell River on the 7p.m. ferry. John and Reubina picked me up and off we went to Dave's place, where a whole mob of kids was already gathered. It was Thanksgiving weekend and Dave's mother was away, so we had the house for a couple of days. We all stayed up all that Friday night and the next day cruised around with John and Reubina in their car. I arrived home late on Saturday night. It must have been after midnight by the time I got to bed and I awoke feeling very refreshed on what I thought was early Sunday morning. What a surprise when I turned on the radio to discover that it was Monday morning! I had slept soundly for about 30 hours and had missed Sunday altogether. From then on, I tried to get more rest and keep my life better organized at home.

I finished harvesting the last of the apples from the orchard and asked Jack Beach if he'd take them to Campbell River on his boat. I had about 20 40 pound boxes that we loaded up on a Saturday morning in mid-October and off we went to Campbell River. Mum met us at the dock and we loaded them into the truck of a man who bought the whole lot. This was a good break for us as we sold them all for $2 a box, a total of about $40, a nice profit for those days. There was one small problem though. We were only paid for half of them and he promised we'd have the balance in a few days. It took me until the following March to collect the remaining $20, getting just a few dollars at a time. It was a good lesson well learned though, and I knew to always be, and always was more careful in the future.

Mum's health somewhat improved and she went to live with Lilly Carlson, who had a small house behind the Van Isle

Theatre in downtown Campbell River, where she worked. Lilly was from Quadra Island and had a son Gary who was about 10 years old at the time. Mum was never pleased about me living by myself on Quadra, and Lilly suggested I move in with them for the winter. It was after that Mum was asked by Mr. Hargraves, who was manager of the paper mill, if she'd be interested in working for his wife as a housekeeper and companion. This was just what Mum had been looking for. It was work that wasn't too demanding and the Hargraves home was just a short walking distance from where we were living.

So once again I found myself living at Campbell River. This turned out to be a very early winter, with extremely cold weather and snow by early November. I was able to drain the water pipes at home on Quadra before they froze solid and secured the boats as best I could at the dock in Campbell River. Mr. Hargraves was very kind to us and Mum enjoyed working for him at the beautiful home that the paper mill provided for their manager.

Living in Campbell River with Mum turned out to be much easier than being by myself on Quadra. The walk up from downtown to school was just a few minutes, and I finally started to settle down to some serious schoolwork in Grade 10. I also made many new friends, one of whom was Bob Stamberg. Bob was about 21 at the time and was living with his parents on their gillnet boat Dagmar. His father was a carpenter who was working on the building of a large hydroelectric dam on the upper Campbell Lake. They had a home in Surrey, on the Lower Mainland near Vancouver, but were living on their boat for the winter in Campbell River, due to the many jobs available in the area at the time. They fished during the summer and worked on construction jobs during the winter.

I first met Bob because of my friend Jack Thompson, who lived with his father, stepmother Jean and his two brothers Bob and Billy. Jack was brilliant at school. The challenges of learning were always too slow to keep his attention for very long and, along with his best friend Don Nelson, he was always getting into some new experiment to test their scientific minds.

One such experiment led to almost total disaster. Jack and Don had mixed up some chemicals to see if they could invent a better type of explosive material. Jack took their concoction home with him in his pocket, and as the family was having dinner, the heat from his body set off an explosion that wrecked their dining room. Jack's father was blown through into the adjoining kitchen, and how any of them survived can only be termed a miracle. Jack ended up in hospital, unconscious and with serious burns to his upper legs. Fortunately for me, Bob Stamberg happened to be in the same hospital room as Jack, and during my visits to see Jack I struck up a lasting friendship with Bob.

The next year Bob went to work for Point Gray Towing, who operated a fleet of small tugs on the Fraser River. From there he worked his way through the marine industry, finally becoming a coastal pilot on the large cruise ships that now sail along the coast from Vancouver to Alaska.

John and Reubina's father had a good season fishing in 1955. The result was a new 1956 Chrysler with all the extras. What a machine! We all had to pool our cash to satisfy its huge and seemingly endless capacity for consuming gas, but what great fun we had just cruising around and doing all the crazy things kids can dream up. Terry Clooten's older brother Gerry had a '54 Mercury convertible at that time that Terry brought to school once in a while. When the Chrysler wasn't available, the Merc filled in very nicely.

During that winter I introduced Bob to Joan Woodcock, a good friend a couple of years older than I was. A few years later Bob and Joan married, but in the meantime, Bob and I hung out together most of the time. We had some great times that will always be remembered.

It was during that spring of 1956 I first met Epor. He was a few years older than the rest of us kids and a genius at just about everything, from science, electronics and mathematics to mechanical repairs. When asked how he acquired his nickname, his standard answer was Epor was 'rope' spelled backwards. What that meant I still don't know. It still doesn't seem to make sense as a reason for his nickname. His real name was Derrick Russell, but few people knew him by that. Television sets were just starting to arrive in Campbell River by the mid-1950's, early sets that were unreliable and the reception poor. This new medium was just heaven sent and hand made for Epor though. He was kept busy rewiring TV sets, and the owners were always amazed with the improvements he was able to achieve. Having cut his teeth, so to speak, with radios, he made this transition to television repair with great ease and one of the most striking things about him was that he always gave a loud commentary while working on a set, on what fools the engineers and designers of these sets were. He would regularly end up with several pieces of wire, switches and tubes left over, but the owners seldom had further trouble with their sets after Epor had finished.

The new radar and Loran navigational systems were just then being installed on some of the coastal tugs and fishing boats during the late 1950's, and Epor could often be seen rebuilding these sets with the same gusto and derogatory comments he had previously reserved for the inventors of television. All this knowledge apparently came to him from reading Popular Mechanics magazine, and an innate, naturally built in ability to quickly grasp how things worked.

Campbell River was a boomtown during the 1950's, with several major construction projects under way. One night some kids broke into a construction shed at the pulp mill and stole some blasting caps. You might have guessed who was included. A bunch of us spent a very happy and noisy weekend gleefully but surreptitiously setting these caps off at various locations around town. We soon became bored with the limits of this particular type of explosion though, and decided some dynamite would be even better, so we agreed some should be acquired. We lifted several cases from a construction site and hid them in the trunk of Doug Hallstrom's '54 Chevy.

Epor was immediately consulted, and he warned us not to store the caps and dynamite at the same place for safety reasons. After some prompting, he was elected explosives leader, and off we set, to try out a couple of sticks out in some suitable spot. The caps were electric, so they were easily set off with a flashlight battery, and by the Saturday night we were gaining some confidence and started moving closer to Campbell River. The police were soon notified though, and the hunt was on to find out who was responsible for all those loud explosions going off around town. By Sunday, the heat was really being turned up to catch us. So we headed out of town with our last case and found a small lake with a dead tree reaching out for about 100 feet from shore.

Epor assured us the electric caps would work just as well under water as above, so we wired up the entire case, ran the wires to shore and took shelter hiding behind a large rock. Doug touched the wires to the flashlight battery and the whole lake turned white from the shock of the explosion. An enormous geyser of water of great height erupted from the depths to shower the guilty dynamiters with cold water. That being the last of our dynamite, we headed back to town, where the search was still on for the noisemakers. Needless to say, we all kept very quiet about how we had spent the weekend and always changed the subject when anyone mentioned the recent bout of explosions around town.

I think perhaps we had been inspired by all the mining activity to do with Ripple Rock, well, that's my story and I'm sticking to it. At the time, the project to defang the twin toothed monster in the middle of Seymour Narrows was getting under way once again. Trapper and his dad both got jobs working on this project, and the Nason family moved from Quadra to Campbell River. It was an exciting time for me living in comparative luxury, but I missed the free lifestyle of the Island. About Easter time Mum had had about enough of me and my friends and our shenanigans, and decided I could move back from Campbell River to the island if I could board at Homewood. The Bayneses readily agreed, so I lived there until school was out in June.

One day in early May, Mr. McLean called to offer me a job guiding that summer. I couldn't believe what I was hearing!

All my energy went into getting myself ready to move into the guides' bunkhouse as soon as school was finished. I had started hanging around with the guides at Painter's in 1953, the last year that Jim had worked there, so I knew a few of the old time guides who lived in the area, figures who were to become part of the local folklore, such as Les McDonald and Joe Painter, but also the guides who stayed in the two bunkhouses. Mostly they were university students who were working their way through school. One of the bunkhouses was an old barn that had been used for milk cows to supply the lodge in the early years. The other one was a three room cabin with two guides to each room. My roommate that first year was Don Hayes who was the local game warden's oldest son.

That was also a year of transition in respect to fishing methods and the types of boats being used at the lodge. Prior to 1956, most all of the fishing was done from the 12 and 14 foot rowboats built by Ed Painter and in latter years by Ernie Lilburne. Outboard motors started to come into widespread use after 1950, but were used mostly to get to and from the fishing grounds. Once there, the motor was stopped and the guide rowed the boat while the guests relaxed and waited for a fish to strike.

Due to a downturn at that time in fishing for membership in the famous Tyee Club, which required, and still requires, rowing boats only, Mr. McLean had acquired a fleet of 14 and 16 foot aluminium boats with 18 horsepower Evinrude motors. Also, the Crown Zellerbach Corporation, which owned the paper mill, had decided to send senior employees and favoured customers to Painter's for week long fishing trips as bonuses and gifts. This really increased business at the lodge, so the new and powerful aluminium boats were well used. The focus in fishing changed noticeably due to this increased business. Production was called for, rather than just fishing long and hard for maybe one big Tyee. The new boats also gave us the ability to fish for Coho and non Tyee spring salmon further from home. The numbers of fish caught increased dramatically now we were able to reach Cape Mudge or Seymour Narrows quite easily within a short time. This was much easier on the guides, as we were able to use these new and reliable motors for fishing rather than having to row all the time.

The Tyee Club of British Columbia, based out of Campbell River, continued though, as it does today, to encourage the traditional methods of fishing for these giant salmon. The rules stayed and still remain very strict, and it was a great thrill to catch these fish on light tackle while rowing in a small boat. The season to qualify for club entry and trophies is still just from July 15 to September 15 each year, and you can use a motor to get to the fishing grounds but after that it has to be tilted up and the boat rowed, with the landing of a large salmon 30 lbs. or more still the main requirement under club rules. The big advantage of fishing at Campbell River continues to be that for the most part during the club season the waters of the club fishing area are sheltered and very shallow. This allows the fishing to be done with very light tackle and small boats unlike deeper ocean fishing from large vessels with rough water.

The one main disadvantage to fishing for these big spring salmon at Campbell River has always been the fact that these fish are heading up the river to spawn and no longer feeding, so it's difficult to get them to strike at a lure.

The rowing was all right as I was young and had been rowing a boat since I was five years old. Two of the guides that summer were on the Canadian Olympic rowing team that were going to Melbourne Australia to compete. The rowing was a good way for them to keep in shape. Some of the new guides fresh from university had never rowed or fished before, so the early season was used to train them before guests started to arrive.

Tyee fishing attracted a variety of sports fishermen from all over the world. Some were very famous people, others were just plain different. Wallace McMillan comes to mind. Over a period of 30 years he probably caught more Tyees than any other person I know of. He lived at the Empress Hotel in Victoria and claimed he had never worked a day in his life.

Another guest who became notorious in a few short seasons

was Richard B. Hovey from Prides Crossing, Massachusetts. He first came to Campbell River at the end of the 1955 Tyee season and caught the last fish of the club season for that year. This prompted him to announce that he would return early the next year to see if he could catch the first one in 1956.

Hovey, as he was known to everyone, was in his early 30's and had never worked a day in his life either, so far at least. In fact, I don't believe he even knew the meaning of the word. He was about 6 foot 5 inches tall, weighed something like 300 pounds, and was an excellent sports fisherman from many years of practice, I don't believe he ever did anything else but fished all year round. He was from a very wealthy eastern family and received an allowance from his mother of $30,000 a year, which was an enormous sum in 1956. This was never enough to keep up with his extravagant fishing habit though, and by the time he reached Campbell River each summer he'd be phoning home to mother for more funds. I believe his mother and probably the rest of the family felt this was money well spent, just to keep him out of their hair.

Hovey arrived about a week prior to the club opening date in 1956, to get some practice in before the start of the season. He was successful in catching the first Tyee of the season, but had gone through three guides in two weeks to do so. The fish was caught the first few days of August, which is normal, so the earlier guides rowed this huge blimp of a man hour after hour, day after day, without anything to show for their efforts except seaweed and blisters. He fished diligently from daybreak, when he could be woken up, until dark each day in a determined effort to get this first fish. It was more than his first three guides could stand, so I was finally appointed by Mr. McLean to be his one and only and fourth guide for the rest of August.

Together, Hovey and I caught a lot of fish over the next few weeks. Guides would be complaining their guests had missed a strike or had lost a fish after playing it for half an hour. Not Hovey. He never missed a strike and was probably the best and fastest fisherman I ever fished with. He was also about as loud and vocal as they come, and could be heard all over the Tyee

Pool telling me his off colour jokes and stories about fishing for stripers (striped bass) in Florida during the winter.

Hovey also claimed to anyone and everyone who would listen that he was one of the few young men chosen as eligible to marry the now late Princess Margaret, but went on to say he'd been roundly snubbed by her after their first meeting. This wouldn't have been too much of a surprise to most of us who knew him. So one day, when a bunch of us guides were sitting around the dock, it was suggested that perhaps a date with a local lady would be more fitting than royalty. After duly diligent efforts by all the guides in the bunkhouse, an agreeable arrangement was finally made with a local lady about his age. I don't know any of the details of their evening out at the movies, but I couldn't help but notice that the lady in question was never exactly overly friendly with any of us afterwards.

So much for Hovey's blandishments and charm, but he had such a good time that summer that after phoning home to mother for more cash, he reserved another visit for August and September for the following year. I guided him again for those two months the next summer and we were to have good fishing once again.

After Hovey left for home that summer of 1956, I guided Mr. and Mrs. Ferguson from Denver. They fished together in one boat, with me on the oars. I never truly liked fishing for Tyee with two people, as I felt it took away from the concentration needed to catch one of these big strong fish. Mrs. Ferguson caught several, but Mr. Ferguson was to wait a full nine years before he finally caught his first. He tried everything he and his wife could think of over those years to try to improve his chances. They got separate guides, traded guides, traded rods, and even traded lures. Mrs. Ferguson continued to catch fish and win trophies, while Mr. F went home 'skunked' year after year. Such is life with the Tyee Club. After he finally caught his big qualifying fish, he said it was well worth the wait, and went on to catch many more qualifying Tyees after that.

In the meantime, Bob Stamberg was fishing on their gillnet boat Dagmar out of Campbell River that summer, so we saw a lot of each other. Bob introduced me to John Humphries, who operated a small tug and barge company and continued to do so for many years. John had met a construction worker by the name of Mike Grohegan, who was a very good long distance swimmer. John asked me if I would follow Mike around with my boat during my spare time, while Mike practised his swimming out in the currents in the shipping channel of Discovery Passage. He told me he was planning to swim from Campbell River to Powell River on the Labour Day weekend, a distance of about 30 miles, and he wanted to practise and get accustomed to the frigidly cold ocean water which doesn't vary much between about 52 and 54 degrees F. all year in the passage. Bob and I took him out several times, and we could tell from early on he had what it takes to be a long distance swimmer. Swimming across Lake Ontario, the English Channel or the Strait of Juan de Fuca was a very popular undertaking at that time, and we could see Mike was capable of making the chilling swim across Georgia Strait to Powell River.

After practising from early May until late August, the time finally came. The weekend was forecast to have fine weather with clear skies and, most vital of all, light winds. Mike plunged into the water at Big Rock on the low water slack early on the Saturday morning, with John Humphries standing by with two of his small tugs in attendance. He was operating one and I was asked to run the other, as the skipper had asked for the weekend off. Mike swam with a kind of breaststroke that sent him surging ahead each time he kicked his feet. He was young and very powerful, and in a couple of hours swimming with a strong flood tide we were abeam of Mitlenatch Island, way out into the central of the northern part of Georgia Strait south of Quadra. The tidal currents become less obvious as the Gulf of Georgia widens out and deepens in that general vicinity and I was sent ahead to find the best direction in which to get the most advantage from the next change of tide, which should also be in our favour. The tidal currents split in the area of Mitlenatch, where the ebb tide becomes a south flowing current towards Victoria and Vancouver.

The slow moving group picked up the southerly current about mid-afternoon and Mike swam on, heading towards the south end of Savary Island. This was the most difficult part of the swim, as several hours had gone by and fatigue was now beginning to set in, and the push from the tides was much less evident. Mike struggled on and on, pushing his way through the water, looking always ahead. Finally, about an hour after dark, at about 11 p.m. that Saturday night, he waded ashore at Sliammon Village north of Powell River, where there was a welcoming crowd waiting to greet him.

We travelled back to Campbell River the next day, and Mike was given a hero's welcome, which was certainly well earned. We didn't see much of Mike after that, as he moved on to another construction job, but I'm sure he found new adventures to pursue. It had been quite an event, and a great achievement.

Chapter 18

Mum suffered a set back in her health during that summer and was unable to continue working for the Hargraves family. It was decided that I would have to leave school and find employment after the summer guiding was finished at Painter's. Mum headed off to California to spend the winter with Jim and Rose, and I found a job on the construction crew building a hydroelectric dam on Upper Campbell Lake. I boarded with the Nasons, who were now living at Campbell River, and caught the construction bus out to the project each morning

I didn't like the work very much, so I spent weekends looking for work around the waterfront on John Humphries' tugs. He was able to give me enough work so I could quit the construction job, and we kept busy towing barges and moving logging equipment around the coast until Christmas. Most of our work was in the Campbell River area, but we did a couple of jobs that were more distant. During one trip we towed a barge to Squamish, at the head of Howe Sound, to pick up some machinery for Loughborough Inlet. This was a round trip of well over 300 miles, and it brought many first time experiences for John and me, including being my first passage through the Yuclataw Rapids, which are located between Sonora and Stewart Islands and the Mainland. I had heard various stories about these rapids which were reputed to be so much more treacherous than Seymour Narrows, and we were able to see an area with the intimidating name of The Devil's Hole while running the rapids safely with a strengthening ebb tide.

My time with Humphries Towing brought me into contact with numerous salvage operations since marine accidents and disasters were much more common in those days, due to the lack and unsophisticated nature of navigational equipment on most small coastal vessels at that time. The M.R. Cliffe Towing Co. operated a large fleet of mostly steam tugs on the coast and had taken over the log towing from Gowlland Harbour from Pacific Coyle Navigation in the middle 1950's. The Morsby was the biggest tug in the Cliffe Towing fleet and one of the largest on the coast at that time, and one of the incidents involved the Morsby after she left Gowlland Harbour with a tow of logs under command of Capt. Fred Johnstone. Fred was a very experienced mariner, with a commendable record of safety and dedication to duty, but even the best of skippers and navigators can run into trouble when things start to go bad.

By 1956, the Morsby, which was built in the 1920's, was starting to show her age. The crossing from Gowlland Harbour to Baker Pass had been made just in front of an approaching southeast gale, which can be some of the worst on the coast. Seeing the oncoming storm, the tug safely made sheltered waters behind Hernando Island, but then, just as the storm started to hit with its full fury, the chief engineer reported the main engine was starving for cooling water and would have to be slowed, due to overheating.

With reduced power from the engine, the Morsby and her large tow of logs started to lose ground. As the strength of the storm increased, the tug and its tow were pushed backwards towards the shore of Cortes Island. Johnstone had to make one of those decisions that tug boat captains dread but are sometimes faced with; save the tug and her 10 man crew and lose the tow, or face the possibility of losing tug, tow and some or all of the crew. Johnstone waited until the last possible moment in the hope that the engineers might be able to solve the problem or that the weather might just moderate enough for him to make Ragged Islands, where shelter and safety were assured. As there were no other tugs in the area to offer assistance, he gave the order to slip the towline. The brake was released and the huge steam powered winch let the 2,500 feet of 1.5 inch steel cable run off into the boiling sea. The tow was quickly lost against the shore of Cortes Island but, free of her load, the tug and her crew was able to limp slowly back into Gowlland Harbour for repairs to the cooling system.

John Humphries and a radio technician named Ted Wakefield had bought a deep sea diving suit, which they had been experimenting with. Neither of them had any formal training in the use of this equipment, so it was very much trial and error from start to finish, but we were called out to make a dive on the Morsby, as the chief engineer had traced their problem to the main sea water inlet valve. There was an obstruction either in or at the opening where the valve went through the hull of the ship. As it turned out, the dive had to be made at night, which was not the best of circumstances, but a plywood patch was successfully nailed over the opening of the inlet valve, which was then dismantled by the engineers. It was found the workings had fallen off, due to corrosion, and that left the valve in a partially closed position. The engineers replaced the defective parts and closed up the valve. Problem solved. The whole repair took no more than about an hour, and we all marvelled at how such a simple lack of maintenance could have produced such a huge loss of property. The good part was that tug and crew were safe. Beachcombers had recovered most of the lost logs within a couple of weeks, at great cost to the insurance companies.

Another salvage incident resulted in our ending up in Vancouver for a few days. It occurred just before Christmas. The fish packing vessel M.C.M. was towing the barge John Davidson from Porlier Pass to Prince Rupert, and both vessels were loaded with herring destined for a reduction plant in Rupert. The barge started to take on water shortly after loading, and by the time they reached Cape Mudge, the situation was starting to be desperate, so we were called out with pumps to see if we could save both the vessel and cargo. We pumped for hours and hours, and by next morning, the barge had stabilized, but continual pumping was still required, so it was decided that the fish boat and tow should be sent to Steveston, rather than heading all the way up north to Prince Rupert.

Under normal conditions, this would have been a voyage of about 20 hours, but conditions turned out to be far from normal. As it turned out, we had a barge to take down to Vancouver with some logging equipment on board. So our barge was hooked on behind the John Davidson, and our pumps were fired up and ready for all the pumping that was going to be required to keep the herring barge afloat. All went well until another of those gales out the southeast forced us into False Bay for shelter. John and I had both suggested to the captain of the M.C.M. that we should travel through Baker Pass and down the Inside Passage, to take advantage of the better shelter there, but the captain was an experienced former deep sea sailor, and he preferred being about as far from land as he could possibly get.

Every couple of hours while under way, we were to come alongside the barge with our tug to start the pumps and make sure all was well. We anchored in False Bay for some pumping and waited there for a couple of days for the weather to improve. Finally, on the third day, the wind shifted to northwest and we were under way again. But by the time we reached the Fraser River, it was well after dark and the wind had increased again to a full on gale. There was a strong ebb tide flowing out of the river, and the M.C.M. couldn't make any headway against the current, so we disconnected our barge tow in heavy seas and started up the river.

This was survival now for us, the fish packer boat and her tow. The M.C.M. was ahead of us, and as we caught up to her, we found they'd wrapped their towline around a navigation buoy while shortening up the tow line. This resulted in the line hanging up on a buoy, with the barge on one side of the buoy and the M.C.M. on the other side. The danger was now extreme for both fish packer and tow, so we called for assistance on the radio, and the tug Sea Cap came out to help, taking our tow from us so we could aid the M.C.M.

LAWRENCE FOORT

The sea was now churning violently and the spray from it was freezing as soon as it hit the deck. Somehow though, we managed to get the two vessels free from the buoy and into Steveston before the barge sank in mid-river. We pumped for the rest of the night to keep the vessel afloat until early next morning, when the fish plant crew arrived to suck out the herring from the barge using a 10 inch pump, sending the cargo directly into the reduction plant.

After securing our barge at Steveston, we took a couple of days off for some rest. It was during this short stay in Vancouver that I first met the Giroday family. Armand Giroday and his cousin Dan operated a sawmill under the Granville Bridge in False Creek, which is now a trendy area of markets and restaurants. Back in 1956 when we moored at the Girodays' sawmill, this area was very much industrial and the headquarters of Harold Clay's marina and boat charter business. Giroday Sawmills had logging operations at Elk Bay and Redonda Bay up near Campbell River, and John had done some towing for them over the years.

The Girodays lived at 52nd and Cartier at that time, and the family consisted of Rosemary, Armand Jr., Janet, Barry, Denise and Michelle, with Carol Ann on the way. Armand Sr. and I became very close friends over the years and I can say without any reservation that he was one of life's 'good guys'. The sawmill was a major business at the time and had been built with hard work from meagre beginnings. Armand, Kay and their family were all to become a major part of my life over the next 10 years.

Rosemary and Janet were having a few friends over the first time I met them, but they invited me to stay at their place, rather than going back on the tug at the sawmill. They had a beautiful home and we had a good time, just a bunch of kids hanging around listening to records and planning the upcoming Christmas holidays.

After a couple of days resting, we were off again, to try to get home by Christmas. As usual at that time of year the weather was poor and we had high southeast winds and rough seas on our way back up the coast. We made several stops at various logging camps, to move equipment on our barge, and finally got home a few days before Christmas.

Tug boating can be monotonous and usually is, but I was learning valuable information that I'd use for the rest of my life. Boats, engines, shipyards and general marine knowledge were to be a dominant factor for the future. I did need more education though, so I decided that in September I'd return to school in Vancouver, where I could enrol in a private school and study at an accelerated rate. I still needed to earn enough money to keep Mum and myself, so I couldn't afford to waste too much time at school.

The spring of 1957 found me leaving my seafaring life for a while to work at Port Alberni and Crofton where new paper mills were being built and it was easy to get work. The pay was all right too, up to $2 an hour, and I saved as much as I could, sending some extra money to Mum, who was still with Jim and Rose in California for the winter. I often bunked in with the Nasons in Campbell River.

By then, Trapper had been working at the Ripple Rock project as a crane operator and was bringing in some pretty handsome paycheques. He decided he needed a boat so we could travel together in style, and he made a deal with Gordy Mason, ordering a new 19 foot beauty with twin 35 h.p. Evinrudes. This was unheard of power at that time. Most boats of that size had the old dependable 25 h.p. motors. This vessel with the twin 35s was something else, especially since the new vessel had some other unique options most of our boats lacked, including a windshield with a canvas top.

That was considered a luxury in those days, and came along with motor controls and steering up front, almost unheard of at the time. The boat lacked a decent sized fuel tank, so we had to depend on two standard five gallon tanks and a couple of extra Jerry cans for the long trips, but at that time there were many marine fuel stations up and down on the coast, so the small fuel capacity wasn't a big problem.

Trapper had not been raised on the coast like me, so I was

appointed captain for the first few months. After a few weeks of local exploring, Trapper asked me if I knew how to get to Vancouver, which of course I did from my time with Humphries. So off we set for The Big Smoke one Friday morning. We had good weather most of the way and made Halfmoon Bay before we had to stop for fuel. The woman who operated the fuel station there had a pet crow she had taught to talk, and she went about her business with this crow sitting on her shoulder making rude remarks to anyone passing by.

By the time we reached Cape Roger Curtis, it was starting to get dark, with a moderate north westerly beginning to pick up. Fortunately the seas were behind us, pushing us forward, and the boat proved herself very comfortable. The lights of Vancouver were bright and twinkling in welcome as we surfed our way into False Creek. This was the best leg of the trip, and after mooring safely at Clay's, we made our way over the bridge to the Austin Hotel. From there we looked down from the Granville Bridge on to Giroday's sawmill, and I explained to Trapper that the owners were friends of mine. He wasn't impressed, and I don't think he really believed me. The next morning, after a good sleep, Trapper said he'd like to explore a little, as he hadn't ever been to Vancouver before, so we were walking down Granville Street when who should happen by but Rosemary Giroday, driving with a friend in her mother's new pink 1957 Mercury convertible. I didn't see them, but Trapper said there were a couple of girls looking back at us from a convertible with the top down. Rosemary did a couple of U-turns though and stopped to see if it was really me. Trapper was a little shy at first, but we soon jumped in with them, and Rosemary said there was a party planned for that night and invited us to go along as her guests. Trapper said he'd prefer to try to find some of his logger friends to drink beer with, so Rosemary dropped us off and said she'd pick me up later for the party.

I spent a very pleasant evening with the Girodays, with Rosemary delivering me back to the hotel at quite a late hour. By that time Trapper had decided Vancouver didn't appeal to him that much and asked if we could head home in the morning. Being early June, it was soon going to be daylight, so we packed up, had some breakfast at an all night restaurant and headed down to the dock to slip our lines and make for home. Campbell River is almost exactly 100 nautical miles from Vancouver and at an average speed of 20 knots we reckoned we'd be home in about six hours, allowing for a fuel stop at Powell River. We had one of those afternoon summer south easterly winds going across from Baker Pass to Cape Mudge. Even though the tide was still flooding, I decided to head across and show Trapper how to avoid the worst of the tide rip off Mudge and the southern end of Quadra. I'm glad to say the boat behaved very well in the steep seas at about half speed, and we crossed the cape into Discovery Passage without any problem at all.

As soon as we arrived home, there was a call from Mr. McLean saying that I should report for work at Painter's as soon as possible. This was to be my second summer at the lodge, and I was looking forward to not being a rookie any more. Some of the university students who were graduating that year weren't returning to the lodge for guiding, and this left some openings for a few new people, such as Ken Dawson, Ken Birch and Jim Sears. I spent some time out on the water showing them how to operate a boat safely, as well as letting them know about some of my favourite fishing spots. Dawson and Birch were from Victoria, and had just finished their year at Victoria College. Jim Sears was from Palo Alto, California, and had travelled all the way up from there on a motor scooter. Jim and Mum became close friends over the years and continued corresponding with each other until Mum passed away 30 years later.

We really were busy that summer. The lodge was filled with guests from Crown Zellerbach, the owners of the paper mill at Duncan Bay, and the new aluminium boats and motors supplied by Gordy Mason worked out very well. These boats, with their speed and additional safety, allowed us to open up yet more new fishing grounds. The only thing that prevented us from having a perfect year was the weather. It started raining about mid-June and didn't stop until mid-August, close to two months of almost solid rains. Someone came up with the catchy phrase 'Forty days and forty nights', but it actually rained longer than that, more like the complete 60 days, and the rain was accompanied by southeast winds. It never really rained hard all that time, but instead was just an annoying drizzle, along with dark and gloomy clouds. But we learned that when the weather doesn't finally break until mid-August, it continues to be nice well into December.

I guided Hovey again that year for two months. We did very well fishing for Tyees and then, during late September, we had great fishing for big Coho in the shallows of Butler Point, off the southeast corner of Quadra. This fishing was done with fly rods, which I think is probably the best fishing one could experience on the B.C. coast, fishing for fighting salmon. Hovey had heard the Brem River in Toba Inlet had a summer run of steelhead trout, and since the Tyee fishing hadn't materialized at that point, he asked me if I knew the waters well enough to take us there. I assured him I could get us there without any difficulty, so we used the largest boat the lodge had, with its 25 hp Elto and also my own 18 hp. Evinrude to give us additional speed and reliability. We set off at daylight so we could make the whole trip in one day if all went well. We stopped in at Hope's store at Refuge Cove for fuel and to buy some extra snacks, then motored up through Waddington Channel and into Toba Inlet. The Brem River is about half way up the inlet on the port side, that's the left for landlubbers! At that time the valley hadn't yet been logged, and the timber growing up along the sides of the river was spectacular. We didn't have any luck with steelhead fishing, but we did sight a grizzly and other wildlife and Hovey said the scenery alone was well worth the trip and the weather. The weather was magnificent and hot, and the water flat and calm.

I guided Mr. and Mrs. Shoemaker and their daughter Wendy for a week in early August. Wendy was about my age and one of those natural blonde beauties that the California sun seems to produce in huge quantities. Mr. Shoemaker worked for a printing company in San Francisco. The family were guests of Crown Zellerbach, and this was their second trip to Campbell River. We enjoyed some excellent fishing in spite of the rain at that time, and after catching our Coho and Chinook limit for the day almost every time we went out, I would take Wendy Tyee fishing in one of the rowboats. It was a little early for Tyees, but we tried hard to luck out as the first of the season to catch a qualifying fish under Tyee Club rules. This wasn't to be, but we sure did our best. We had a great time together and I was sad to see them leave and have to face Hovey for the next two months. Wendy was from Palo Alto, and attended the same school as Jim Sears, one of our new guides. I was to see a lot of them over the next few years when we visited my brother Jim in California.

I guided into early October that year and saved enough money to be able to attend school in Vancouver. Trapper was logging for CCM in Heming Bay, and one evening I decided to take my boat and run up there for a visit. On arriving, I was given dinner with the crew at the logging camp, which was owned by Henry Carney. His oldest son, Lorne, was a good friend of mine, so we had an enjoyable time sitting around visiting and chatting on a fine autumn evening. Henry was quite surprised when I said Goodbye and started to leave, since it was well after dark and he didn't think I should be out in a fast boat at night. I assured him I would make the low water slack at Seymour Narrows and it'd be all right. It was one of those rare nights when there was a full moon, flat calm seas and a nice warm offshore breeze. I passed the S.S. Cardena northbound at the Maude Island light, and I think that was probably the last time I saw that faithful old ship while she was still in service. I remember thinking how fortunate I was to be alive but also a little sad at the approach of yet another winter and the prospect of having to move to Vancouver.

The next day I packed up, said Goodbye to Mum, caught the bus to Nanaimo, and then took the Canadian Pacific Ferry to Vancouver. I stayed at the Amos Hotel on Cordova Street, just across from the CPR docks and railway station. This was a part of the city I was familiar with from my childhood trips aboard the Union Steamships vessels. The next day I opened a bank account at one of the banks, to deposit some of my summer earnings. Up to that point I had been packing them around in the big city in my pocket! The headline news that morning was all about the Russians launching Sputnik, the first satellite sent into orbit around the earth. Later that day I found a boarding house on Barkley Street and moved in that afternoon. The Barkley Manor was an old mansion from earlier days and my rent was $16 a week, including breakfast and dinner.

I still had to enrol at the private school up on Broadway to start my Grade 11 classes, and as I was late enrolling, I could only find space in afternoon and evening classes. This worked out all right though, as I had mornings free to roam around the waterfront and explore the downtown part of the city. I accelerated my studies, so Mum and I could go to California at Christmas to stay with Jim and Rose. This all worked out very well for me. I spent some weekends with the Stambergs where Bob and I hung out with his friends in New Westminster. Joan Woodcock, one of my friends from Campbell River, was also attending school in Vancouver and Joan and Bob were seeing a fair bit of each other at that time and talking about getting married the next year.

The old steam tugs, mostly of the Pacific Coyle and Cliff Towing fleets, were moored along the waterfront west of the foot of Burrard Street at that time and held some fascination for me. Most had definitely seen better days and would never sail again, but many were familiar to me from the days when they towed log booms out of Gowlland Harbour. I would prowl around the engine rooms and inspect the crews' quarters. The telegraphs in the wheelhouses were still hooked up, and I would ring them at will, delighting in listening to their clanging responding signals deep down in the hull of these ancient vessels.

The hull of the tug Active was moored at the Canadian National Railroad dock at the foot of Main Street. Active was a famous old steam tug at that time, and had been repowered with an 800 h.p. Enterprise diesel. She was a real beauty, but unfortunately she later met with disaster near Cortes Island, grounding on a reef and breaking her back. All was not lost, however. After being salvaged, the engine was used to repower the tug Sea lion. I happened to be on board the Sea lion a few years ago and that old engine was still providing valiant service.

One day as I was walking along Granville Street, and I met up with Bob Davis, a friend from Campbell River. He wasn't doing too well and had absolutely no money or even, apparently, the prospects of finding a job. I brought him home to the boarding house and booked him and a friend in for a week, then fronted them ferry and bus fare back up to Campbell River. We had some good times together during that week, further exploring the city and each enjoying having found a friendly face.

Vancouver was like an overgrown small town in the 1950's, and it was not unusual, even for me as a stranger, to meet up with people I knew. One evening I was out to a movie with a young lady I had met and what a surprise it was to spot Peter Stanley working at the theatre. He'd been laid off at Vancouver Tug where he had been working as a deckhand. Peter was from Quadra, where his father was skipper on a purse seiner. Peter and his brother Kayo both went on to work at Vancouver Tug before eventually becoming coastal pilots.

Another day I met Tom Toynbee, who had guided at Painter's and was from Saltspring Island. Bob Groulx was another guiding friend I spent time with while in Vancouver that year. Bob got married that fall and moved to San Francisco to work for Mr. Larry Odell, the husband of Marie Odell, whom Bob had guided for several Tyee seasons. The wedding was well attended by former guides and many other people I knew from up the coast. While I missed the island life, I wasn't lonely or homesick during my time in The Big Smoke and I made many new friends there.

One highlight of life in the city was the arrival of the Pacific & Oriental (P&O) passenger ships every few weeks. Huge crowds would wait at the CPR docks at the foot of Burrard

Street for these beauties to dock. The liners would leave from England and circle the globe, making stops in numerous different countries. When they reached Vancouver, they'd either be 'inbound' back to England from Australia or departing for Australia and New Zealand via Hawaii and Fiji. The arrival and departure of these ships was always marked by a huge outdoor party, with bands playing, streamers flowing, family and old friends meeting and reuniting once again. The ships usually stayed in port for at least a day, with hundreds of passengers from a whole variety of nations and nationalities, and a broad mixture of languages roaming the downtown area. I usually tried to meet these ships whenever I could, and collected many happy memories as a result.

Looking back, I suppose my stay in Vancouver that year before Christmas was rather like a wandering nomad, drifting the streets and different events and activities with the assurance of a few dollars in my pocket and a place to sleep at night.

When I had completed my schooling, I caught a ride back to Campbell River with Bob Groulx in his old Morris Minor, and a couple of days later Mum and I left for the trip to California.

Chapter 19

Mum wanted to visit some friends in Vancouver for a few days on the way south to California, so I made my way out to Jack Anderson's, where I had a standing invitation to stay whenever I wanted. Wes, Stan and I hung around with some friends in New Westminster and did our best to get into as much trouble as possible over the next day or two. Stan had recently bought a brand new suit which was way too big for him, and as I didn't have a light suit to wear down in California, I bought it from him for the princely sum of $15. I stayed with them a couple of days until Mum was ready to resume the journey then I met her at the Main Street train station.

We rode the train down the same way we'd gone in 1951. Jim met us at the Berkeley train station, and we spent another happy Christmas in California. It was good to see the Aboumrad family again, as well as Heather and Michael, my niece and nephew.

Aunt Sarah had moved from the family home on 61st Street to a smaller place in East Oakland, so I somehow didn't ever get to see any of my friends again from my time at Washington school. The whole area had also changed, and most of the families I knew had moved away. I roamed around the streets I had once known so well, but it was so different now. I decided instead to explore San Francisco, as I had three weeks ahead of me staying with Jim and Rose.

Jim had bought a home in the Berkeley Hills, at 93 Sunset Trail. This was a most unusual area, as the homes there couldn't be accessed by road at the time. Instead, a short but steep hike up from the parking area brought one to a beautiful wooded trail lined with houses on each side. The view was truly spectacular, with the Golden Gate and Bay Bridges in the background and the huge gleaming white Claremont Hotel directly below, with its well groomed gardens and flowering trees.

The street railways were still in use at that time, and the "E" Train to San Francisco terminated at the end of Claremont Avenue, a short distance from Jim's house. Almost every day I'd take the train to the city and go exploring this fascinating seaport. I always enjoyed the train rides through the East Bay, then over the bridge to the terminal downtown. I took full advantage of my leisure time to go poking around the waterfront and look up some of the people I'd met guiding at Painter's Lodge the previous summers.

My first call was at the newly constructed Crown Zellerbach building on Market Street, in the heart of the business district. I stopped at the reception desk and politely asked for Mr. Bob Connors, whom I knew quite well. He was their public relations director at the time. The receptionist asked if I had an appointment, which of course I didn't, but she was kind enough to ring him up to see if an appointment was possible for the next day. I heard her say "Yes sir, right away!" and then she asked me to please take the elevator right on up to the boardroom. There I was greeted at the elevator by a secretary who very nicely showed me through into a huge walnut paneled room where many of the executives of the company were seated. Lunch was promptly served, with me as a guest of these high ranking executives. Just about every salmon that had ever been caught by these men, their wives and their guests were re-caught over lunch, related in great detail with much humour and gleeful enjoyment over the next couple of hours. I was certainly given a royal reception beyond anything I had even thought or dreamed of. I had hoped to be able to just say a brief hello to Mr. Connors and here I was being accorded the full red carpet treatment.

A few days later I called up Mr. Shoemaker, Wendy's father, who immediately invited me to come and visit him at his office. He showed me round the printing plant, then phoned Wendy at home in Palo Alto to let her know I was in town for Christmas. I spoke with her for a few minutes, and she very quickly extended an invitation to me to come and spend the weekend. As Jim Sears also lived in Palo Alto, this was a great opportunity to see the pair of them. They said if I could make my way to the Cow Palace in South San Francisco, they'd pick me up there Friday afternoon.

This promised to be a great treat for me, so as planned, they collected me at the Cow Palace and we drove south on Highway 101 down to Palo Alto. It was good to see my two friends again, and we had a wonderful weekend together. I slept at Jim's house but we spent most of our time over at Wendy's, where her mother, father and two sisters were most gracious hosts and showed me a fabulous time. Sunday came all too quickly, and I rode the train back to San Francisco, then on to Berkeley, since it was now almost Christmas.

I spent a few more days exploring San Francisco, which to me is still about the best city on the West Coast to be a tourist. We visited with Aunt Sarah and her family a few times. It was good to see Bill again. He had a newer Olds convertible now, but I still preferred the old '48 model best, mostly, I guess, because of all the great childhood memories.

After Christmas, I said goodbye to the family and caught the bus 'home' to Vancouver. This turned out to be the only really long bus trip I've ever taken by myself, and I must say that as far as I'm concerned once was more than enough. The best and most memorable part was that I sat next to a U.S. Navy recruit who was headed for a radar station near Kamloops and had some friends in Seattle. So we stopped off there overnight and caught the bus north again the next morning, arriving on New Year's Eve. I had a date for that evening, and we went to a party at the Anderson's to welcome in 1958.

After a few days, Bob Stamberg drove me downtown to catch the first C. P. R. ferry of the day back to Nanaimo and then take the bus home to Campbell River. As it happened, John Humphries was in need of some help right away on his tugs, and since I was at a loose end and didn't have anything else to do, it was back to work for me.

After two months with John, George Parsons asked me if I'd come to work for him skippering a log yarding tug they had, a 34 foot vessel they used to gather up small log booms from the various logging camps in the area. Jack Williams from Egmont was my deckhand, and we'd gather up enough logs for the larger tug Sea Imp, which would then haul the whole tow down south to Howe Sound.

Together, Jack and I gathered up logs all over the coast. We moved them through the notorious Hole in the Wall, Welbour, Green Point and Yuclataw Rapids to where they were assembled at either Siwash Cove or Raza Island, making up gigantic tows of hundreds of logs in about 30 sections. This system was used by most of the log tow companies, as it saved a lot of time for the much bigger tugs, whose operating costs were of course much higher than ours.

We learned by listening to others and paying attention to our instincts and experience. I was just 17, and here I was, skipper on a tug, doing some of the most dangerous towing to be had on the coast. I found my well honed instincts served me well, as the fast waters we navigated were by now very often a kind of part of me. I had become used to them from early childhood. Learning the towing trade from others and experience came later, to be passed on to the next generation. John Charlton, who did the same work for Maritime Towing, also showed me some of the things he'd learned over the years, which was also very much appreciated and taken to heart.

One day that spring we passed the CPR passenger ship Princess Patricia southbound off Kelsey Bay. She was painted white rather than her traditional array of colours, and was all decked out with flags. This was the start of a new career for this ship and her sister Princess Marguerite. The two ships had previously been on the triangle route between Vancouver, Seattle and Victoria during the summer season, and then the

Nanaimo-Vancouver route during the off season. Now, while the Marguerite took on the Victoria-Seattle run for many more summers, the Patricia was placed on the Alaska cruise service, which was then just the start of all the Vancouver-Alaska cruising we see today, serviced by some of the largest and most luxurious passenger liners in the world.

As this cruising to Alaska is seasonal, the Princess Patricia was sent south to Los Angeles in the winter, beginning what is now known as Princess Cruises run from Los Angeles south to various ports in Mexico.

Spring, with its long days and warm weather, tends to bring out the adventurous spirit in young and old alike, and it certainly always did, and still does, for me. Some of us were sitting around one Saturday night that spring wondering what to do with ourselves, when someone mentioned there was going to be a regatta on one of the lakes near Port Alberni, on the other side of Vancouver Island. Vic Graham, Gerry Clooten, Trapper and I decided immediately this could well be a worthwhile experience for us to go off and explore. We invited along some of the girls to accompany us, but for some reason they all firmly declined. So off we set, the four of us, leaving Campbell River about 1 a.m. I was driving Vic's '54 Chevy, as I hadn't been among the drinkers at the previous party. We took our time, as we were all tired by that time of the morning, stopping for gas along the way, and the chauffeured passengers continued indulging in the odd beer or two as we talked and travelled. We arrived safely outside the Arlington Hotel in Port Alberni about daybreak. There was still some time to spare before the start of the regatta, so we just snoozed and used the hotel facilities to freshen up.

The regatta was great, with numerous thrilling races by high speed boats around a course on the lake. It was the first time I'd ever seen a boat travelling at more than 100 miles an hour (160km/h), and we'd also made some new friends with some local ladies who appeared to be much braver than the girls at home and were evidently prepared to put up with our company, probably in part because Trapper slept most of the day on the grass.

As time went by, Vic noticed our supply of beer wasn't keeping up with the demands placed on it by the expanded group and our new found friends, so he started to look for two bottles of lemon gin he knew we'd stashed somewhere in the back seat.

"I know where they are," said Gerry. "They rolled out onto the street in front of the Arlington when we stopped there this morning."

The girls immediately suggested rather haughtily that Gerry should be given "a darned good beating for his careless and thoughtless behaviour", but instead we all piled back into the car in a reasonably friendly manner, to head back into town and then begin heading home at day's end.

Amazingly, when we stopped in front of the Arlington, there were our two bottles of gin still sitting right in front of the hotel! My passengers promptly polished them off in short order, and then, as some of us had to work the next day, we deposited the girls on the sidewalk and headed home. That was a regular occurrence in the short nights of spring. Beach parties often went on well into the night, with most participants arriving home just in time to get ready for the day's work. We were young and carefree and we lived each day as it came.

Bob Stamberg and Joan Woodcock were married that June. This was a particularly happy occasion for me, as they were both good friends and I had introduced them to each other, so I felt a greater than normal attachment to this marriage. The good times Bob and I had together in the past seemed to mature somewhat after that, but we still maintained a close friendship for many years afterwards.

The job I had with Parsons Towing at this time was a good one, and it gave me a chance to get some of that much needed experience I would require to draw on in the future. Soon though I had to decide whether to stay with it or go back to guiding at Painter's Lodge. I knew jobs would always be available for experienced boat skippers who knew how to work the rapids in the area, so I decided to return to Painter's for this one final fishing season.

When I had some time on my hands that summer, I'd often hang around with Stan Palmer at the Tulloch-Western fish plant, and one day Stan told me my father had called and wanted to let me know he was in Vancouver and would like to see me if possible. I guessed he'd phoned home to Mum, and she'd tried to reach me by leaving a message with Stan. Laurie Myers was skipper on the Tullcrest, which was due to leave the plant for Vancouver in a couple of hours, and Stan said I was welcome to ride down with them. I hadn't seen Father for eight years, and I really agonized over whether to get my gear together and get on board for the overnight trip, but in the end I decided not to go after all. I've regretted it ever since, since that was the last time I was ever to have contact with him.

Although still in my teens, I was a senior guide at Painter's now, so I began about May 1 and was soon kept busy for the whole season, five very full months right into early October. The early season was great that year, and we had some truly spectacular fishing at Copper Bluffs during May and June. Q Cove also 'turned on' fish wise during July, with daily catch limits regularly being taken by guests each evening.

Ken Birch and Ken Dawson were my roommates again that summer, and we sure had a good time together. Dawson often wondered if he'd be able to swim the couple of miles in the strong currents across Discovery Passage from the Vancouver Island side. I encouraged him to give it a try, and one evening we set off on the first of the ebb tide. There were just the two of us, and being a strong guy, he made it across from Painter's dock to Steep Island, just north of Gowlland Harbour on the Quadra side of the channel, with ease. I kept the boat close alongside, as the water is always very cold in that area and I was concerned he might get cramps.

Ken had a 1950 Ford convertible that we used to enhance our social life. Driving around with a car full of teenagers and the top down on a warm summer night is just about as carefree as one can get, and we had a great time cruising the town.

The fishing season suffered a bit of a blow for me that year though. About the last week of July, Hovey called to cancel his two month fishing trip to Campbell River. This was a bit of a disappointment, not that I can honestly say I was all that eager to guide him again for a third time, but it had always been good sure money until the end of September.

As it turned out, I was appointed to guide Dr. Julian Benjamin, from Cincinnati, Ohio, whose name later went on one of the major perpetual trophies open for competition in the Tyee Club each year. We had a wonderful time fishing together and became life long friends. We'd make every early morning tide in the Tyee Pool. This meant being out on the water before daylight. We'd come in for breakfast about 7:30 a.m. and then go out again at about 10 a.m. or the next favourable tide. Mrs. Benjamin didn't fish, but enjoyed coming with us for the morning trip after breakfast. She'd sit in the boat, looking out over the water at the scenery on the Quadra Island and Campbell River shores, watching the boats and doing her knitting. We'd sometimes take a lunch with us if the tides were favourable at noon and we didn't want to miss out on the opportunity of a possible fish. As a result, often we fished four tides a day, going from daylight until after dark. It was great fun and paid off with a good catch of Tyee that year.

We made a trip one day with Larry Odell, who was being guided by renowned Tyee rower Les McDonald. On that occasion we used a couple of the new fast boats to make a trip all the many miles north up to Adams River, about 20 miles north of Kelsey Bay. We tried our hand at doing some fishing at the mouth of the Adams, but we only caught one lingcod, and it poured rain for the entire trip. It was an interesting trip, but we weren't experienced at fishing those waters and our disappointing catch proved it.

Although this was to be my last year as a guide at Painter's, I would continue to spend time with Dr. Benjamin each summer until he passed away in 1975. I still have a tackle box we won together at the annual 1958 salmon derby, in which we placed 2nd with a 54 pound Tyee. Dr. Benjamin continued to fish at Campbell River each summer for over 30 years, and in his honour the Tyee Club named after him its annual trophy for the rowing guide whose guests catch the most qualifying fish during the club season.

September always brings shorter days of course, and most of the Tyee fishing is starting to wind down following the summer holidays. The guides who were university students had to leave for home to get ready for classes mid-month. That year, Dawson and Birch talked me into coming home to Victoria with them for a few days after Dr. Benjamin left for another year.

Birch and I drove down in his old Austin and I stayed at Dawson's place, where his mother and father were kind and generous hosts. On the Saturday night, we went to a party at the old Crystal Gardens with a group of student nurses. We all had a great time, and it was with some feeling of loneliness that I returned to Campbell River and the empty guides' bunkhouse. I was still kept busy guiding until the first week of October though, and managed to put away another good nest egg to share with Mum.

Chapter 20

1958 Was a year to remember in the commercial sockeye fishery. A huge unexpected run of Fraser River fish passed through Johnstone Straits during August, and some of my friends who were fortunate enough to have jobs on boats in the area came home with $8,000-$10,000 as their share of the catch. This was an unheard of amount for a few weeks of work and represented about two years wages at the time. This windfall generated some very amusing stories, and one that represented many was the saga of Raymond 'Daylight' Smith.

Bill Roberts was skipper on a Canadian Fishing Co. vessel named Otard. It was probably the smallest, lowliest and most humble of the small boats in their large fleet of seiners. Bill was to leave Steveston one Saturday night, but was delayed when one of his crew was late for departure time. There was no time to waste, as the boats had to be ready to fish by opening time of 6 p.m. the next night, so it was decided a replacement crew member could possibly be found at Campbell River, on their way north as they sailed for the fishing grounds.

As fate would have its way, according to the story, Daylight Smith was sleeping off a substantial amount of rum he'd drunk on the Saturday night and when Bill docked at Campbell River early that Sunday morning, Daylight was found passed out on the end of one of the floats. This was too good an opportunity to pass up. He was known to be an experienced deckhand and there he was for the taking, so they loaded him aboard, threw off their lines and headed off to catch the tide through Seymour Narrows.

Quite a few hours later, Daylight was still snoring away on deck when it was decided a bucket of cold water was needed to get him up and at least partially ready for work at the approaching deadline. Daylight awoke quickly under the water treatment and gazed around in wonderment as to how on earth he had ended up with Bill and his crew, who were making ready to cast their nets. He was also more than a little angry at the trick that had been played on him and demanded in no uncertain terms to be taken back to Campbell River immediately. This of course wasn't about to happen, and after some threats from the crew Daylight set to work with the rest of them.

Fate is a wonderful thing when it goes your way. Bill and the Otard crew caught so many fish that week that they ended up being one of the highest scoring boats for the entire season. Daylight hit town on the Thursday, drew most of the massive sum of money he was due, and by Saturday was wearing a huge diamond ring, a set of new and expensive clothes and sporting a young lady on each arm as he entered the Willows Hotel bar on the waterfront.

Now Daylight was nothing if not generous and he was sharing his newfound wealth in a most open handed way with all his friends. His social standing moved up several notches as he refused to let anyone other than himself buy a round of drinks, so by the time the next week rolled around, he was more than eager to go back to fishing with Bill and his crew again. Sadly, fate had turned its head in another direction. The run of fish had passed, and no more big money was to be made. Everything was back to normal again. So there was Daylight once again, sleeping it off down at the dock on the end of a float, minus his diamond, fancy clothes and most of his friends.

Others who were lucky enough to have received a portion of the marine bounty were more careful with their sudden affluence, making use of it to continue their educations, purchasing homes, upgrading their boats and starting businesses. It was a good thing they did, for the following year and several more to follow after that were about as poor in their catches and yields as at any time in recent memory. But that season of 1958 will always be remembered as the year that a number of fortunes were made.

Another milestone in the history of the area was the final removal of Ripple Rock from Seymour Narrows on April 5, 1958. As mentioned earlier in this telling, this made history as the largest non-nuclear man made explosion up until that time. Police patrolled the area around the perimeter the night before the blast to keep everyone at least five miles away, I know because Trapper and I made several attempts before we were finally able to penetrate the perimeter. We slept out in the bush all night awaiting zero hour, but as it turned out, we didn't manage to get as good a view of the explosion as others did outside the line, due to a heavy fog that had rolled into our area. The explosion was, however, effective in taking off the tops of the two submerged mountaintops, removing this great navigational hazard and making the Narrows much safer for larger ships.

About a month before the rock was blown up, Life Magazine sent up some underwater photographers to get some pictures of the underwater phenomenon. This was technology that was fairly new at the time. They used the same camera that took the pictures of the sunken Andrea Doria as she lay on the bottom off New York. I asked to go along on the expedition, but they said there was no room for me on the diving vessel. I had my doubts whether they'd be able first to locate the rock and then, if they did, whether they'd be able to get enough time at slack water to get the pictures before the growing current forced them to surface.

The first few days of the photo shoot were evidently a failure, and one day I was asked to come along with my boat, after assuring them that I could find the rock. I located the rock with ease, as I had many times before, and Life Magazine got their pictures. For many years afterwards, I'd still quite often drift over the rock at tide change to see if it was visible, and it always gave me a creepy feeling I can't explain to see this once ferocious monster lurking so close to the surface.

After what was to be my last summer at Painter's as a guide, my sister Ruth was married to Mr. Ron Allen, of Rio Dell, California. The wedding took place at Homewood on Quadra, with Kathy as bridesmaid and my brother Bill giving away the bride. They moved to Portland, Oregon, where Ron was working, purchased a house, and settled down to domestic life.

About this time I first met John Michael Nash. I had an agreement to share an apartment in Vancouver with Dawson and Birch while they attended the University of British Columbia, and this was an inexpensive way for me to have a foothold in the city whenever I needed one. I was due down into Vancouver after Ruth's wedding to see what work was available on the tugs there to further my experience, and I called Dawson to pick me up from the CPR ferry. He said he'd send Mike Nash to meet me. I had heard my friends speak of Mike during the past two summers, but had never met him and we hit it off right away. Little did we know that many years later he'd wind up as my brother in law. Mike's father was a doctor in Victoria and his mother had just passed away in June of that year at the young age of 48, so Mike was on his own, working at Safeway, sometimes attending UBC, and living at our pad located at Fourth and Trimble.

Rosemary Giroday used to pick me up when I was in town and I'd spend Sundays with the family, watching football with Armand on their television. I again managed to get a job with Cliffe Towing on the Joan I, but it only lasted for a couple of trips. In off times, I'd spend time with other tow boaters hanging out at the Invermay, Georgia or Niagara pubs, swapping tales with them and listening to their latest voyages and exploits. I learned a lot, but I was also getting nowhere in a hurry.

A couple of years before, in the autumn of 1956, my brother Bill and I had made a trip in his speedboat to an area just east of Bute Inlet, where he wanted to have a look at some timber available for harvesting. We spent the night in sleeping bags around a campfire on the beach, so we could start early to cruise the timber. During the night, I awoke to hear Bill digging into the gravel under where he was sleeping. He produced the largest frog either of us had ever seen. It was at least four or five inches across the body, with huge eyes and big, long legs. I suppose it had been hibernating, and with winter fast approaching the heat from Bill sleeping over it had made it think that spring had arrived early.

We cruised the timber, along with another patch outside Village Bay, and Bill put in a bid to the Forest Service for both locations, eventually succeeding in obtaining the Village Bay cut block. It was in the winter of 1958-59 that he asked me if I'd help him harvest it. I had never worked in the woods before, but I readily agreed to go with him. We built a small building on a float at Hyacinthe Bay and towed it across to Village Bay with one of Bill's boats. This was to be our home, where we lived while at work on the timber. John Humphries barged a Caterpillar tractor belonging to Ralph Wilks across for us to use. We'd skid the logs to the beach, and make them up into booms there for towing.

This logging was about as 'gypo' as you could get. We lived in a shack on a float, sustained by a wood stove, gas light and battery radio for keeping in touch with world events. One of these events was Fidel Castro winning the revolution in Cuba with the overthrow of Batista, and I only mention that event because it would have an impact on my life in a few years time.

Ben Fellows skinned the cat as we called driving the Caterpillar tractor, Bill felled and bucked the timber, and I set the chokers, washed dishes and did some cooking. When we had sufficient timber at the beach, all three of us would stow the logs into booms for towing to the storage grounds down the coast at Howe Sound.

Bill Keats was our log broker who handled the sale of our production to the mills in Vancouver. He'd advance funds as needed to keep production flowing, as he did for most of the small logging operations in the area, but it was dreary work. We did have some good times together that winter though. The beach at Moulds Bay produced some of the best large butter clams I've ever seen. We'd jig up a couple of Yellow Eye Rockfish and make what was some of the finest and tastiest seafood chowder anybody has ever eaten. There were so many butter clams in the area that we'd simply scoop them out from a few inches down as we didn't have a shovel to dig with. One day while at the post office at Heriot Bay, we read a notice that the whole area was officially closed to clam harvest due to shellfish poisoning. We just kept on eating them anyway as we figured they'd been well tested by us over the past few weeks.

Though we didn't have a shovel, we did have a gun, and from time to time we'd shoot a deer for a change of diet. It was a life we adapted to easily and it stands out in as one of my most memorable winters. We came home for a couple of weeks at Christmas, but Mum was once again with Jim and Rose in California, so I just stayed on Quadra Island. We spent pleasant evenings with Herb and Dorothy Hope, who were living near Heriot Bay. Herb was a partner of the aviator radioman Jim Spilsbury in the early days of marine radios, and can be credited with inventing and building some of the early Spilsbury and Tindell radio sets. Francis Dikie and his wife Suzanne were old family friends with whom we frequently exchanged visits. Francis was an author, writing mostly children's stories and magazine articles, and my family had lived at their place for a time after moving from Surge Narrows.

Also during that winter, Bill Hall bought a new ferry to replace the Victory II which had served Quadra Island and Campbell River faithfully for 10 years. The new vessel was the Uchuck III, which had previously been used on the West Coast of Vancouver Island. This was a much larger vessel, with twin Cat diesels which gave an added safety factor compared to the Victory as she plied the swift flowing waters of Discovery Passage. Neil Watson was hired as engineer, and Tom and Bill Hall were alternating captains. This ferry served Quadra Island well until a Highways Department car ferry was introduced in 1960. Tom Hall was appointed as senior captain of the new car ferry, and remained in that position until his retirement.

The New Year of 1959 was welcomed in traditional style at the old Quadra community hall located at the south end of Gowlland Harbour, marked with the same good fellowship that has always prevailed among islanders. But soon it was back to Village Bay, the bitter cold weather and renewed efforts to get the logging finished.

Shortly after getting back to work we experienced some trouble with the tractor. Ben couldn't seem to get his repairs to last more than a few hours, so Bill asked me to take the boat, go over to Viner Point and see if Old Pete was in residence. Old Pete had earned quite a wide spread reputation for his Gerry rigging repairs and he had that to maintain, so he readily agreed to come over to repair the problems with the cat. It proved to be no problem at all to him and he soon had it finished the next day. I think Pete was a little tired of his own cooking, because he showed no readiness to have me take him back to Viner Point. Then, the next day, a strong southeaster blew up and prevented us taking him home, so he just hung around, helping out where he could. During the long evenings he told great stories, drank huge amounts of coffee, and was quickly using up the can of tobacco he'd brought with him.

I was starting to get a little anxious to get him back to Viner Point, as we only had three bunks, which meant I had to sleep on the cold floor when we had guests. But he kept on just hanging around and dining like a king on our clams, fish and deer meat. The southeast wind continued to prevent travel by sea in our small workboat, and after a while Old Pete's tobacco was starting to run as low as our dwindling coffee supply. On his final morning with us, I mixed Old Pete some tea with the coffee to make it last a little longer and that was the last straw for him. Now being totally out of tobacco, he announced he was going to hike overland to Hyacinthe Bay, the southeaster could blow forever as far as he was concerned.

We didn't worry too much about Old Pete's abilities to

survive the 10 mile trek, even though it was mid-winter. He had lots of coastally generated savvy about wilderness survival, and being without tobacco for a day unquestionably made him more than a match for any passing cougar or wolves that might have considered taking him on as a possible meal. We heard that in an amazingly short time he arrived at Hyacinthe Bay, pounding on the door of Bill's house. When Sheila and the kids ran to see who was kicking up such a ruckus at the door, they were greeted by this soaking wet, tired old goat whose only urgent desire was for a cigarette and a hot coffee. After smoking everything he could get his hands on, Sheila drove him on to Heriot Bay. I guess that inhospitable mixture of coffee and tea and the lack of tobacco were just too much for old Pete, as he related my outrageous culinary skills to anyone who would listen for months afterwards.

Back at camp, we managed to accumulate ten sections of logs behind Breton Islands in Moulds Bay, so Bill called Maritime Towing to send a tug. The Green Cove arrived the next day to tow our winter's production to Vancouver. The skipper helped us secure the booms with swifters and they quickly disappeared down south on the trip to Howe Sound. Buddy Jones was deckhand on the Green Cove at that time. Captain Jones went on to be a senior coastal pilot in later years. We packed up camp over the next few days, called John to barge out the cat, and headed for home. Thankfully, the logs sold at very good prices, and spring was just around the corner.

Bill and family and I took a trip to Vancouver to see Bill Keates the broker and get their business settled. Keates, who had an office in the Standard Building on Hastings Street, had our cheques waiting for us when we arrived and treated us like long lost friends. I spent some time with Mike Nash, Birch and Dawson at their place for a few days, and I was surprised to find Mike knew the Girodays from the days when he went to the same church as they did. I spent some time visiting with my friends, but was soon ready to get back up the coast. I caught the ferry to Nanaimo, and stayed a couple of days with Roy Sharcott, who had recently moved to Nanaimo from Campbell

River. We met Bill and Sheila a few days later and drove them to Tony Hornby's place in Roy's new '58 Thunderbird. Once back home, I went back to work with Parsons Towing, working the rapids again. As much as I liked the challenge though, I couldn't see myself spending my whole life there, as some had done before me. I needed to get in some time on larger vessels, doing other types of work to gain more experience.

Chapter 21

Stan Palmer was the new manager for Tulloch Western Fisheries in 1959 when he suggested I come to work for them on one of their fish packing and freight vessels. Their fleet consisted of two converted navy fairmiles about 110 feet long and several smaller vessels. Most people aren't familiar with fairmiles, so I should perhaps explain they were a kind of motor launch built for in shore escort, anti-submarine and rescue work during the war. They were designed in England by the Fairmile Company, hence the name they became known by. Mostly the 80 or so built in Canada were built in Great Lakes boat yards but 14 Class C vessels were built on the west coast and seven at Weymouth, Nova Scotia.

It was about the first week in June that I got the call from Stan to see if I was interested, since there was a deckhand job available on one of their small chartered vessels. He told me he thought I should take this job for a start, with the chance of moving up to one of the larger company vessels when an opening occurred.

So, after saying goodbye to Mum and my friends, I was off once more for The Big Smoke, to join George Georgeson as his mate, deckhand and cook on the Georgeson Bay. George picked me up with his boat right off the end of the CPR ferry dock and this was the start of a long and interesting relationship with Andy Tulloch, Ed Moir and the B.C. fishing industry.

The Georgeson Bay was a 45 foot boat used to collect and hold fish delivered each day from the fishing vessels. The catch was iced down in the hold and picked up every few days by a larger packer boat, for transportation to the company's processing plant at 2199 Commissioner Street in Vancouver, the present location of McMillan Fisheries and the Cannery Restaurant.

The Georgeson Bay was an older boat powered by a five cylinder Gardiner diesel. We had no navigational equipment other than a compass but that was not unusual for small coastal vessels at that time, and George was a good shipmate from a well known family who lived on Galiano Island in Active Pass, between Vancouver and Sydney, on southern Vancouver Island. He had started his career with Victoria Tug, and had many interesting stories to tell of his tow boating days. One of his uncles was a well known captain with the Union Steamship Co., and his family had been light keepers for many years at Georgina Point.

We caught the ebb tide out through the First Narrows, where George turned the wheel watch over to me. I think he'd had too much of Big City life the night before and it had started to catch up with him and he needed to get some rest. I was a little tired myself, but set a course for Cape Roger Curtis, then up the gulf for Balleanas Islands. The weather was good, with a bright moon and calm seas, and we maintained about eight knots until, about daylight, we were abeam of the Sisters light station, when George took over from me at the wheel. We were headed for Alert Bay to start tending some of our salmon purse seine fleet, which were to begin fishing upper Johnstone Strait that Sunday at 6 p.m.

We stopped at Campbell River to wait for the tide, then set sail again on the first of the ebb. If one can be at Seymour Narrows at slack water, a fair tide can be enjoyed all the way right up to Alert Bay. As often happens in the summer months though, a strong westerly wind was encountered at Salmon River near Kelsey Bay, so George decided we'd spend the night at Port Neville, rather than fight the heavy seas all night long.

We were a couple of days ahead of the scheduled arrival time at Alert Bay, so there was no need to hurry. Bart Web, with his vessel B.H. II, was also sheltering at Port Neville. He was towing a camp barge from False Bay up to Rivers Inlet, where he was to work for the next few weeks tending the gillnet fleet. Bart and his wife Jenny were long time employees of Tulloch Western. They used to start their fishing season at False Bay, where they collected fish from the gulf troll fleet in that area. The camp barge served several different purposes, for ice and fish storage, as well as a fuel station, store and living quarters for their crew. The company had many of these well equipped barges, known as fish camps that they moved to strategic locations as the fishing season progressed. The vessels were tended twice weekly by the larger packer boats that delivered ice and supplies, as well as picking up their fish for delivery back to Vancouver.

We departed Port Neville the next morning as planned, reaching Alert Bay by early afternoon. This was my first of many visits to Alert Bay. I had been in the general area a few times before but never had an opportunity to spend some time ashore. When I was employed by Tulloch Western, I was to be mate on a larger vessel named the Grand. I was slated to meet the Grand at Alert Bay, as she was southbound from Rivers Inlet, and the regular deckhand, Stuart Henderson, who worked with George on the Georgeson Bay, was to be picked up at Port McNeill where he was living at the time. We were never able to contact Harley Brown, skipper on the Grand though, so I stayed with George for the first two weeks.

When we arrived, Alert Bay was a beehive of activity, with many boats making a fuel and supply stop on their way north to Rivers Inlet. I met with a few fishermen I knew from home and started making some new friends among those who regularly stopped in at the Government dock for what was usually an overnight stay. The Union Steamship Company had gone out of business the previous year, but the coast was still being serviced by Northland Navigation and Packers Steamships. The passenger vessel Queen of the North was still in operation, and made Alert Bay a stop for passengers and freight. There was no reliable or paved road north of Kelsey Bay on Vancouver Island in those days, so these vessels were still very much in use in 1959.

Packers Steamships was owned by B.C. Packers, which was then the largest fishing company on the coast. They operated two freight vessels, the Teco and the PW. These vessels mostly serviced the company canneries and the ports where their fishing fleet was stationed, Quathiaski, Alert Bay, Namu, Klemtu, Butedale and Prince Rupert. They carried all kinds of fishing gear, general cargo and cannery supplies northbound, and brought back mostly canned and frozen fish.

We had almost a week in Alert Bay before fishing was to open, so we had plenty of time on our hands. We worked on the boat until noon, then took the afternoons off to just loaf around. One morning, George, who slept in the main cabin, awoke to find all our lockers open and most of the groceries we'd bought the day before missing. I can't imagine how he could have slept through all this going on just a few feet from his bunk but apparently he did. Then we recalled there had been a decrepit gillnet boat from Churchhouse moored alongside the previous evening, and George was sure they were the guilty parties. The crew on this old tub consisted of the skipper, his wife and three raggedy looking kids, so we decided they needed the food more than we did and took no further action.

In passing, I might mention that about 1956 Alert Bay had acquired a liquor outlet, and although beer was in plentiful supply from the hotel and at Minstrel Island, no other alcohol other than beer had been readily available until this new store opened.

The area between Alert Bay and the Mainland was known as The Jungle. Newcomers to the coast date themselves now by referring to this as the Broughton Archipelago, but to everyone who lived on the coast during the heyday of the 'gypo logger', it was and will always remain The Jungle. If one looks at a chart of the area, it's quite clear how the name evolved. The coast is a maze of inlets, bays, islands and channels, a jungle of narrow winding passages that were alive with small logging camps almost beyond count. So this new liquor store was a major attraction for the loggers and others in the area, and Alert Bay swarmed with them on weekends. This brought a lot of business to town, but not without its accompanying social problems.

The trip across Queen Charlotte Strait from the Mainland shores to Alert Bay can be treacherous for small boats at almost any time of year. In the summer, fog and prevailing northwest winds can be expected pretty much daily. In winter, strong southeasters lash the strait virtually continually. So to transit the strait at night with mostly inexperienced and well oiled loggers in small outboard powered craft is to court a disaster just waiting to happen. The result was that the resident RCMP patrol vessel was called out on numerous occasions to search for missing and overdue boats. Sometimes they were found and all was well, but all too often only an overturned boat or some floating wreckage was left to remind us of the fate of the passengers.

In the end, the crew on the police patrol vessel grew tired of this exercise in catastrophe and decided something needed to be done. After much hard thought, they came up with a novel solution. On their next weekly patrol, they stopped in at Sullivan Bay to have a talk with the lady who ran the store and fuel station. The officers asked her if she'd consider selling liquor there, as the bay was strategically located to supply the area. The storekeeper refused the offer and firmly reminded the officers that it would be against the law, but the officers reminded her they were the law and she'd be doing everybody a great public service if she'd be kind enough to assist them in trying to control the booze traffic flowing between The Jungle and Alert Bay.

The next problem that almost trashed the idea though, was to come up with a solution to how she would haul the merchandise from Alert Bay to her remotely located store. Shortly afterwards, the police boat was seen making the trip at regular intervals, hauling suitable quantities of booze up to Sullivan Bay. The loss of life and the incident of marine accidents to which the RCMP were called dropped considerably, and all was well again.

The 1959 fishing season finally got under way, and we received orders to run down to Parsons Bay to pick up fish from Neilo Erickson, who was fishing that area for springs and early sockeye. Neilo lived at Sointula and owned a small table seiner which he fished in the upper strait, with a four man crew. Parsons Bay was a little known secret fished only by fishermen with local knowledge, but the amount of hulking salmon taken out of that bay by Neilo and his crew was sizable. We would pick up his fish every other day, dress or clean them, then ice them down in the hold. On alternate days we'd run down to Port Neville to pick up fish from Dave Moon, who was seining there with the Anna A. These were the only boats we had to service at that time, as it was still early in the season and most of the fleet were heading for Namu to fish for pinks.

Because of the large area we had to cover, we picked up Stewy at Port McNeill and I stayed on as the third crewmember until I could join the Grand on her next trip south. We were slated to unload our fish on to the Grand, but somehow or other we missed her once again. On the next conference call, we were ordered back to Vancouver to unload, as our fish were a few days old and needed to be processed. The 18 hour run south proved gratuitously uneventful, with warm sunny weather allowing the crew to sleep out on the foredeck while off watch. Upon arrival, I was called up to the office, where I first met Andy Tulloch. He apologized for the mix up in not meeting up with the Grand and said he had to hire a mate for her, which meant I was laid off. It was a bit of blow but I took the opportunity to tour the plant, as I had never been in a large cannery before. I helped George and Stewy ice up the boat for their return trip to Alert Bay, packed up my gear, and made a few phone calls.

John Humphries happened to be in Vancouver for a few days, and he drove down to the cannery to meet me, as we were invited to Girodays for an afternoon at their pool. John had a Campbell River newspaper on the front seat, which I glanced at as we drove through town. We had lots to talk about, so I wasn't paying too much attention to what I was reading. I asked John if he had seen Trapper lately. He stopped the car and looked at me.

"Read the headlines in the paper again" he said. There it was. "Frank Nason presumed drowned." Cape Mudge had claimed yet another of my friends. The rest of the day was not a happy one for me and I got John to drive me to the ferry so I could get home. Trapper's body was never found but his boat was recovered drifting up side down near Village Bay.

The next day I was back in Campbell River again and Stan Palmer told me Andy Tulloch had called him to let me know he would take me back at the first opportunity. That opportunity came only a few days later, when a long time employee retired as mate on the Amboyna. When I got back to the plant on Commissioner Street again, Capt. Bill Zelley and the other two crew members were there waiting for me. We sailed immediately, as the crew had already taken on 30 tons of ice, fuel, empty fish boxes and supplies for a trip to service the eight company fish camps located around the upper Gulf of Georgia. This turned out to be one of the best jobs I could have wished for in the maritime industry.

We made a circuit of the camps twice a week, delivering fresh fish back down to Vancouver every Monday and Thursday morning, taking on another 30 tons of ice each trip, and as many empty boxes as we could load on the after deck.

First stop was Pender Harbour, followed by Egmont, Westview and Lund along the Sunshine Coast. We delivered ice and empty boxes, but left their fish there until we could pick them up when we were southbound. Next we stopped at Refuge Cove, Stuart Island Landing and Big Bay, where we delivered more ice and boxes, picking up the boxed fish at these locations as we had delivered enough ice to make room aboard for cargo. We stayed over for about six hours at Stuart Island then, left for the major camp at Campbell River so we arrived at about 7 a.m.

The Amboyna was about 90 feet long, with two holds. The

main one was aft of the deckhouse, with a capacity of 20 tons of ice, while the smaller hold was forward and held the remaining 10 tons of ice. The vessel was very narrow, with a steady speed of 10 knots fully loaded and about 11.5 knots when empty, which of course we seldom were. The living quarters were very comfortable with three staterooms for the four man crew. The vessel had a wheelhouse and skipper's cabin topside, with the galley, two staterooms and toilet facilities on the main deck. There was a towing winch aft, which we used to tow the various fish camps around the coast as required, and each hatch was serviced with a standard mast, with single boom. The lifting gear consisted of the towing winch aft and the anchor winch forward, both run by hydraulics. Like so many of the other vessels, as explained, she had no navigational aids other than an old AM two way radio and a compass; pretty rudimentary equipment and inadequate by today's standards, especially considering the conditions we regularly encountered as we and other members of the commercial fishing fleet plied the coast.

We were powered by a new turbo charged Cummins diesel that developed 225 horsepower, which had recently replaced an eight cylinder Vivian of 150-hp motor. By our standards in those days though, the Amboyna was ideal for the work we performed, although she was also a terrible sea boat other than bucking straight on into a head sea, at which she was excellent due to her long waterline. The vessel had a certain amount of fame attached to her, as she was the first vessel built in the United States with diesel power. The registry showed her date of building as unknown, but most who knew her agreed she was probably launched about 1914 as a ferry on Puget Sound, running between Seattle and the nearby islands.

The heart and soul of the ship was her captain, Bill Zelley, who was born nearly 20 years before her, in 1895, in Nanaimo, and had lived his entire life in that area. His father was a sailor, and Bill said he could remember his dad taking him to sea at a very young age. Bill landed his first job as a fish packer skipper in 1912 and had been in the industry all his working life. He had joined Tulloch Fisheries in 1944, and was the senior captain in the much expanded Tulloch Western Fisheries after the company merged with Ed Moir's Western Fisheries in 1955.

Bill was a very small man who was easy going and good to get along with, but very deliberate and serious about being on schedule. He never got excited about anything no matter the circumstances, smoking the cigarettes he rolled himself then stuffed into the mouthpiece of an old pipe he had smoked at one time. The deck of the wheelhouse was always covered with tobacco that had been lost during this cigarette rolling exercise that went on without break day and night. He was always careful not to bring his tobacco container too close to the compass for fear of the metal swinging our only navigational aid off a few degrees.

Bill kept an amazingly detailed log of compass courses, distances and times that he made sure we used when under way, so that during times when the fog or storms rolled in and reduced visibility for us, we could be fairly certain of our position. He checked this log constantly against actual times and the compass courses on every trip, to make sure they were accurate.

When we arrived at Campbell River, which would be every Sunday and Wednesday morning, we unloaded all of the 10 tons of ice in the forward hold on to the camp so we could take on the boxed fish for Vancouver. Then it was off to Lund, Westview, Egmont and Pender Harbour to pick up the fish there. Often we had quite a deckload, as there was a huge fleet of trollers working Gulf of Georgia at that time. We'd arrive at the plant about midnight, so as to be ready for the unloading crew starting at 7 a.m. The iced, boxed fish were unloaded by the cannery crew, dumped on a grading table for sorting as to species and size, and then most would be repacked as graded and sorted into 50 lb boxes for shipment by refrigerated truck to Los Angeles. These shipments left the plant every Monday and Thursday afternoon for the 24 hour ride to California, and every Monday we'd reload with supplies and head back up north to start the whole thing all over again. On Thursdays we'd reload and sail for Nanaimo, where we had Friday as a day off. Then, early Saturday morning, it was off for Pender Harbour to begin the process once more.

This routine went on from April 15 to November 30 each year while the fishing was open at that time. We'd start towing some of the mobile camps out in March and at the end of the season bring them home again, finishing up by December 15. It was hard work with long hours, but I was young and enjoyed the job, the outdoors and the hard work very much. The pay was great, almost $30 per day with benefits, which was a substantial amount of money at that time, so I was able to put away most of my earnings into Mum's bank account. I earned over $8,000.00 that first year, which was very big money indeed.

Tulloch Western was a great company to work for. They had become a major fresh fish supplier as they had camps in the lower gulf as well as the West Coast of the island. The lower gulf camps consisted of Deep Bay, Ford Cove, French Creek, Nanaimo, Silva Bay, Porlier Pass and, once a week, a pickup from a couple of cod fishermen at Active Pass. This run was serviced by the vessel Palmersyl, with Rod Fredricks as skipper. Sometimes we'd fill in on this run as the Palmersyl was a much smaller vessel and the fish were mostly lingcod, which had a longer season than salmon. The Gulf camps were usually picked up twice a week, with Nanaimo south three times, as they could be serviced in one day out of Vancouver. The camps on the West Coast were located at Bamfield, Ucluelet, Tofino, Nootka, Nuchatlitz, Kyuquot and Winter Harbour. They were major operations and were serviced each week, starting at Bamfield and finishing at Winter Harbour, then round Cape Scott and on down into the Big City via Johnstone Strait, or during peak production periods, doubling back to unload the camps once again.

The rest of the fleet consisted of the Randy, which was a sister to the newly commissioned TW Islander and of course the always elusive Grand, five vessels in all, with several other privately owned charter vessels and collector boats mostly used for dealing with the net fishing fleet. The two converted American fairmiles were brought into Canada after the war.

They had both been built in 1945 and were never commissioned or used for naval purposes prior to arriving in Canada. Dolmage Towing chartered the Randy before Tulloch Western built enough volume to keep her busy. The Islander had been the former Jervis Express, operated by Union Steamships. She was bought by Andy Tulloch and Wes Parry and re-commissioned in 1959, with a new deckhouse installed to make her identical to the Randy. They were both powered by twin eight cylinder Cleveland diesels built by General Motors, which could shove them through the water at speeds of up to 17 knots, but usually cruised at 14.

The speed of these two fine vessels enabled them to keep to the weekly schedule around Vancouver Island. They both carried 60 tons of ice and a crew of six, and were workhorses year round, as they were both rigged with powerful towing winches. During the winter months, when fishing was closed, the Randy was usually chartered by Straits Towing for weekly trips towing freight barges to Kitimat and Prince Rupert. The Islander was used to haul dynamite from a factory at James Island near Victoria to various coastal destinations. This meant that when fishing was closed and the Amboyna was laid up for a rest, I could work as a spare on the one of the two sister ships while their crews took time off.

I made two trips on the Amboyna before we were laid up by a strike over the prices paid for fish. My half brother Ted was an organizer for the Fisherman's Union. I would often see him over the next few years, as he would come down to the docks to meet me when we were in Vancouver. Due to the strike, we took the boat home to Nanaimo, and I caught a ride home to Campbell River with Steve Assu and his wife Sissy who were also heading home to sit out the strike leaving their vessel Patty G. in Vancouver.

Jim and family were visiting Mum for a couple of weeks at that time, so it was nice to be able to spend a few days with them. I asked Jim if he'd be interested in renting a rowboat boat at Painter's and trying for a Tyee. I didn't have to ask twice. We immediately got our fishing gear together and headed over to collect the wooden boat. Jim had taught me in 1953 how to fish the flood tide at the corner of the bar, in the Tyee Pool just south of the Campbell River mouth. We arrived a little late for the tide, and I had a difficult time getting a good position, due to the 30 or so other boats trying to fish the same corner.

Jim soon had a Gibbs #8 spoon over the side, set the tension on the reel, and started chatting with Les McDonald, who was rowing beside us. In no more than a minute or two, we had a strike. Jim handled it well, and I was quickly able to work our way out from among the cluster of boats. The usual thrill of catching a big Chinook salmon with such light tackle was intensified by our having been on the fishing grounds for less than five minutes. Within an hour we were back at the Painter's dock with a big fat 45 pounder. We changed boats and sped back to Quadra with our prize. Mum immediately canned most of it so that Jim and Rose could take it home with them to California. Looking back, I think it would have been nice, though rather less sporting, if Tyee fishing had been like this more often!

As I was going to be working for Tulloch Western again as soon as the strike settled, I called Roy Sharcott, a friend of mine who was living in Nanaimo, to see if I could bunk in with him on my days off. Roy was living with Blaney Paul in a house on the C.I.L. property, located above the Black Ball Ferry terminal at Departure Bay. Blaney was manager for C.I.L. on the property, where there was once a dynamite factory in the golden days of coal mining around Nanaimo. The factory had been moved to James Island near Victoria, and their Nanaimo property was only a wholesale outlet for serving the logging and road building industry with dynamite and blasting caps. The property covered more than 100 acres of beautiful waterfront, with only the three of us and Blaney's dog Jigs in residence. Roy and Blaney agreed I could stow my gear with them and stay as long as I wanted. As I was only in Nanaimo Thursday and Friday nights, this was a good arrangement for all of us.

In a few days the strike was over, and the crew and I sailed from Nanaimo at midnight for Vancouver to take on the usual ice and supplies for the camps. There was a heavy summer westerly blowing as we left Nanaimo, and the ship being empty in a beam sea, rolled like a drifting log. Bill took her out of the harbour while the rest of us stowed everything as well as possible for what promised to be a lively crossing. Bill turned in as soon as I took over the watch and asked me to call him at Point Atkinson. I don't know how any of them stayed in their bunks that night as we rolled our way across the gulf with a moderate quartering sea. Very seldom did we experience travelling with a completely empty ship since we were nearly always loaded with something, and I enjoyed my watch that night as the moon was out full and the radio crackled with other boats heading over to take on supplies for the opening of fishing in a couple of days. As requested, I called Bill abeam of Atkinson, and we made our way through under the Lions Gate Bridge and moored at the ice machine, ready for loading at 7 a.m.

Our orders were to re-supply and ice up all the camps and then get back to Vancouver a soon as possible as there was no fish at any of the camps. We wanted to get them all ready for when the fishing started again. All the camps were totally empty of ice since it was mid-August and their supply had all melted during the week long shutdown. Vancouver was ready with another shipment when we got back, so we wouldn't fall behind, as fishing would be heavy at what was now the peak of the season.

In late August of that summer, a large run of pink salmon appeared in Blackfish Sound north of Johnstone Strait. We had a camp at Double Bay, and the company dispatched us there to help move the huge volumes of fish that were being caught. The Double Bay camp was seasonal, just for a few weeks every other year, so was a very temporary installation. Roy and Jan Pardiac with their baby boy Kenny were operating the camp. This was the first time I had met them but we have remained life long friends ever since. The water supply at Double Bay was very poor though, so we set to work to improve the pipeline and re-anchor the barges, floats and other equipment. The oil tanker Imperial Namu stopped in to fuel up the operation so gas and oil would be available to the fishing boats.

Unfortunately Roy had quite a bad accident, cutting his hand quite seriously on an aluminium bucket used to weigh fish. Stan Palmer, who was area manager for the operation, thought we should take Roy to Alert Bay to see Dr. Pickup for some medical attention, particularly since the fishing had just been closed for a few days due to the huge volumes of fish being landed. So it was all right for Roy and Jan to leave the camp for a few hours. I recall this as the first time anyone could remember an area being closed for trolling, which was usually open seven days a week in those days.

We arrived at Alert Bay on the Saturday afternoon, right at the peak of the fishing season. Everyone had lots of money to spread around and it seemed that everyone was drunk, including, apparently, Dr. Pickup, whom Roy had gone to see. He managed to get Roy patched up though, and we took on fuel while waiting for Roy and Jan to return, using the opportunity to do some shopping for groceries. They were still off on their errands, when I noticed a gillnet boat about 30 feet in length leave the B.C. Packers dock, its Easthope engine barking away and obviously at full throttle and full speed. The skipper was steaming straight for the fuel dock where we were tied up alongside and I could see there was going to be a collision. There was. Luckily though, the vessel managed to hit us only a glancing blow, and just bounced along our starboard side. Bill was hanging out the wheelhouse window with his cigarette holder tightly clenched between his few remaining teeth, while the inebriated skipper of the gillnetter was hollering up to him to "Get your f-blanking boat out of the way!", only he filled in all of the blanks quite colourfully!

After the final bounce off our bow, the skipper of the gillnetter announced loudly he was going to Port McNeill, and started to make off across the channel. A Canadian Navy destroyer happened to be southbound in the channel at reduced speed at the time, and the two vessels were on course to meet in mid-channel. The destroyer captain could see a collision was almost inevitable and instantly ordered full astern, while sounding a warning blast to the gillnetter on his whistle. The fishing boat didn't miss. It hit the stopped destroyer squarely amidships, folded up like a paper bag and promptly started to sink. It was quite a sight. The crew of the navy ship quickly threw a Jacob's ladder over the side to the gillnetter and the skipper promptly scaled the rope ladder to the deck, then proceeded to chew out the assembled naval crew for being in his way, in much the same manner, tone and language as he'd done with us at the fuel dock. The police boat was summoned to remove this much insulted fisherman from the destroyer and deposit him in the already overcrowded jail to sleep it off for a while.

Fortunately there wasn't much damage to our boat. Bill, I have to say, didn't see much humour in the incident though, and gave orders that we were to cast off as soon as Roy and Jan returned. Alert Bay was obviously in a riotous weekend mood, and he didn't want to hang around any longer than absolutely necessary. We returned to Double Bay late Saturday, to set up for the expected volumes of pinks when fishing resumed next day.

As most of our trolling fleet had left the Gulf of Georgia to fish Blackfish Sound, we had reduced volumes of fish to move from the Gulf camps. After three weeks, the run of pinks moved on, and our schedule returned to normal once again. I spent my 19th birthday coming of age at sea that October 9, 1959, as we settled in to our twice weekly trips around the upper Gulf.

Chapter 22

After the lingcod fishery closed in the gulf in November that year, we towed the camps that weren't permanent structures up the Fraser River for storage in fresh water for the winter. I then had some months off until fishing reopened again in March, 1960, so we moored the Amboyna at the company docks at Nanaimo and I headed home with a nice little bank account to turn over to Mum, which we were able to use to shut up the house and go back down to California to visit with Jim, Rose and family.

We took the old familiar route by bus to Nanaimo, CPR ferry to Vancouver and then train to Berkeley via Seattle and Portland. I then spent some days exploring some new areas of San Francisco I hadn't seen before. Bob Groulx kindly invited me to stay with them for a couple of days, and I would wander round town while Bob was at work. I called on Mr. Shoemaker, who was surprised to see me but immediately invited me to Palo Alto for the weekend, as Wendy was due home for Christmas. Bob and Joyce drove me over to Berkeley after a couple of days, so they could visit with Jim and family, and we all had a good time swapping stories about fishing experiences at Painter's Lodge. Then I took the train back to San Francisco and rented a car, producing a driver's license I happened to have found on the street in Vancouver. There seemed to be no problem with that, so off I went down the Bayshore Freeway to Palo Alto. It was great to see Jim Sears, Wendy and her family again. I had a wonderful weekend with my old friends and Mrs. Shoemaker treated me as a very special guest, as always.

Sister Ruth, Ron and baby Esther all spent Christmas with the family down in Berkeley, where we also celebrated Esther's first birthday. Then after New Year, Ron and Ruth drove back to Portland where they were living. I caught a flight back to Vancouver while Mum stayed with Jim and Rose until spring.

A few days after my return I checked in with Andy Tulloch and was put back to work on the Randy, towing freight barges from Vancouver to Kitimat and Prince Rupert. We'd leave Vancouver on Thursday night with two and sometimes three barges. One barge would be taken off at the head of Whale Channel by a Straits Towing tug for delivery to Kitimat, then we'd then carry on to Prince Rupert, deliver our load, refuel and pick up our tow for the return trip. On the way south we would meet up with the barge from Kitimat that we'd dropped off on our way north.

Kitimat was the site of a huge aluminium smelter built during the early 1950s. The town is located at the head of a long inlet, and at that time I don't believe there was a reliable all weather road to the 'outside world', so supplies for the residents and aluminium products going out had to be transported by barge or ship. This was big business for the marine transportation industry.

Depending on the weather conditions, we'd plan to be back in Vancouver for the following Thursday morning, to be ready for a possible crew change and to pick up the loaded barges for the next journey north that night.

Not surprisingly, we experienced some terrible weather on these winter trips with high winds, fog, snow and freezing temperatures. The Randy was well suited for this work, with her twin engines and a good length, and we could average eight knots with two barges in tow, since they were much smaller than the huge barges used today. One disadvantage though, was our fuel capacity which was quite severely limited and usually necessitated a fuel stop at Beaver Cove on both legs of the voyage. We finally installed extra fuel tanks in the forward hold, to give us enough fuel to complete a one way trip without the stop at Beaver Cove.

During one evening ashore in Vancouver that winter, I went out to dinner with a few friends, and when we left the restaurant at about 10 p.m., someone turned on the radio, where the evening news was being read. One item reported that a fish packer was ablaze down on Commissioner Street, so we hurried to the scene just in time to witness the end of the beloved M.V. Grand. According to the report, a heavy southwest wind had blown the vessel ashore from her moorings at the cannery, and somehow she had caught fire and was a total loss. We knew Gerry Del Seco had his new seiner Tiber, which was in the final stages of completion, moored there also, so we raced over and assisted the firemen and Gerry to secure the vessel out of danger and save her from grounding. Rod Fredricks and Billy Rapita were unable to save the Grand. Fortunately nobody was injured but the Grand was beyond repair.

With the cod fishing due to open in March, this put me back to work on the Amboyna towing some of the camp barges to their summer locations. We completed the work in late February then, prepared the vessel for the coming season tending the northern gulf locations. Billie Rapita joined us for what started out initially as a short term and ended up being for two years. Billie was from Kipling, Saskatchewan, and had worked for Tulloch Western for several years previously. He had served on almost every vessel in the fleet, and we considered his deciding to stay with us on the Amboyna as an important seal of approval for the way we operated. Bill Zelly, as senior captain with the company, as always was a pleasure to work with. A few days before the March 1 opening we sailed into Vancouver, loaded the usual 30 tonnes of ice, a bunch of empty boxes and supplies for the camps, then headed out for yet another season of tending the camps twice a week, with Friday off each week in Nanaimo.

As Billie is one of my lost at sea shipmates, I'll take a little time to tell the story of the loss and salvage of the tug Emerald

Straits under his command some years later. Billie had left Tulloch Western in 1965 to join Straits Towing, and by 1968 he had worked his way up to be the captain of the Emerald Straits, one of their smaller tugs. On a trip from Squamish to Vancouver towing an empty chip barge, they were somehow pulled under by their tow in a strong northerly wind. The only survivor was the mate, Barry Gordon, who managed to swim ashore through the chill waters. The vessel was eventually salvaged using the undersea submarine Pisces, which had been developed by Don Sorte and Mac Thompson. The cause of the sinking was never definitely established, but it's known there were heavy winds and with the empty barge in tow it can be assumed the lightweight tug was pulled under by the wind force against the barge. Billie's wrist watch was found in the wheelhouse stopped at 01:30 on the morning of April 19, 1969.

Salmon fishing opened for trollers later in the spring of 1960 and by mid-March the Randy and T.W. Islander were once again making the rounds of the camps each week. The company purchased the W 6 for the lower gulf operation to replace the gutted Grand, and by May, other fishing companies had also established new fish buying camps in the gulf, due to the heavy landings in the Deep Bay area near Hornby Island. We were kept very busy, and had to take on a fifth crew member, using one of the plant workers on a temporary basis.

One trip that spring the fishing was so heavy south of Cape Mudge that we had to make a direct run from Vancouver to Campbell River, where Stan Palmer and 'Buddy' Recalma had been collecting fish with the Tulcrest in the area of Mittlenatch Island. We stopped to pick up the fish they had on board and supply them with ice and the money to purchase yet more fish. This was the first time I met Buddy and we became fast friends, also with his wife Diana and their family. They had settled at the Indian Reserve just south of Qualicum Bay shortly after their marriage in May, 1952, and were starting to build the beginnings of their fine family home.

I should mention more about Arnold Patrick (Buddy) Recalma in passing. The U.S. Marines have a reputation built on the buddy system, whereby the marines are paired up to look out for each other. This system and the rigid training that goes with it have helped mould the Marines into a formidable and renowned fighting machine of worldwide fame. Buddy lived up to this adopted name as a true buddy to all who have had the good fortune to have known him. Over the years he worked to overcome injustice suffered by anyone regardless of colour, race or whatever native tribe one might be descended from. In his quiet way he has succeeded in making governments aware of their failings to the little guy on the street, and he helped make life better for many because of his tireless dedication to his ideals and dreams.

Buddy started in the fishing industry at 14 and retired at 60, when he sold his modern Matsumoto built seiner to his son Mark, who carried on in his father's footsteps as a superb fisherman and someone I've been proud to know, along with the rest of the family, for so many years.

During that spring, I once again met up with Jack Thompson, who was in school with me but whom I hadn't seen for a few years. The family had moved to Vancouver as Mr. Thompson's work had ended in Campbell River. Mr. Thompson was a skilled machinist who was mostly employed by large engineering companies to oversee the installation of sawmill and paper mill machinery. Jack obtained his commercial pilot's license and was flying out of Vancouver to various locations. He had also taken up skin diving as a hobby. Through him, I met Don Sorte who was a fully trained professional diver and operated a dive shop on Kingsway with his wife and a partner. They taught diving in a swimming pool and manufactured wet suits for their graduates. I could write a whole book just on everything that went on between Jack, Don and me but suffice it to say we ended up sort of living together, along with Don's German Shepherd pup, Caesar. I say sort of, because all of us were always on the move due to our jobs, and were seldom all together for more than a day or two, except during the winter months.

Don and his new partner Mac Thompson, no relation to

Jack, were building a small submersible in a steel shop on the east shore of False Creek. Mac lived in Seattle and came up to Vancouver every week to oversee the construction of the sub. The construction was very slow due to the highly complex and sophisticated technology involved, that and a chronic lack of money. Don tended to be very secretive about the project until I suggested one day that I maybe might be able to help them out financially.

Down we went to the steel shop, where we were shown what looked to be a steel ball about eight feet across. Mac was the genius behind the project and was one of those people, much like Epor, whom I mentioned earlier, who had more smarts than the rest of us. I don't believe he had any formal training as an engineer, but he was still able to design and build what was to become one of the first small submersibles in the world. Don said they already had about $25,000.00 sunk into the project and couldn't proceed any farther without more funding. As I was the only one with any surplus funds at the time, I agreed to advance them $5,000, a fair bit of money for those days. I didn't expect to see any return on my investment, let alone have the principle repaid, but in hindsight, I know I'd do it all over again, just for the great experience it turned out to be.

There have been numerous stories told and written about Don during his years in Vancouver. Many of them contain some truth, but a lot of them are pure fiction which has been added to and enhanced over the years. Yes, he did always have a table at the Cave Supper Club any time he showed up, regardless of how many were in the party. It wasn't that he had a permanent reservation, but partly due to the bandleader, Fraser McPherson, and his wife Helen being friends of mine, as well as my next door neighbours. It was also because the cigarette girl, whom Don was madly in love with, was the wife of Ray Paris, a good friend of Don's. So any time we showed up they always made room for us.

The Cave wasn't really one of my favourite spots to spend an evening, but it certainly did attract a lot of the most popular entertainers of the day, who used The Cave as a proving ground for their acts before taking them on to Las Vegas. One afternoon, Jack and I were at loose ends and wondering how to spend the evening with a couple of young ladies we had dates with when Norm Pittam, a friend from Victoria, showed up at our place with four free passes to The Cave. As Norm had to return to Victoria that evening, he wasn't able to use the tickets. He had been having a beer at the Georgia, when a stranger asked if he could join him. Norm said "oh, sure," and they spent most of the afternoon chatting and drinking beer. During their conversation, Norm asked this guy what he did for a living and he said he was an entertainer, and would Norm like some free passes to his show? Norm of course accepted but then passed them on to us. It turned out that he had spent the afternoon with Johnny Cash, though Norm had never heard of him before. These were some of the hottest tickets in town that week, and I'm sure we could easily have got $100 each for them. We had some of the best seats in the house to see one of the most popular entertainers of our generation. Between acts, Cash came over to chat with us when he found out we were friends of Norm's. Jack Beban, who was one of the big time logging operators on the coast, joined our table, and we all had a great evening with the famous Johnny Cash, who came back and joined us after he'd finished performing for the evening.

****

The years from 1959, when I started with Tulloch Western, until 1964 when I started my own business can only be described as fast, exciting and non-stop. I was making more than enough money to look after Mum, put some in the bank, and also live the life of Reilly to the fullest. I always made between $8,000 and $12,000 a year, which was extraordinary money at that time. I had investments in blue chip stocks, due to good advice from Armond Giroday, and making money seemed as easy as falling off a log. Vancouver at that time wasn't the city it is today. It was still sort of "small town" in its feel and culture, and somehow my circle of friends turned out to be some of the 'movers and shakers' of that period.

Through Armond, I met John McDermid, whose father was one of the principals in the stock brokerage house of McDermid Miller McDermid. John helped me invest some of my surplus earnings during a time when a major bull market was in progress. He was married to one of the McLean daughters. Bowell McLean was a large General Motors car dealership, and John later joined the company, along with Peter Birks, who was married to McLean's other daughter. I really liked John and we used to spend time together talking business whenever I was in port for a few days.

Another good friend of that period was Buster of Buster's Towing, who had a contract with the City of Vancouver to tow and impound vehicles for traffic violations. Our friendship certainly came in handy whenever we were about to have our cars towed for some minor parking infraction.

Although I could always stay with Roy and Blaney whenever I was in Nanaimo, I was more or less homeless in Vancouver. Don Sorte had split with his wife and was then living in the basement suite of a friend's house on 41st Avenue, just east of Fraser Street. He suggested Jack and I move in with him and Caesar, as he was very seldom at home. The free rent was part of the $5,000 I had invested in the submersible program, an enjoyable fringe benefit, but we did have to look after the dog. That task fell mostly to Jack, as both Don and I were away a good deal.

Don was always trying to save every penny he could in order to keep the submersible project afloat so to speak. Besides working on that, he was employed at the time as a diver on the new sewer outfall being installed at Victoria. I stopped in to see him one evening in Victoria and he was living at the YMCA in a room barely big enough for both of us to fit in. Certainly there was no room to swing even the most stunted cat. He and I had dinner at the Y, which was just terrible, but Don thought it was just great since the Y only cost him a total of $25 a week. I pointed out to him that he was earning about $750 a week, and suggested he should at least be eating well due to the long hours spent diving. But he was firmly fixated on his plans for the sub and living as cheaply as possible had to be a part of his plan.

During that summer, Don and Jack were contacted by a group of scuba divers from California led by Ray Carey, who were on a trip up to some rivers on the north coast, where they planned to dredge for gold. Unfortunately, the venture was a total failure, but as they all bunked in with us, we had some good times together. One of the group, Jose Rodriguez, was a Mexican living in Oxnard, just north of Los Angeles, and the next year, he took me on my very first of many trips to Mexico.

So that summer, on we sailed around the gulf, until the last week in June, when we were sent to Rivers Inlet for a load of sockeye. This was to be my first trip across Queen Charlotte Sound on the Amboyna, which, as mentioned, had no navigational aids other than a whistle and compass. Bill's book of courses and times continued to be checked constantly as a reference while we travelled north and, as always, proved to be extremely accurate. We stopped at Christie Pass overnight, as Bill preferred to cross the Sound in daylight. The Canadian Fishing Co. had a fish camp and fuel station at the pass, and Black Pete was the resident manager. He was an old friend of Bill's and we spent a pleasant time listening to the two of them chat about bygone events.

We departed the pass about four in the morning and cleared Scarlet Point light before picking up a fog bank about half way to Pine Island. Our compass course to Pine was dead on though, as we picked up the lighthouse fog horn to starboard. Then we set course for Egg Island, 28 miles ahead, and settled in for the next two and half hours. Egg Island light station is one of the more isolated and lonely outposts on a coast that has several which are notorious for their exposed locations and sometimes very hazardous waters, many of them located a long way from the nearest civilization.

We picked up the booming foghorn on Egg Island right

on schedule as expected then set a course for Cape Calvert. The fog lifted somewhat before reaching there, so we changed course for Clam Bay, which was the location of our Rivers Inlet base. This way of navigating is not too difficult, as long as one understands the problems that can arise. One of those is other traffic in the area. Without radar, we had to depend on other vessels equipped with it to spot us and start sounding their whistles at timed intervals to fill in the gaps when we were sounding ours.The other problem that can arise of course is from wind and tidal effects which can be generated over a long distance of unsheltered water and can quickly put a vessel into danger.

Our base at Clam Bay consisted of several barges and floats secured by anchors, with one barge as living quarters for the crew, and an ice house on the main deck. A covered barge was used as a net loft and fuel barge. There were also numerous floats used as shelter and moorage by the fishing boats and others that were net racks where the fishermen mended their nets. Several small collector boats left port each morning to collect the previous nights catch from the fishing boats. This fish was then delivered to us back at Clam Bay, where we iced it down in our two holds. We then loaded a small amount of ice on to the collector boats for the next day's pickup.

Will Mitinen was the manager at the time, and he also owned the Aldofina, one of the collector boats. I was familiar with the Adolfina, as my brother Bill had been a skipper on her when it was first built about 1945 and I told Will that as we travelled up the inlet to Bickle Pass and Beaver Inlet to pick up fish from the camps. Will had spent many years in the industry, and he told me some of the history of the various canneries that operated during the earlier years.

We were soon loaded with 110,000 pounds of sockeye salmon and sent south to Vancouver with all possible speed. The distance from Rivers to Vancouver is about 250 miles, but even fully loaded, we were still able to maintain our 10 knot speed. We reckoned if we hit the tides properly at Alert Bay, we could make Vancouver in 24 hours. Bill always had us keep two hour watches at the wheel, so three of us spelled each other off two hours on, four hours off. Tony, the fourth crewmember, didn't stand watch as he wasn't familiar with navigation or the area and had only been at sea for a short time.

On most trips north, we'd ice up the northern gulf camps and sometimes pick up the boxed fish as a deck load on our way south. This of course would stretch the return trip into almost two days, and sometimes that worked out better, as we could time our arrival for when the cannery crew started work at 7 a.m., rather than arrive at mid-day and cause the crew to work late. Rod Fredericks, with the W6 was able to take up the slack for us, as the gulf fishing dropped off by mid-July, when most of the fleet moved north.

After Rivers Inlet was closed for the season, the fleet moved up into what was called the Central Area, from Addenbroke Island north to Millbank Sound. The fish changed from sockeye to pinks and chum salmon. We also had troll fishery camps at Spider Island, St John's Harbour and Hakai Pass, where large Chinook and Coho salmon were caught and landed. We would go for long periods with no time off, but we enjoyed the work and learned the approaches to some very treacherous bays and harbours where few people had gone before us in vessels the size of ours.

One weekend found us at Bella Bella awaiting the next opening which was due to start at 6 p.m. on the Sunday. Mrs. Martin, the owner of the general store, asked us if we'd like to attend a dance at Shearwater on Saturday night. She said some of the off-duty nurses from the hospital would be there and she thought it would be nice for us to attend. Bill and Tony had no interest in this, but Billy and I agreed to be there. We were picked up by Mrs. Martin and a mob of nurses in their launch, and set off for Shearwater.

Shearwater is often referred to as "New Bella Bella", and is located on Denny Island directly across from "Old Bella Bella". I was very interested to go there for the first time, as my older brother Jim had been stationed at the Air Force base there during World War II. Most of the old buildings were still in use for various purposes in 1960, and the dance was to be held in one of the old aircraft hangers. We all had a fun time Quadra Island style, and it put me in mind of the country get togethers back on the island. But the best part was the ride back to the ship, as it was one of those rare warm mid-coast August nights under a full moon. We passed the CPR liner Princess Louise, which was southbound from an Alaska cruise, probably one of the last voyages for this beautiful old liner before she was retired and became a floating restaurant. The ship was ablaze with lights and looked very regal making her way slowly through the narrow channel.

On the Sunday we did our tour of the troll camps and picked up some high quality fish, but due to restricted space on board and large volumes of net caught fish expected by Monday night, we layer iced the troll fish in separate bins in the forward hold, instead of packing them in boxes. The camp at Spider Island serviced the boats that fished out on the Goose Island banks, and was a navigational challenge to find if any fog developed. We usually left St. John's Harbour past Cape Mark, then on to Spider Island. Inbound, we'd pass Iron Rocks on the way into Hakai Pass, then head up the Inside Passage, returning to Bella Bella. This was all very good experience for me to test honing my navigation without any aids but a compass.

During November of that year, I finally decided to buy a car. I had saved most of my earnings and even after sending several thousand to Mum, I could still afford a used vehicle. Tommy Williamson told me his nephew had a 1951 Chevy for sale and I should have a look at it. The car turned out to be in very good condition and ran well, so I bought it for $800 cash and drove it away.

Later, I happened to mention to Rosemary Giroday, as I was showing off my new acquisition, that I had been invited by Ken Dawson to a fraternity party at the University of B.C. Rosemary really wanted to go to the party, as she had some friends who were also invited, but I already had a date for the evening. I told her that it would probably be all right if she came with me and Donna Marie. Donna Marie wasn't nearly so keen when I told her my plans. Eventually though, all three of us arrived at the party, after I'd had to change a flat tire in the pouring rain.

I drove home to Quadra after the fishing closed for the winter, to show Mum my car, and also to finally get a driver's license for our annual Christmas trip back to California to visit Jim and family. In the meantime, I spent some time with Bill helping out around his sawmill. He'd just paid $200 down in Victoria for a 1932 Packard sedan, which sported a plaque on the dash saying it had been custom built for Louisa Todd. The Todds were a wealthy Victoria family who owned fish traps at Sooke, as well as fishing vessels and processing plants around the coast, so that was a noteworthy feature of the vehicle, which was in extremely good condition even though it was almost 30 years old. Bill wasn't interested in the vehicle, only the motor, which he wanted to power his sawmill.

So the V-12 motor was removed and hooked up, and the body was sent to spend its final days at Pete Cradock's junkyard. Looking back it's always so easy to see an alternative course of action. Today that car would probably be worth several hundred thousand dollars. But we saw it only as a source of cheap power for a sawmill.

Quadra had a major development that year. The Quadra Queen, a new ferry with a capacity of about 20 cars, came into operation to replace the Uchuck III. This vessel was operated by the Department of Highways and was a huge success and great convenience to islanders. The crew at the time came under Capt. Tom Hall, who was the senior captain, with John Oswald as the other captain and Gilbert Krooks and Ralph Hendrickson as mates. The deck and engine room crews were also local islanders who all had long experience at sea over their lifetimes.

When the time came, I had an appointment with the driver license examiner to finally get my license. I borrowed Alan McPherson's 53 Chev and $5 later I had my first legal permit to drive. The next day Mum and I left on the long journey down to California. This trip turned out to be a very happy time for

Mum. She was very excited to be travelling with me in our very own vehicle, and we made the most of our time together.

After leaving Vancouver, we made Roseberg Oregon the first day. We stopped at a small motel overnight where we were to stay several times on future trips. We took our time through the mountains of northern California stopping at Lake Shasta and exploring the redwood forests out towards the coast. On our fourth day we reached Berkley where we settled in with Jim and Rose.

My niece Heather had found herself what turned out to be her future husband. His name was Arnold Griller. The Grillers were from England and Mr. Griller was dean of music at the university. They had a daughter Katherine who was about my age and we spent some time together exploring San Francisco. Arnold was well liked by mum, and the rest of the family, and she was pleased that Heather had met such a fine young man.

The Grillers lived in north Berkley and their next door neighbour was Admiral Nimitz who was commander of U.S. Pacific forces during the war with Japan. One day when I had stopped by to see Katherine, the Admiral was sitting in his back yard reading a book. Mr. Griller introduced me to him and the Admiral invited me over for a short visit with him. This was the one time waiting for a lady to get ready was not going to be a problem. I was surprised at what a soft spoken and relaxed man he was. He was enjoying his retirement after a lifetime of serving his country. He didn't mention his time in Hawaii as commander of many thousands of men and ships during the war. I would liked to have talked to him about this time in history but felt he would mention it if he wanted to. We did talk about salmon fishing and he seemed very knowledgeable on the subject.

Mum and I spent some time with Aunt Sarah and family over the Christmas holidays. Her daughter Dorothy was living with Aunt Sarah to look after her as her health was failing.

Early in January, Jack Thompson and John Humphries flew in from Vancouver for a planned trip to Mexico. I picked them up at the airport and after a couple of days showing them what I knew of San Francisco we headed for Los Angeles. Our plans were to meet up with Ray and Jose then drive down to Ensanada, which is about a hundred miles south of the Mexican border. On the way south we stopped at Santa Barbara to give Mrs. Ripley a call. She invited us up to their mansion in the hills where I met her new husband, Mr. Fargo. Only Robert was still living at home but Polly was in San Francisco so I got her phone number for when we returned. From Santa Barbara we took the coastal route through Malibu arriving in L.A. well after dark.

Ray gave us directions to where he and his mother lived in Long Beach. We found their home without any trouble and Mrs. Carey welcomed us to her home even though she didn't know any of us. We spent a pleasant week there just hanging out during the evenings when Ray was able to be with us after work.

Jose arrived on Friday afternoon from Oxnard so we started off for Ensanada. The drive from Long Beach south to San Diego was along the old Pacific Coastal Highway through all the seaside communities. San Diego was still somewhat of a small city compared to L.A. with some of the wartime factories still standing along the waterfront. The navy was very much in evidence with many ships at anchor in the harbour. We crossed the border at Tijuana from the orderly streets of San Diego into the squalor and confusion of T town. From there we drove to the pleasant seaside town of Ensanada where we spent a most wonderful weekend returning on Monday night. This was my first of many trips to Mexico that I have made over the years. Mexico is a country that I always enjoy visiting and look forward to returning whenever possible.

Chapter 23

Soon another fishing season got under way and I was called back to work. Around and around the gulf twice each week we went again, with Fridays as our day off. Jack and I found a very nice apartment in a new building owned by the Wosks at 40th and Cambie. Fully furnished, it cost us $160 per month. This was a huge improvement over Don's basement suite, complete with the luxury of an elevator and swimming pool.

We moved in February 1,1961 and a short time after, disaster struck. Jack had been doing some scuba diving with John Humphries trying to salvage an old tug of John's. The dive was deep, and due to the strong tidal currents, Jack was swept up to the surface and was unable to decompress properly. He seemed to be all right when he surfaced though, and decided to go back down again so he could resurface more slowly, to dissolve the nitrogen build up in his body that is one of the results of breathing air under pressure. A short time later, John found him floating face down on the surface again. He quickly pulled him on board and, with Jack apparently unconscious in the boat, quickly made for the seaplane base at Campbell River. There Jack was loaded aboard an aircraft and flown into Vancouver, landing near a site where Northern Construction had a decompression chamber. Don Sorte and I had already made arrangements to have the chamber activated and ready for their arrival, and Don climbed into the chamber with Jack, who at that point was just starting to be semi-conscious. This meant that Don had to stay in the chamber for the whole time of decompression, which is done by slowly building up the pressure inside the chamber, holding it at an elevated level for a set time, and then bringing it back down to the same level of the surrounding air. After many anxious hours, the pressure inside the chamber was slowly released, and both men were removed. Unfortunately, as it turned out, Jack was paralyzed in both legs and was to remain that way for the rest of his life. This was not a good start on life for someone just 22 years old with so much promise and intelligence. I must say he handled it well, and after a long stay in hospital, he was back on stream again with two crutches to help him get around.

Jack was always one who accepted the cards that were dealt to him, and he carried on with his life with remarkably little interruption. He could still drive a car, fly an airplane and use his better than average intelligence to find a job as manager of a chain manufacturing plant, eventually starting his own house construction business.

That turned out to be a great year for me, with money rolling in, a nice apartment and many new friends. The volume of fish being caught in the gulf was dropping off though, due to many boats moving north earlier than usual. This meant we spent a lot more time on the run up to the central coast, which was all right with me, as I was able to navigate in many new places with Capt. Bill as a very much appreciated teacher.

One of the new friends I made that year was Joe Prosser, who was a neighbour of Norm Pittam in Victoria, and was skipper on the Canadian Navy sailing vessel HMCS Oriole. What a dream job, having a 102 foot sailing ketch to cruise around with. The Oriole was the fourth vessel to bear that name, and was built and launched on the East Coast in 1921 for George Gooderham. Most of her early life was spent on the Great Lakes, with Toronto as her homeport. Acquired by the Navy sometime in the late 1930's, she was sent out to the West Coast in 1954 and Joe became her skipper in early 1957.

For some reason, Charles Arthur Prosser was unknown to

most people by either of his given names, and was just Joe to everyone. Born in 1918 in Newfoundland, he spent his early days as a cod fisherman working the Grand Banks in sailing schooners aided by their little dories. At the age of 21, Joe joined the Newfoundland Commandos and was sent to England as part of the British forces over there during the war. He took part in a raid on the Norwegian coast and was captured by the occupying German forces. Somehow he managed to escape and found his way back to England. Having been wounded during the escapade though, he was discharged as unfit by the Commandos, and promptly joined the Royal British Navy as an ordinary seaman. He saw action in several war zones and finally ended up as a lieutenant commanding a frigate on Atlantic convoy duty, a dangerous and unpleasant duty which meant braving not only ghastly storm conditions but also German submarine packs out to attack the convoys of merchant vessels.

Discharged after the war, Joe came to Canada with his wife in 1951 by sailing their yacht from Europe to the East Coast, where he promptly joined the Canadian Navy. He was later sent to serve in the Korean War. That's what brought him to the West Coast of Canada, as the ships serving the war were based in Esquimalt B.C.

I never met his wife and family, as a divorce was under way about the time that we first became friends. Joe's wife was reputed to have been from a family of great wealth and I wouldn't be surprised if Joe's spending habits, as I saw them, had a good deal to do with their going their separate ways.

After Joe and I became friends, HMCS Oriole became the center point of my social life whenever she was in Vancouver for a few days. Joe would have me on board whenever he was entertaining various dignitaries, which was frequently. During the day, whenever possible, I'd sail on that great little ship, as cadets were being trained. In various aspects of seamanship, Joe tried his best to convince me to consider the Navy as a career, as he'd done as a youth, but times were changing and I couldn't see my future in the armed services.

As the 1961 fishing season began to draw to a close, Jack and I decided another trip to Mexico would be a good way to spend the cold winter months. I had bought a better car that spring, a 1957 Ford hardtop. I got it from Rod, a friend of Norm's, for a very good price of $1,200, though truly that was a lot of money in the old days. It had very low mileage, as Rod had the use of a company vehicle, so he decided to sell the Ford, since he didn't need two cars. Jack had a brand new 1961 Pontiac convertible though and we decided to use that for Mexico.

After the Amboyna finished her season securing the gulf camps, I worked up until the middle of December on the Randy making the barge run to Prince Rupert. By then, Mum was ready to roll as soon as I got home, and we quickly loaded up our baggage and headed south for California. I left my '51 Chev with Barry Giroday to sell for me, as I didn't plan to be back in Van' until the end of February.

Jack drove to California in his car, with his brother Bill, and met me at Jim's place in Berkley. We left immediately in Jack's car, with a quick stop at the Mexican Consulate in San Francisco to get our visas. We decided we needed to put some serious miles behind us as we left San Francisco about 12 noon and drove overnight to Phoenix. We had the usual rotation system all worked out, with one of us driving for two hours and the relieved driver then moving to the front passenger seat for the next two hours to act as lookout and to keep the driver awake and happy with snacks, conversation and suitable tuning of the radio. The third person would be in a sleeping bag in the back, resting up for his next turn at driving. We only stopped when we needed gas, and after leaving Bakersfield, we made terrific time across the desert, arriving in Phoenix at six the next morning.

From there it was on to Tucson, and then to the Mexican border at Nogales. Driving into Mexico was always an interesting event, as there didn't seem to be any set rules, other than those dreamed up on the spot by the particular customs official on duty in that particular slot at that moment. There were no real formalities other than that one must import the car into the country. This requires much paperwork and time, but we were well prepared, with the numerous copies of the licenses, insurance and registration that were required. On this occasion though, our copies were unacceptable to the customs agent, who said only copies that were from a place next door to the customs office, at 10 cents a copy, made by the fair hand of a very attractive senorita were acceptable.

Standard procedure at the time, though not recommended these days, was to place an American one dollar bill in each passport, as this had a way of somehow speeding up or eliminating the tedious process of paper work and red tape. As this was our first trip into real Mexico, we didn't know this was only the first of many more borders and obstacles that lay ahead of us. After leaving Nogales with all our papers finally in order, we were commenting on what an easy procedure the 'dollar per passport' routine had been.

Little did we know that nothing is easy in Mexico, as we approached the first of many road blocks about 20 miles south of Nogales. The border itself may not have been a serious affair in Mexico at the time, but these roadblocks certainly were. They were run by the army or Federales as they were commonly called, machine guns and all. They completely blocked the road, with a couple of machine gun nests located up in the trees sighted down on the blockade, and a spike belt across the road, manned by a couple of privates hiding in a ditch a few hundred yards down the road just in case one felt the urge to move out before the senior officers said it was okay to do so. That's not something I'd recommend unless one has absolutely no regard for one's life. Just because the previous army officer says it's all right to proceed doesn't mean the next one will agree your papers are in order, or that you can proceed without a complete search of the vehicle and your baggage. We were certainly surprised by the frequency and thoroughness of these roadblocks, but fortunately we didn't experience any real problems, other than the two parties trying to understand each other, since we had only a very limited knowledge of Spanish.

By evening though, we had reached Hermisillo, which in 1961 wasn't the huge industrial city of today. We met some nice senoritas who spoke a little English, and they were kind enough to take us to a friend who spoke English very well. He was very good to us, as is the Mexican way, and gave us many helpful tips on how to conduct ourselves during our stay in their wonderful country.

After a very pleasant evening spent over dinner, we headed out of town and passed the night in our sleeping bags rolled out under the open sky in the desert. We lit a small fire to keep warm, lay down gazing up at the stars and felt very sorry for all of the friends we'd left back home who weren't sharing the experience.

The next morning Billy suggested that maybe sleeping out wasn't such a good idea as he said he thought he'd heard a snake going by during the night. One has to be careful of snakes and scorpions in the northern parts of Mexico, as a person keeping cosy warm in a sleeping bag can attract a snake also looking for somewhere cosy and warm for the night, with unpleasant results for the sleeper as he or she wakes up to the movement of the snake. Still, we packed up feeling very refreshed after the long drive from San Francisco, and headed south with Mazatlan in our sights.

Along the way, we stopped at a roadside cantina for some coffee and breakfast, where, apart from an American beatnik from New York, we were the only patrons. This guy was apparently also on his way to Mazatlan to spend the winter, as he had several times before. In chatting, he passed on what sounded like some good advice, and we offered to give him a ride, to allow him to travel in style rather than trying to hitch-hike the whole way. Surprisingly, he politely refused, explaining that he wanted to finish the chapter of the book he was reading before hitting the road again. We couldn't believe someone could be so independent and carefree as to turn down a ride of almost 700 miles because he wanted to read for another half hour or so, but we headed out without him and sure enough, he did show up in Mazatlan a few days later.

We sighted the beautiful blue waters of the Gulf at Guaymas after driving another couple of hours. It was good to be out of the desert and back on the coast again. Highway 1 down the West Coast of Mexico was built in the 1950's and was still under construction in some parts. It was very heavily used by everything from large transport trucks to donkey carts. Cattle roamed at will, and night driving was as hazardous as it is today. There was no marked centre line, and if one went off the so called pavement, it would result in a flat tire for sure and possibly much more damage to your vehicle than that.

The drive from Hermosillo to Mazatlan was a very long one and we arrived well after dark on December 20, 1961. Today there is a toll freeway and this same trip can be made with ease, though the tolls can add up to a substantial amount of coin. The old highway remains still in use and the last time I was down there it was still as narrow and treacherous as it was in 1961. It probably still is.

We had made it from San Francisco to Mazatlan in two days and one night of driving, with one night spent sleeping in the desert. This was good time even on today's highways, but we sure were tired and ready for a good sleep upon arrival. We obtained a large room at the La Siesta Hotel for the three of us for the princely price of $12 a night. The room had three double beds and was considered expensive by the standards of those days, but we decided economizing could wait until after Christmas.

The next day dawned bright and sunny, with the sound of surf rolling gently in on the beach. I headed up to the hotel where Jack Beban was staying and had breakfast with him, before he caught a flight home to spend Christmas in Nanaimo. We talked to some of the beach boys who hung around the tourist hotels to entertain the wealthy widows who frequented such places, and after 'interviewing' several, we hired one called Ricardo to be our amigo for the duration of our stay. We feasted on Camerones and Langosta at some of the beach cantinas, and everywhere Ricardo took us he collected from the owner a nice little commission for bringing us to the establishment, so it was quite a profitable little venture for him.

The whole period of Christmas through New Year's is one huge fiesta in Mexico, and the La Siesta Hotel was alive every evening, with families and many children dressed in traditional costumes, all kinds of boisterous parties, much loud music and the noise of laughter and conversation. One day we were having such a good time swimming that when some new friends invited us to have Christmas dinner with them, we looked at each other in total surprise. We had completely forgotten it was Christmas Day.

When dinner was over, I thought I'd phone home to my girlfriend, to tell her what a horrible and miserable time we were having. That proved quite an adventure in itself, as calling from Mexico continued to be until quite recently. One possible way of telephoning at that time was through the Publico Telephono, which cost about $50 and was a complete rip off, even though they did have enough people paid off for you to be able to get through quite quickly. That meant the public telephones were out of the question, so I thought I'd try going through the hotel front desk. They did manage to get through after about six hours of effort and waiting, only for me to find my girlfriend's sister was the only one home at the time of my call. I should have known better and I don't think I've ever phoned from Mexico since, even though there is now a very modern telephone system.

We soon tired of the non-stop action at Mazatlan and left the day after Christmas for San Blas, quickly learning yet another of Mexico's many lessons when we stopped for gas. Small boys wanting to clean our windshield immediately swarmed the vehicle. We hadn't yet learned not to let them do this with the dirty, oily rags they used, as their efforts only made things worse rather than better. Despite that, we let them check our oil and water. That was another big mistake. A few miles out from the station, the radiator boiled over, as the kids had thoughtfully left the radiator cap off. This is all planned of course and soon someone showed up with water in an old beat up truck, to lend a hand. Naturally there was a price for that also, so after much negotiation over the price, we were filled up again for another $2, and I made sure the cap was put securely back on again. Down the road we stopped and bought some bananas and other fruit at a roadside stand and were happy to be on our way again. There were many iguanas sleeping near the road, and although we tried many times to catch one, they were very quick and always got away.

A few miles before Tepic, we turned off the main road and down to San Blas. This area is a mass of dense jungle, with many colourful and noisy birds and an enormous assortment of different kinds of animals. We stopped a few times to listen to their raucous calls after the sun had gone down, finally reaching San Blas well after dark and checking in at The Buccaneer where we were met by Jungle Jim. Thirty years later, when I spent another night at The Buccaneer, Jungle Jim was still taking tourists on his canoe trips up the river that flows down through the swamps behind the village. Jim still remembered me from that previous visit, and it was good to see him and other long lost amigos from that happy time.

San Blas was a major Spanish Navy base during the years of discovery on the west coast of North America. There's a large lighthouse on the promontory overlooking the ocean and many years later it was still the sleepy little town that had changed very little since it fell from prominence during the 1800's. There was only one other hotel when we got there. It was located on the beach, and was a new modern building, which was empty except for a young couple who happened to be from Vancouver. This establishment never gained any popularity, and years later it stood in ruins, even though the dilapidated old Buccaneer up in the village is still going.

The Buccaneer was just $2 per night, and was like something out of Treasure Island, complete with a very beautiful senorita and an appropriately noisy parrot. To have a shower, one had to go out back, light a wood fire under an old boiler, then go up to the village square for breakfast while the water heated.

We had breakfast each morning at a little place run by an elderly couple who lived in the kitchen area. They had chickens in the back yard, so fresh eggs were readily available, along with fried potatoes, coffee boiled in an old jam can, and fresh oranges from the property's tree. Sometimes if we were early, we had to wake the proprietors up and had the coffee boiling for them by the time they were dressed.

The first day at San Blas we decided we'd float down the river to the beach, as this would be easier than walking for Jack, who due to his injury was on two crutches. We wondered why so many people were watching us as we drifted down the very slow moving stream. The senorita from the hotel, who met us at the beach, told us they were all waiting to see what would happen when the alligators found us in their river. Jack walked to the beach after this and the senorita kept a much closer eye on us and our activities over the next couple of days.

Ross and Eunice Hunt were a young couple also staying at the Buccaneer. Ross was from South Africa while Eunice was from Edmonton. Ross was a geology student and had spent the summer at Granduc Mines in northern B.C. His father was president of Newmont Mining, one of the largest mining companies in the world at the time, and we had a fun month together and had many amusing adventures.

Ross and Eunice told us they were planning to travel further south, maybe even as far as Costa Rica, and we decided we'd tag along, so we packed up most of our belongings, leaving the rest with the senorita at the hotel. This way we would have room for everybody in one car. We had to wake up the breakfast makers early so we could get a good start and they told us they thought we were 'loco' travelling so far, but I don't think they'd probably ever even been away from San Blas. The hotel senorita had evidently developed some affection for us, as she gave us a tearful goodbye as we set off for Mexico City.

We made Guadalajara the first day, and promptly had some things stolen from the car overnight, but down at the market the next day we managed to buy most of them back at reasonable prices. We didn't bother about the hubcaps and a few other odds and ends and ornaments that the car could do without. That's when Ross said we should see if there was a Canadian Consulate in the city, so he could get his visa renewed. At that time, the only Canadian Embassy was in Mexico City, but there was a British Consulate in Guadalajara who could look after Canadians and other British subjects. Since Ross was South African, he thought that would work out all right.

That evening we thought it would be nice to take Eunice out to an expensive restaurant as a special treat after hanging out with four boys in the wilds of San Blas. We found a very nice place near the city centre and settled in for a very exciting evening. We had bought a few new clothes so we wouldn't look like bush men, as Eunice was dressed to kill, in a lovely dress.

Courting in Mexico at that time was still conducted under the chaperone system and possibly still is in some of the more old fashioned and older Spanish families. A young man would ask permission from the father of the house to call on one of his daughters, and if this was approved, at some later date decided by the father or older brothers, some time was spent with the family. Perhaps a movie or walk in the plaza, with most of the family in attendance. The next step would likely be a movie or some other social event, with the mother or grandmother as chaperone, and maybe after a year or so, a social event with another couple, with a chaperone still along to keep an eye on everyone. Next would be a double date, with a young married couple from either family, and finally, after a proposal of marriage, the lucky couple might be allowed to go to a theatre and perhaps dinner together by themselves, provided of course that they agreed to be home early! The whole community would be expected to keep a firm watch on them and report any suspected wrong doing to the two fathers involved.

That night, the young couple at the table next to us in this very fancy dining room were on their first evening together by themselves. It was indeed a first class and expensive place, with Mariachi music, low lights and excellent food. The music in Mexico is truly infectious, and the young man had a good singing voice. In celebration of their first evening together, he had also had taken on board on a sizable amount of wine. His betrothed was getting more agitated with each passing song, and the musicians spent a good deal of time at their table, urging him on, as did the rest of us.

Finally, it was all too much for her and she stormed out of the room, but not before giving her beau a good dressing down in the most exquisite tones. This of course was just too much for the young suitor's sense of pride. He promptly picked up a wine bottle, broke it over the back of a nearby chair, and in full dramatic fashion made moves to slash his wrists. Several of us jumped on him and prevented him from doing too much damage, but there was blood everywhere. Someone chased down the departed senorita, who promptly returned and soon I'm happy to say there were more tears than blood. It was all very beautiful in a melodramatic, sad kind of way and very much in tune with the extremes of the Latin temperament in just about everything they do.

The next day we had an appointment with Mr. Stevens, the British Consul. We arrived early and were shown in to his office to wait for him. In a few minutes, the two young ladies who worked there wheeled in the consul, who turned out to be at least 90 years old and evidently barely alive. We attempted to explain to him our needs, but soon had to give up, as he had fallen asleep in his wheelchair. His secretary said that was the first time he'd been called to the office in several months, and he had really been looking forward to meeting someone he could speak English with. We couldn't quite believe that and even wondered whether he'd make it home without an ambulance. We decided a visit to the Canadian Embassy in Mexico City might be more productive.

We arrived in Mexico City the next evening, and weren't in the least prepared for the huge size of the city. We stayed right downtown in a moderate hotel. By then it was coming up to the New Year's holiday, and as a result, we weren't able to get to the Canadian Embassy. So we moved on to Acapulco, but that was so crowded we came back to Cernuvaca, which is a mountain city about halfway between Mexico City and the Pacific Coast. There we welcomed in the New Year of 1962 as part of the many festivities already well under way. Many wealthy Mexicans have holiday homes in the city and it is very neat and tidy, with no industries of any size. The mountain air is pleasantly cool, especially in the evening and it is a most relaxing place.

I paid a small boy $2 and an ice cream cone for a clay jug, which was way more than it was worth. The young lad and his father sat with us while the youngster thoroughly enjoyed the ice cream, but the jug is still sitting on my desk over 40 years later, and I can still see the happy look on that little boy's face as he sat with us that night so long ago. I often wonder where he is today.

New Year's Day was spent exploring the large pyramid just outside the city, where we killed a coral snake we found on the trail. Coral snakes are very poisonous, but are quite small and don't pose much of a danger if one is wearing shoes and long pants. We didn't want to take a chance with this one though, as there were a lot of people on the trail who weren't dressed appropriately for hiking among snakes.

The next day we headed back to Mexico City and we were surprised to find frost on the road, with the Mexican senoras all bundled up against the very cold temperatures. Mexico City is about 8,500 feet above sea level, so the mountain pass to get to it must have been close to 10,000 feet. It's not unusual to have snow on the hillsides around the city, and the higher volcanoes have snow on their tops much of the year.

My brother Jim had a friend who lived in Mexico City, so I called him and he came to our hotel to meet us. His name was Dr. Ruiz, and he kindly gave us a fine tour of the university and Chupultepec Castle. I was very impressed with the beautiful architecture at the university. The next day, the Embassy was open, so Ross got his papers in order and we decided we'd had enough of what is now one of the largest cities in the world, with a population of over 20 million and really has to be seen to be appreciated. It was already a very large conurbation, and there was a huge barrio right next to the modern international airport, where people were fighting to scratch out an existence on a daily basis. There was no water, sewage or electricity at that time, and I've heard little has changed since.

One thing that was interesting was that a British Airways Comet aircraft was parked at the airport. This was the only time I ever saw one and I was very impressed. Bill caught a Canadian Pacific Airlines flight back to Vancouver shortly afterwards, as he had to be back at school, and we struck off for Guadalajara with an overnight stop at the beautiful city of Morales.

Late the next night we were turning off the main highway for San Blas when a policeman who lived on the corner waved us down. We weren't going to stop, but he immediately pulled out his gun and fired a warning shot in the air. Blasting off that gun did the trick, and we quickly stopped. When he walked up to the car, we recognized him as the night patrol at San Blas. He was clearly very drunk and apparently hadn't been able to get a ride into the village about 20 miles away. He promptly climbed in the back with Ross and instantly passed out. The next morning he was very hung over and was trying to get a ride back home again after a night shift spent asleep in the back of our car.

It was certainly good to be back in the friendly community of San Blas after the big city life we'd experienced over the past 10 days. After a few days at the beach, the senorita from the hotel asked us if we'd take her to Tepic, since she had some business to do there for the hotel and some friends she wanted to visit. Dressed in our best clothes, we headed for Tepic, which is about 20 miles south of the turn off to San Blas. Tepic is another of Mexico's mountain cities and one of my favourite places in the whole country. As always in these elevated townships, the air is sunny and warm with cloudless skies in the day and pleasantly cool at night.

After the young lady had finished her business, she suggested we have dinner with some of her friends at one of the fine restaurants downtown. The specialty of this place was chicken. I knew this was going to be a mistake, as we were always very careful not to eat most fresh meat anywhere in Mexico, but I didn't want to be rude. So I picked away at the wonderful looking chicken dinner. By the time we arrived back at San Blas, I was a basket case. The local doctor fixed me up with some anti-toxin the next morning, and this was the only time that Montazuma has ever had his revenge with me while in Mexico.

One day a group of American tourists asked us if we'd like to join them on a boat trip down the coast towards Puerto Vallarta. They wanted to do some hunting for ducks and maybe a jaguar if one could be found. So we packed up our camping gear and headed off in a miserable old boat with a little putt putt four cylinder gas engine, which proceeded to quit about 10 miles down the coast. Not unexpectedly though, the long suffering skipper knew how to take it apart and coax it back to life again. We stopped at a small village about half way to Guyabitis to make camp. We had brought along a couple of canoes to get us ashore after we had anchored the boat behind a sheltering point of land.

It was some fun coming in through the surf in one of those canoes, but after a few flips we eventually got the hang of it and Jack, Ross, Eunice and I made camp while the Americans went off with the skipper to do some duck hunting. There was one small cantina in the village of about 100 people overlooking the beach with scenic views of the ocean. The cantina had a dirt floor and the largest hog I have ever seen. It wandered amiably around begging for scraps from the clientele. If it got to be too much of a pest, the owner would throw down a handful of maize. Today there is a road along the ocean between San Blas and Guyabitis, and I have looked for this village several times without success. My Mexican friends have warned me not to drive this road at night, as banditos on horseback will rob anyone driving this wild, unsettled part of the coast after sunset.

The Americans soon arrived back at camp with a good bunch of ducks. We managed to borrow a large cooking pot from the cantina to cook them along with some corn and potatoes. As I was throwing a piece of wood on the fire, a scorpion jumped out of a knothole and landed at my feet, its stinger raised to attack. I promptly kicked it on to the fire and was a little more careful where I reached in the future, as these nasty little creatures tend to live under dead wood and rocks.

The duck stew tasted wonderful, and many of the village residents came to join us, since there was plenty for everyone. We slept out under a bright star filled sky with the Southern Cross showing above the horizon and a jaguar grunting in the trees behind the village. Despite that sound, I look back on this as probably one of the best times I've ever had camping, with the nice warm days, cool nights and very few bugs or mosquitoes.

We spent the next few days travelling down the coast ending up at Puerto Vallarta. There was no road that was usable into the town at that time, and the fame it gained from movie star visitors Richard Burton and Elizabeth Taylor was still a few years away. The then small fishing village sported a large cathedral as a prominent landmark, as it still does today. Soon though, we headed back up the coast, and after a couple of days, arrived back home at San Blas. This was the first time that I had ever been in the water with sharks, a new experience to be sure, but we learned to swim along with them and keep a look out for any sign of aggression.

As we were arriving at San Blas, a fishing boat was landing with a large sea turtle, which the crew cut open, passing around the eggs from the poor, still struggling animal. The eggs were eagerly devoured, while the tortured animal looked on in pain. I've never eaten any part of a turtle since, though turtle stew had previously been a favourite of mine.

I think we all felt we could happily have stayed at San Blas the rest of our lives, but all good things must come to an end and Ross had to get back to Tucson, where he was registered to finish his course in geology. I also had to be back to work by late February. So we started north in the two cars, Ross and I in his Volkswagen, Jack and Eunice in the convertible. We spent our last night in Mexico camped out on the cement cover of the

Guymas water reservoir, which was on a hilltop overlooking the town.

The next day we stopped in Hermosillo for haircuts and a general clean up before crossing back into Arizona. We visited with Ross and Eunice at their Tucson apartment for a couple of days then drove across the southern desert to San Diego. Sadly, I've never seen or heard from Ross and Eunice since that time. I've been back to San Blas a few times over the years, but it's not the same, and I always get a feeling of sadness and nostalgia for that wonderful time we spent there so long ago.

We drove non-stop as usual through Yuma, Death Valley, San Diego and up through Los Angeles. We had planned to take the central route north to San Francisco, but the mountain pass between Los Angeles and Bakersfield was closed for snow and we had to turn back and take Highway 101 up the coast instead. We arrived at Jim' place in Berkley early in the morning. Jack rested up for a day then, drove back up to Vancouver by himself in 19 hours. Mom and I left shortly afterwards, with a stop in Eugene, Oregon, to visit Jim Sears, who was attending university there.

Chapter 24

As soon as I had Mum safely home on Quadra Island, I was called back to work and joined the Randy on a trip out to the west coast to pack herring for Nelson Brothers. It was a terrible trip, with poor weather and heavy seas, but we loaded up with 200 tonnes of herring, towing a barge with about the same load from Quatsino Sound around Cape Scott and up to Prince Rupert. We took a real licking in those heavy seas, with large waves sweeping us as we rounded the cape, and on arrival in port I recall we found the pounding had even managed to shift part of the superstructure slightly.

Shortly after arriving home from our trip to Mexico, Jack had decided he wouldn't be able to share the apartment with me any more, due to financial problems brought on from restraints to his earning power from his injury. Instead, an old friend from up coast said he'd like to take Jack's place, as he needed a place to stay when he was in Vancouver. So Ed Bomford moved in with me. As we were both away most of the time, this arrangement worked out just fine for both of us. Ed had a logging camp at Hall Point, at the north east corner of Sonora Island. He had a home in Duncan, just north of Victoria, but also spent some time in Vancouver on business to do with his logging operation.

Ed was a big man and we referred to him as the great snowman, a name Don Sorte hung on him. He had long red hair with a large, bushy beard and an impressive personality to match, which seemed attractive to almost everyone he came in contact with. Overall though, he was a quiet man, with an easygoing manner, and I certainly met some interesting people because of our friendship.

My next trip was back on the Amboyna, to start getting the Gulf of Georgia camps ready for the lingcod fishery. It was good to be back with the old crew again and to be back on the familiar old camp run for the fourth season.

Andy Tulloch had a big surprise for us that spring. The business was growing and had purchased three new vessels that were former U.S. Army personnel carriers that had been used as tugs since their arrival in Canada in the late 1940's. With the French names of Le Prince and La Fleur, operated by Vancouver Tug, and the P.B. Anderson, owned by Kingcome Navigation, they had to be readied for the coming season. Billie Rapita and I were assigned the task. Peter Stanley, who was working for Vancouver Tug and had experience in the fishing industry, had decided they would make excellent fish packers, and Andy agreed to buy them.

These three vessels were born to be cargo carriers. They were about 90 feet in length, with a good beam and high freeboard. The crew accommodations were definitely above average, and the trio were all capable of maintaining a good steady speed of about 10 knots. They had a large forward cargo hold and a smaller one aft, with the accommodation amidships. We rigged them with forward twin booms that were run by electric winches, and the aft hold was serviced by a single boom. They all had excellent towing winches, since they had been used as tugs for the last 15 years.

Two of the vessels reverted to their original names, both preceded by the initials TW. Le Prince became the TW Sea Prince, Le Fleur became the TW Sea Queen, and the PB Anderson became the TW Zelly in honour of Bill, who was the senior captain with Tulloch Western Fisheries.

Billy Rapita and I quickly got to work to fix them to go back to sea. We painted them in their new company colors, renewed the rigging and lifting gear, and docked them for underwater work such as painting the hull below the water line with anti-foulant.

I was helping the shipyard crew take the propeller off the Sea Queen one day, when an older man in work clothes came by to watch.

"Is this your vessel?" he asked.

"No," I said. "I'm just an employee, a boat this size is beyond my pocket."

He then told me he owned the vessel over in the next slipway, the Wild Goose, a converted U.S. Navy mine sweeper. He was John Wayne, the famous actor who was still continuing to star in untold numbers of Western movies. My visitor seemed like an all right guy and the two of us sat and talked for a while about his planned trip up the coast that summer to do some sport fishing with friends. (Bob Hope and Phil Harris)

I really enjoyed that spring, working around the new vessels and being on shore at the same time, rather than months at sea, which would come soon enough. Joe Gillis was manager of the shipyard, which was then located at the foot of Denman Street. I learned a valuable lesson one day that spring, that I still call back to mind each time I get too sure of myself.

The vessels had to go through steamship inspection and it fell to me to expedite this procedure. Mr. Moorcroft was the government inspector assigned to handle the inspections and we had always got along well together. I recall he was later to become chief inspector for the whole West Coast, a very competent marine engineer. One day he asked me if the main sea valve on the Sea Queen was sound and had I taken it apart for him so it was ready for him to inspect. I had, and I assured him that it looked in first class condition. He went down to the engine room with his little hammer in hand and hit the valve a few times. This good looking piece of equipment completely fell apart after the third hit. The valve was completely eaten up with metal fatigue and electrolysis. He gave me a knowing look and said that he'd be back as soon as I had installed new valves on all three vessels. It was a good lesson for me. Things are not always what they appear to be, and there is no substitute for experience. The valves are very expensive, and Andy Tulloch wasn't pleased with this turn of events. However, we did get the new valves and the vessels ready for sea by the first week of May, and I gathered the Vancouver waterfront was suitably impressed with the new look these vessels had taken on at Vancouver Shipyard.

To fill out these new vessels while continuing to crew the old fleet, there was some rearrangement of existing employees and hiring of new personnel. Rod took over the Amboyna, while Bill Zelly was to start on the Sea Prince, as she was the last vessel to sail and he needed extra time at home with his wife who wasn't doing too well with her health. A new skipper, a very capable Ernie Fisher, took over the W #6.

I was assigned to the Sea Queen, and our first job was to pick up two new camp barges that were built at Star Shipyard. Magnus was previously mate on the Randy and this was his first trip as a skipper. He was Norwegian and had spent a few years on deep sea ships before coming to Canada. He was a very capable man, but I think he tended to worry too much. No matter how grim a situation might be, I always rather prided myself on being upbeat and sure everything would work out all right in the end. This attitude tended to give Magnus nightmares, but everything always did manage to work out all right for us.

Our orders were to tow these new camp barges to the west coast of Vancouver Island, one for Kyuquot Sound and another for Winter Harbour. We also loaded up with 60 tonnes of ice to deliver to some of the camps and got under way. All went well, and we were very pleased with the performance of the vessel. After delivering the second barge, we towed the old barge from Winter Harbour around Cape Scott and then on down the Inside Passage to Vancouver. The weather was fine down Johnstone Strait, but this did not stop Magnus from worrying, as the old barge we were towing wasn't in good condition.

This of course was the start of yet another season of continuous round the island voyages. We'd leave Vancouver Thursday at midnight with a load ice, empty fish boxes and supplies for the camps. Our first stop would be Bamfield, then on to Ucluelet, Tofino, Neuchatliz, Nootka, Kyuquot and Winter Harbour. Then we'd double back, stopping at all the camps again until we arrived back at the start in Vancouver the next Thursday morning. The TW Islander was on the same run, except that her trips were staggered with ours, and she left on Mondays.

Wes Parry was the manager of the West Coast of Vancouver Island operation and often drove out to Tofino on the logging road from Port Alberni, so he could catch up with us to ride up to the northern camps. On one early trip we had to stop over at Bamfield for a few hours to do some repairs to the barge. The woman who ran the camp was overseeing the repairs as we tried to carry out her instructions. Magnus asked her to have lunch with us on board, to which she readily agreed. But the whole time she was complaining about Wes Parry and saying what a terrible manager he was. She just couldn't say enough bad things about him and the way he ran the operation. On and on she went until we all got thoroughly fed up with her complaints and criticism. When lunch was over, she looked over at me.

"You're new to me," she said. "We haven't met before. Who are you?"

I kept a straight face as I told her I was Wes Parry's son and we were going to pick up my dad at Tofino in a few hours. I wish someone had had a camera handy, because the look on her reddened face brought howls of laughter from the rest of the crew. I don't believe anyone ever put her out of her misery and told her the truth.

Bill Zelley came back to work early in June that year. He made the first trip on the Sea Prince and was clearly impressed with the vessel's fine performance. He had never used radar before and said he found it very useful getting into Port Neville one dark night. We had also installed radar on the Amboyna earlier that year, but Bill never sailed on her again, even after being her skipper for more than eight years. When we got back to Vancouver, Bill transferred over to the Sea Queen and remained with her for the rest of his illustrious career. It was good to be sailing with Bill again on this trip, with Tony, Billie Rapita and me together with 3 new crew members to fill out our crew of seven. We spent most of our time packing seine caught fish out of the central area.

That was also a year to be remembered for one of the largest pink salmon runs in history returning to the central coast. All the plants were overrun with these small fish averaging less than two pounds. The fishermen were put on a quota by the canning companies, as they couldn't keep up with the huge volumes of fish flowing into their facilities. The Sea Queen could hold about 325,000 lbs of iced fish, and we loaded her up many, many times during that memorable season.

On one trip we pulled into Kwakume Inlet in the late afternoon, to be met by a fleet of seine boats waiting to unload. We worked right through the night and were fully loaded by daylight, but then we were sent to Bella Bella to deliver some supplies before heading south back to Vancouver. Bill said I should get some rest and he'd stand watch on the three hour trip north. Dane Campbell was one of the new deckhands on board, and he was so tired by that time, he fell asleep on the wet and slime covered deck. He was sleeping so deeply Billie had to turn the wash down hose on him to wake him up. I recall I lay down on my bunk, closed my eyes for what seemed like a few seconds, and found the three hours had passed and we had arrived at Bella Bella.

After we unloaded our cargo and set off south, I took over the watch from Bill as we were heading through Lama Pass. At Pointer Island, we passed Joe Prosser on the Oriole, who was heading north to Alaska with a load of cadets. We dipped the flag in salute and had a good chat on the radio as we parted in our different directions.

Towards the middle of August, the fishing started to slow down, as the pinks had passed through on their run to the rivers to spawn. On one of these late summer trips into Vancouver, we had stopped at Deep Bay to pick up a small amount of troll fish when a Mayday call came in over the air from the government radio station at Comox, saying that the Loretta B. was sinking off Porlier Pass. The boat was under charter to our company and had left Porlier with a full load of boxed fish, a crew of three and two passengers. The night was quite clear, with a light westerly wind, but for whatever reason, the craft was apparently taking on water and sinking rapidly. We were just south of Qualicum Beach when we received the Mayday call and Bill instantly ordered all possible speed from our faithful Enterprise diesel engine. The engineer cranked her right up to 420 revs a minute, which was 20 above her normal running speed, and off we went to see what we could do to help. We could see flares being dropped by rescue aircraft called in to assist in searching the area. As we were still about three hours away though, we couldn't do much but hope the people on board could manage to survive until help got there.

In the meantime, the Sea Queen pushed on through the night too, cranking out 12 knots while her anxious crew readied the lifeboat for launching if needed and got blankets, food and first aid supplies laid out in the galley. The cook had a huge pot of soup in preparation for any survivors who might come aboard from the chill outside, in need of a hot meal and warming showers.

We got to the search area just at daybreak, with heavy hearts but still trying to be optimistic some or all might have survived the night. Shortly afterwards, a fisherman who hadn't heard the alarm call came on the radio to ask if a vessel had sunk during the night, as he had just picked up a young woman clinging desperately to a wooden fish box in the water. This was one of the two passengers who had hitched a ride from Porlier Pass to Vancouver. Our spirits rose when we heard the news, and all hands were on deck on the lookout for any further survivors. We even sent one deckhand up the fore-mast with a pair of binoculars to get a better view. By this time there were many boats scouring the water for anything from the vessel, but in the end we only found broken remains of the Loretta B and no sign of any of the other four missing men.

It was a very sad occasion, and I've often thought about

this one young woman who was able to survive the wreck. She was reported to have been well along in her pregnancy at the time of her rescue and the baby would be over 40 years old now. I've often wondered where this child is and whether he or she was ever told what the mother had gone through on that summer night so long ago.

During my early years at sea, we took part in many rescues and salvage jobs. Before radar and other navigational aids became widespread, accidents were much more common than they are today. I picked the Loretta B incident solely as an example of so many other accidents, simply because of the unique outcome of this young mother to be and her survival.

After so many weeks without any time off, we were scheduled to make a stop at Nanaimo to drop off some supplies to the camp there. Bill said it would be all right if we wanted to have wives and girlfriends aboard for the short 35 mile trip from Vancouver. Most people took him up on his offer, so we had a load of assorted females aboard that night for the crossing to Nanaimo. We weren't really supposed to carry passengers except for company employees, but as Bill was the senior captain with the company, he could stretch the rules once in a while, as he sometimes did. We arrived in Nanaimo just in time to wake up the sleeping females and drive them to catch the 7 a.m. ferry back to Vancouver. Bill spent some hours with his wife, who was ailing, then we set sail once again at noon heading north to start towing the fish camps south into Johnstone Strait for the late summer fishery.

During October we made a trip out to the west coast of the Island to pick up a load of chum salmon needing to be delivered down to Bellingham in Washington State. This turned out to be a real trip to remember, as the weather was extreme for the entire week, ending with Hurricane Freda lashing the coast during the memorable night of October 12, 1962. We stopped in Victoria on the way north, as the weather was poor and Bill wanted to wait for some of the smaller packers to catch up, so we could travel together for everyone's safety.

I called Joe Prosser and found out the old Newfie fisherman

had been elevated to Master of Ceremonies at a dress ball for cadets at the Empress Hotel that evening, to be attended by the Lieutenant Governor and other dignitaries.

This was an opportunity too good to pass up. Billie and I dressed in our oldest, most worn out clothes, complete with heavy gumboots and rain gear, and walked up the sidewalk to the grand old granite hotel, which was just a few blocks from where we were moored. We'd show old Joe who his real friends were, by crashing this fancy party and causing him just as much embarrassment as possible. We hid behind some bushes until the doorman was occupied, then made a dash for the ballroom. We certainly did manage to put poor Joe on the spot as we suddenly appeared out of nowhere in our ancient fishing gear, but the joke was just as much on us, as most people thought it was a prank Joe had put on himself, as he was famous for that kind of practical joke. After appropriate introductions, he hustled us outside and promised he would get even with us when we least expected it even if it took him the rest of his life.

Rather than make a pest of ourselves any further, we returned to the Sea Queen and had the crew in stitches as we regaled them with the story of our appearance at the ball all kitted out as we were. About midnight, as we were getting ready to turn in for our early start that morning, we heard a sharp whistle from someone on the dock. It was Joe, all dressed in full military attire, with a couple of Military Police, who came on board demanding to see the captain. Bill chomped down on his cigarette holder and declared that would be him, and what was it they were wanting? Joe promptly announced that he had brought the MPs to arrest Billie and me for indecent exposure, and continued he didn't want any trouble from anybody. Old Bill just looked on in total disbelief, as Joe then proceeded to produce a bottle of rum and a tot was poured all round.

Joe and Bill became instant friends and set about talking about their early lives at sea, Bill on the west coast and Joe on the east. We all polished off a few more tots of rum Navy style, out of mugs, before daylight arrived. Bill then ordered everybody ashore who didn't intend making the trip up the west coast with us, and Joe departed with the MPs. Evidently he felt we still had some pay back coming for our prank, because he departed uttering dire threats. He'd deal with Billie and me "in the very near future."

That was the start to October 9, my 22nd birthday, as we pulled out into raging autumn seas to escort the arriving fleet of smaller packers up the west coast of the Island. It was quite a ride, with 60 to 80 knot gales running up a huge following sea. We rode it all well, but one of the smaller boats couldn't make the turn safely into Tofino, so we stayed with it until the crew could get it into Nootka Sound. We ended up in Hesquit Harbour, unloading some of the smallest tattered wrecks of seine boats I've ever seen. We finished off our load a day later at Ucluelet, then sailed through the islands to re-enter the still raging storm at Cape Beale.

As we entered Imperial Eagle Channel, the tide was ebbing against the prevailing seas, resulting in a huge tide rip right off the cape. Someone called us on the radio for a weather check out there, and Bill told them to stay where they were if possible, as the seas were huge just where the tidal stream met the open Pacific Ocean. We had rough and heavy going all the way back down to Victoria, where we cleared customs for the trip to Bellingham. In spite of the heavy weather, we felt perfectly safe (or at least I did), as the Sea Queen had fine sea going qualities, and we were as comfortable as we could be in such stormy conditions.

Arriving in Bellingham, we sailed finally into calm and sheltered waters, and it felt good to be in port for a few hours while we unloaded. Soon after, I got a call from the office in Vancouver that I was to catch the bus back there as soon as possible, to join the Randy, which was due to sail that evening for Prince Rupert with two freight barges. It was quite a scramble, and I had a real hassle with Canadian Customs at the border as they accused me of working in the U.S. It finally took a call from Andy Tulloch to get me and the whole bus released by Customs, and I still don't know to this day why they should have had any problem, even if I had been working in the U.S.

I joined the Randy on time down at, ironically, the Immigration Dock at the foot of Burrard Street. The crew already had her all fuelled up, and we were ready to pick up our tow at the Kitsilano Buoy. As we were hooking up, we noticed that there was a two to three foot chop blowing in with heavy winds at the mooring buoy. This was unusual, as the buoy is located in what are usually very sheltered waters protected from southeast winds. The wind was gusting and the buildings along Beach Drive were quickly plunging into darkness. Transformers were flashing as power lines were torn from their poles and the wind was continuing to pick up speed. It didn't look good, but we started out into the gulf with our tow, with all hands on deck to try to see what the heck was going on.

As we left the shelter of Point Grey to port, the night was perfectly clear, with no rain at all at that time. We could even see the lights of Nanaimo off in the distance about 20 miles, and they looked like they might be just a mile away. A delayed hurricane warning had been posted, and the seas were building by the minute as we came abeam of Cape Roger Curtis. The radio was alive with chatter from boats seeking shelter. But since the heavy-gale warnings earlier in the day, most vessels that needed shelter had made port, leaving the rest of the larger vessels to ride out a normal early winter gale.

Drydie Jones was skipper on the Island Sovereign southbound abeam of White Islets with a loaded log barge that night. Drydie was a tough tow boater from the old school, who spent his entire life on large tugs. We could see his three white towing lights very clearly in the distance, due to the unusually good visibility. Every few minutes these lights would turn a shade of light green. We called Drydie on the radio to ask him if he knew his white mast lights were turning green.

"Oh that'll probably be the green water coming right over the wheelhouse," he replied. "I guess the waves are over 30 feet high. I've never seen anything like it in the gulf."

Fortunately, in our big boat we made fairly good weather

of it, with the giant following sea. Don Burben was the skipper that trip, and he kept enough speed on the engines to keep ahead of the barges, without putting too much strain on the towing gear. We made 14 knots all the way from English Bay over to Cape Lazo, where the winds started to drop off. By the time we had got up to Cape Mudge, the wind had started to come around to northwest and the seas had flattened with a nice favourable ebb tide to take us through Seymour Narrows.

Dick Kiyama was one of our fishermen we picked up fish from at Active Pass each Sunday evening during the lingcod fishery. Dick had a new boat just built that year, and he was very pleased with his fine new purchase. The vessel was anchored out during the hurricane, when Dick became concerned about her safety. He launched his dinghy from shore, and headed out into the blackness of the night to make sure all was well and the anchor was holding. Sadly, this was the last anyone ever saw of Dick, and although his fish boat survived, we have to assume he was swept out of the somewhat sheltered waters of Active Pass into the boiling turmoil that was the open gulf.

Such was my experience of Hurricane Frieda, which struck with such force and fury on October 12, 1962. Many people were injured in Vancouver, and one person was killed by a falling tree while driving the causeway into the city's famous Stanley Park. So many of the old mature evergreen trees were blown down in the park during the hurricane that it took about two years to clean up all the fallen timber. It kind of reminds me of a similar loss of large numbers of tall evergreens in the park in another heavy storm just a few years ago.

The storm marked the end of the year for the Sea Queen, as she was tied up at the dock for the balance of the year. I spent my time between the barge run to Prince Rupert and Kitimat, and some time with Rod on the Amboyna. Joe Prosser brought the Oriole into Vancouver to take part in the annual Remembrance Day Parade. He had the usual gathering on board and I met Glen McDonald, the Vancouver City Coroner. Glen was an old sailor who had started his career as deck boy on the Empress liners, on the run from Vancouver to the Orient.

He had a very interesting life but his first love was reserved for the times he spent at sea as a youth.

Joe told me at that time he was thinking of leaving the Navy, and had been offered a job as skipper on the Eaton family yacht, which was based out of Miami, down in Florida. He had an interview set up the following week, and if accepted, he wanted to take two crew members from the West Coast, to fill vacancies from retiring crewmembers. Would I be interested? I said I'd have to think it over, as I had my mother to look after, and wanted to talk this over with her before making my final decision. I talked this over with Mum, and fortunately for me, she thought this would be a very good experience for me, provided of course that Joe was successful in being hired on.

With this in mind I gave notice at my apartment and moved in with Mike Nash, who was to be my future brother in law, though none of us knew that at the time. Joe was offered the job with the Eatons, and I decided one bleak morning while crossing the gulf on the Tomte, one of our smallest packers, with Rod Fredricks as skipper, I would head down to Miami with him. In the meantime, I went back to school to brush up on some courses I needed to upgrade my certificates.

Joe called me in early January 1963, asking me to meet with him and Mr. John David Eaton at a suite in the Hotel Vancouver. I had never seen such luxury. Someone said it was a suite which was regularly reserved for the Queen, royal family and certain other distinguished visitors when they were in town. I have to admit I was a little nervous being questioned by Mr. Eaton and Commander John Lawrence, who was manager of the Eaton's store in Duncan. Commander Lawrence was a retired Royal Navy type, who was in charge of the yacht, and it was said he was the highest paid company employee west of Winnipeg and a great friend of Mr. Eaton.

I'm glad to say that apparently Mr. Eaton took a liking to me right away, and told me he had plans for me. Believe it or not, he told me I was to serve on board the yacht for a couple of years, then return to Vancouver to take over as manager, where he had plans to build a marina in front of their store at Park Royal.

This planned marina never took place, as the environmental damage would have been too much to contemplate even at that time in history. But the plans did do something for me, as I had always dreamed of being involved with a marina. It took a long time, but 20 years later I was to start building a marina of my own at Deep Bay. But that's another story for another time.

Chapter 25

Naturally, such a trip called for a farewell party with my friends, which was held at the Harlem Nocturne. Then in early January, I was off to Miami. One interesting note about my farewell party was that Mike Nash invited his sister Betsy to attend. She was on her way from Winnipeg to Victoria to visit her father, and this was the first time I had met her, even though I knew the rest of her family. I noticed she spent the whole evening in deep conversation with Mike's girlfriend, Louise, and that left me with the impression she was a bit of a snob.

After leaving my car with Barry Giroday, I caught a plane for Seattle, with a stop in Victoria to pick up Joe Turcott, who was the other crew member picked from the Canadian west coast. We had never met before, but we soon became fast friends, and, not surprisingly, he was a very capable seaman. We changed planes in Seattle for the night flight to Chicago. This was my first flight in one of the new jetliners, and we were both very impressed with how quiet they were compared to prop driven aircraft.

Chicago was reached in the early hours and was very cold and windy. We had to wait a few hours for our flight to Miami, but we decided not to leave the airport building due to the cold weather. Finally we boarded the flight and were on our way to the sunny south. It was a nice flight with window seats, and we were able to look out at the landscape below as we flew on ever southward into ever increasing sunshine. Luck turned out to slip from the aircraft as, on the return flight from Miami to Chicago, the pilot became lost during a violent thunderstorm and crashed into the Everglades. There were no survivors. What a thin thread we all live by. Every day should be treasured and treated as something very special.

On arriving, we took a cab straight to the docks in downtown Miami where the motor yacht Hildur was moored. The vessel was about 110 feet overall and was built in 1958 by Sam Matsumoto at Dollarton, a small community on the north shore of Greater Vancouver. I had some dealings with Sam while I was with Tulloch Western and I recall seeing a model of a yacht in his office. I had no idea we'd be joining that same work of art. The Hildur was very well built, mostly from local yellow cedar, which has some very good qualities quite apart from the wood being very oily and rejecting most oil based paint. I'm sorry to report though that the Hildur, which was designed by Bill Garden, was the worst sea boat I ever had the misfortune to ride on. She was all right in a head sea, but if the sea was on the beam or it was a following sea from the back, we rolled around like a log in one of those logger competitions. Of a modified trawler design, she looked like the ultimate ocean going yacht, and the construction was excellent. Her fittings were all stainless steel or chrome plated. The decks were solid teak and she was rigged as a motor sailing ketch with the two masts able to be lowered by hydraulic rams so she could pass under the many bridges along the waterways leading to the Great Lakes, where she spent each summer.

The Hildur was powered by two Rolls Royce diesel motors which were plain junk and were located in the very stern section of the ship, with a V-drive so that space could be saved. We also had a couple of smaller Rolls Royce motors for generators, and a water maker that ran off the heat generated by the main engines. All this worked all right, but it was very complicated and altogether it took up a lot of space. The fuel capacity was large, and her accommodations were excellent, for both passengers and crew. The ship was air conditioned throughout, with an old style system located on the boat deck.

There were two very beautiful launches also very heavily built using yellow cedar. Their unnecessary weight up high in the vessel contributed greatly to the excessive roll of the vessel. Not unexpectedly, we were fully equipped with the very best, state of the art navigational equipment of the day. Included was a Decca 202 radar, which somehow never seemed to work properly despite numerous attempts by Decca personnel.

We also had a console navigational system, a gyro compass, a Sperry autopilot, which was the best autopilot I've ever seen, two chronometers, and the usual other bits and pieces that make up a modern wheelhouse.

I have to confess I've always had a great dislike for boats designed by Bill Garden ever since, mainly because of the Hildur. Mr. Garden is now recognized as one of the premier designers on the west coast, and at the time of writing was a very old man, but still active in the industry. Based on my experience, I think he should have been made to ride the Hildur until he was able to cure its unceasingly annoying ability to dip her rails under. I'm happy to admit that the vessel proved to be safe enough at sea, she was just a bit uncomfortable.

Joe hadn't arrived from the west coast yet, so we were welcomed aboard by Captain Ed Sylvia, who had been with the Eaton's for about 12 years by that time. He had served as master on the previous Hildur, which was a war surplus vessel of which there were several still in use as yachts in the Miami area. The chief engineer was Art White, who was from the west coast and was related to Henry and Fred Johnston, who were well known west coast mariners. Art had also been with the Eaton's for more than a decade, and had supervised the construction of the new vessel in Vancouver. Capt Ed was going to stay with us for one trip while the new crew got used to the vessel. The rest of the crew was comprised of Gerry, who was a deckhand from the Deep South and had been with the vessel for many years, George Blok, the chef, Ken Thompson, the steward, Joe Turcott and myself. I found myself appointed as mate and assistant engineer at a salary of $300 per month, which wasn't much, but I had a good bank account with enough saved to look after Mum for a couple of years or until a raise would be in order.

Capt. Ed was already at retirement age and told us a good many yarns of his years at sea. He was from Martha's Vineyard and had been master of liberty ships as well as T-2 tankers in the U.S. Merchant Marine. His sea going experiences started with the U.S. Coast Guard on board lighthouse tenders, where he served until the war, when he was placed on convoy duty. He had lived in Miami for many years, and that was the main reason the yacht was home based there. He loved the races, horses, dogs and Jai Alai games, for which he had worked out a system to clock up regular wins. He taught some of us the system and although we didn't win big, we seldom lost and our small wins did add up.

We also soon had a system worked out for ship's maintenance. Capt. Ed went home each afternoon and came back aboard at about 8 a.m. He made a point of not interfering with the workings of the ship, which were looked after by Art as the chief engineer. We kept the ship as a gleaming showpiece, with teak decks, polished rails and bright work in mint condition at all times. Our duties were usually easily completed by noon, after which time I started to explore Miami.

The Cuban Missile crisis was still in high gear at the time, with the southern Florida area flooded with military personnel of all ranks and stripes. The city was also starting to be invaded by Cuban refugees, and some of them were most interesting people to talk to about their escape from their island homeland. There was an old cabin cruiser moored near us with a very distinguished looking man on board. I learned from my conversations with him that he had owned the Bacardi Rum factory in Cuba and was left with nothing but his boat when the country was taken over by Fidel Castro. He escaped with his life, his family, his boat and not much else. It was the same story that could be repeated many times by others Cubans that I met around the waterfront.

We were not due to set sail until the end of January, so I

had plenty of time to become familiar with the ship, the crew and Miami. Just about everything on board was high quality, but not always what I would have chosen. The air conditioning was a nightmare of outdated machinery that had been poorly installed on the boat deck. This was quite a surprise, as cool air is certainly desirable at sea level in the tropics. The system didn't do anything for the crew's quarters, so we relied on wind scoops through the port holes while in port and just sweltered while at sea. When we returned to Miami after our first voyage, we installed a separate modern air conditioning unit for the crew's quarters. The launches were another problem I spoke to Art about. He nodded in agreement with me, but no action was taken. They should have been replaced with lighter craft, which I'm sure would have helped ease the top heavy nature of the vessel.

The yacht was ketch rigged and looked like she should sail, but she wouldn't, not even a little. Art said the sails were always raised while at sea, but only to try to keep the vessel from rolling. She wouldn't make any time at all under sail alone. I found this difficult to believe, but try as we might after Captain Joe took over, she would not move through the water under sail except sideways.

Miami was an exciting place in winter, with the hotels overflowing with snowbirds from the northern states and eastern Canada. I spent weekends exploring all the way from Key West to Fort Lauderdale, meeting many interesting people and having some great fun on the sun drenched beaches. The nightlife was positively extreme, with something for everyone. My favourite place to hang out was the Bamboo Bar in Hollywood. All kinds of Canadians used to meet there in the evenings, and I'd go there once or twice a week when we were in port.

A week before departure, Captain Joe arrived. I met him at the airport and he must have brought everything he owned along with him. We had to put most of his luggage in a cab he had so many personal artefacts and pieces of heavy clothing. It was good to see him again, and we settled down with Captain Ed to get ready for sea. I took him around to meet some of my new friends, but truth be told, he seemed to be a little down about his impending retirement after so many years of navel service.

Departure day finally dawned. We cleared customs late in the afternoon and set off across the Gulf Stream for the island of Antigua, a non-stop voyage of about 1,200 miles. Captain Ed was in command, with the idea that this would be a tune up for the new crew members before his retirement upon our return to Miami. Mr. Eaton and three of his friends were to fly in Antigua from Toronto in the new Jet Star aircraft the company had just bought. They would be with us while we cruised through some of the islands and made our way slowly back to Miami.

We soon found out just how much the vessel could roll, as we crossed the Gulf Stream towards the Bahamas. The Gulf Stream runs northeast up through the Florida Strait against the prevailing winds and this can be the cause of high, sharp seas that are a real trouble for small vessels. There's a huge fleet of pleasure boats that travel these waters with Bimini and Nassau as favourite destinations for weekend travel. Without the U.S. Coast Guard, which I have a very high regard for, there would be many more accidents than there are and many more lives would be lost, especially in that area.

We soon regained our sea legs, and even though the crossing was uncomfortable, I felt the vessel was certainly safe and reasonably well suited for ocean travel. The main, jib and mizzen sails were all set, and they did help keep the vessel more or less upright. We averaged between seven and eight knots, which was slow compared to what I was used to but reasonable, and never seemed to vary regardless of sea or wind conditions. Captain Ed said we'd set a course for the Hole in the Wall, a name given many passages throughout the world and in this case a passage through the Bahamas. Of course this one was much different from the one of the same name I was used to at home, and I took the opportunity to relay to Ed some of my experiences towing log booms through the tidal rapids of the B.C. Coast. Ed had sailed the west coast during the summer of 1956 on board the previous Hildur, so he had a good knowledge of the area.

Soon we had crossed the busy Gulf Stream, with its endless traffic of large tankers, freighters and other vessels of every size and shape. The sharp seas moderated as we plunged into the Bermuda Triangle, through the Northeast Providence Channel leaving Spanish Wells to starboard. Darkness quickly came upon us as we set a course for San Salvador. I wasn't due to come on watch again until midnight, but I decided to stay up most of the evening to make sure that I didn't miss anything. Captain Ed and Captain Joe took six hour watches each and I was due on watch with Joe. This was good, as we had lots of time to talk, but I also enjoyed being with Ed, as he had so much experience in the waters we were to sail over the next two months.

San Salvador is a high island as islands go in the Bahamas, the highest of which is Cat Island at just 206 feet above sea level. San Salvador has a lighthouse that can be seen for many miles during clear weather due to its height. The island is supposed to be the landing place of Christopher Columbus who reached there in 1492 after a voyage of discovery, which originated in Spain. The many islands of the Bahamas were inhabited by Lucayo Indians, whom Columbus mistakenly took to be inhabitants of the Indian sub-continent of Asia. The islands were eventually made a British Colony in 1717 gaining self government almost two and a half centuries later in 1964, and independence nine years after that, in 1973.

San Salvador was our first landfall after leaving Spanish Wells. Joe and I were on watch as we left this desolate place well to starboard. We were already bucking head on into seas of about 10 feet, and it was hot. To enter the engine room, one had to wear gloves or use a rag to prevent being burned by the heat of the steel ladder. Each sea sent spray over the bow, and occasionally one came over green to wash the decks. Many flying fish landed on the deck which resulted in fresh fish for lunch. We trolled a fishing line behind us but only caught barracuda, which were in the same category as spiny dogfish back home in B.C.

After leaving San Salvador we continued to encounter head seas, heat, squalls and flying fish until we made our next landfall at the northern end of Puerto Rico. Captain Ed decided we should go through Mona Pass, between the islands of Hispanola and Puerto Rico, leaving St. Croix to port, then on to Englishman's Harbour on the island of Antigua. It took us six days to arrive.

I had never visited the West Indies before, but I found it was very much as I imagined it would be. Hot, windy and poor. The Nicholsons had a yacht chartering business based in the harbour at Antigua, and the restored Nelson's dockyard was a major tourist attraction for the guests at the fancy hotels on the other side of the island.

We dropped our anchor and moored stern to at the cement jetty. There was some motion from the ocean as we came through the narrow entrance, so we had to be careful to make sure we had good fenders to prevent damage. The harbour was the home to the British Fleet during the 1700's, and the base was known as Nelson's Dockyard, named after the great naval commander of that time. A small white cottage overlooked the harbour where Princess Margaret was reported to have spent her honeymoon. The harbour was full of yachts of which Lady Docker's was the largest, with ours the next biggest.

We all turned in for a much needed rest, with one of us on watch at all times to make sure nothing was stolen or damaged. Mr. Eaton was due to arrive in a couple of days, so we spent the early cool hours of the next day tending to the ship's requirements. Tom the taxi driver soon arrived, as he was paid by Mr. Eaton to be on standby at all times while we were in port. He drove a fairly good car of British design with the steering wheel on the right hand side, since this was a British colony and followed the British rules of the road, with traffic driving on the left side of the road. Tom became a great friend, but we never allowed him aboard as this might have cause problems with other residents. Tom understood this and perhaps had even initiated it, but we did keep him well supplied with food and drink as we told him tales of the far north.

Tom was quite a character. He told me he thought he and his lady had about 10 kids, as far as he could remember. He wasn't married but said his lady had told him she would marry him if he bought her a white dress. He had never been able to afford this luxury, so he had stopped asking her a few years back. He thought that was after child number eight. His life was simple but better than most of his friends', due to the small taxi business he managed to maintain. The winter months were good, but during the off season, he had to work the sugar cane fields to keep his ever expanding family in basic necessities.

The day came for the arrival of Mr. Eaton and Joe put on his best uniform and drove with Tom to the airport to meet him and his three friends. They soon arrived in two cars piled with all their gear and settled in for a month of good times. The guests were Dr. Sharpe, an elderly doctor from Toronto, Mr. Powell, a middle aged lawyer from Parry Sound in Ontario, and of course Commander John Lawrence, manager of the Eaton's store in Duncan, a small town on Vancouver Island. Commander Lawrence was supposed to be in charge of all workings on board, but left pretty much everything for Art to look after. He was easy going and very jovial and after a few days he let us know he and Mr. Eaton were well pleased with the new crew members.

The Eatons were a very wealthy family at that time. John David was the grandson of company founder Timothy Eaton, and had taken over the business around 1940. He was a very private person and stayed away from usual tourist places and society in general. His close friends were mostly just what you could describe as 'ordinary people' such as the guests we had on board. One evening, Mr. Eaton was asked to attend a party on Lady Docker's yacht and he apparently only agreed with the greatest reluctance. Lady Docker was about 70 years of age at that time and known in many parts of the world as a real character. She could be seen out water skiing most afternoons, and the rumour was that she had been expelled from Monaco for 'disorderly conduct'. Quite what that was wasn't clear but she was anchored up in Antigua serving her time until Prince

Rainier of Monaco and his former film star wife Princess Grace, previously Grace Kelly, were convinced it was time for her to be allowed back into the country.

Mr. Eaton returned from this party very disgusted and let it be known that never again would he feel duty bound to attend such an affair. Commander Lawrence told me there was a young Canadian niece of Lady Docker's on the yacht and, amazingly, she had indicated she'd very much like to meet me. Mr. Eaton got wind of this and said he'd phone my mother if I ever dared go near that dreadful, sinful ship. I never heard much about Lord Docker, but I understand that he was a quiet old gentleman who had made his fortune in British shipyards and just went along with pretty much anything his wife said and did 'for the ride'. The Dockers' yacht was an older ocean going vessel of about 150 feet, with two heavy duty diesels. Sure enough, one day word came through that Princess Grace had forgiven all, and they immediately weighed anchor and headed out to cross the Atlantic back to the Mediterranean.

One evening in Antigua, three of the crew had Tom the cab driver take us out for a conducted night on the town. He dropped us off at a nice beachfront hotel where a lively party was in full swing. Limbo dancing was all the rage at the time, and I had a girlfriend back home who was the best I had ever seen at it. That is, up until this time. I actually saw a six foot tall, very black man go under a limbo pole supported by two Coke bottles, not the large ones but the small ones. And he did it while wearing a 10 gallon cowboy hat. I couldn't believe my eyes. I asked him if he could do it again, and to much applause he agreed. He continued doing so until too much rum took over and he called it off.

The three of us had such a good time we decided to go back the following night, and much to our surprise, we weren't allowed in, as we were not properly dressed. All the men were sweltering in suites and ties, and the ladies were wearing evening gowns. We explained that we had attended the previous night and dress hadn't been an issue at that time, only to be told in the strongest of British accents that last evening had been a special slumming night held once monthly and proper dress was a requirement at all other times.

That finished me with Snobsville, and I asked Tom where the locals hung out. He took us to a hilltop out in the country where a party was in progress. We were the only non-blacks present, and Tom thought we were probably the only whites who had ever visited the place. The reception was a little subdued at first, but after Tom assured everyone we were his guests, all went well, things started to take off, and we had a wonderful time.

Two things stand out in my memories of Antigua; the music and the people. I had never seen real steel drums played before. They're just old oil drums, rust and all, but the music they produce is beyond belief. The people are very poor, with very little chance to improve their living conditions, but they are so spontaneous and friendly and clearly enjoy themselves despite their poverty. I recall one day I was in St. John's, the capital city, when a minor traffic delay took place. One of the stopped vehicles was a flat deck truck carrying a steel band. They immediately started playing some music on the drums, and instantly everyone around got out of their cars and joined the pedestrians in dancing to the rhythms. The dancing continued even after the traffic started moving again and the truck drove slowly along the main street.

That same day I had to see a doctor, as something was in my left eye, and I couldn't seem to get it out. The doctor's office was in a large white house and the waiting room was his front lawn, under a shady tree. There we at least 30 people, mostly women with squawking kids, waiting to see the doctor. I had just sat down for what I thought would be a very long wait, when the nurse came running out to say the doctor would see me right away. Before I could say anything, I was seated in front of him, with the nurse looking for the cause of the problem. It suddenly hit home. I was being seen ahead of all the others because I was white, the others would just have to wait. That's the way their world worked at that time. The doctor had trained in Toronto and spent the next hour talking with me about his time in Canada, while everyone else just had to sit around waiting on the lawn.

All too soon though, we said our goodbyes to our new friends in Antigua and set sail for Guadeloupe. This island is a French colony and we were headed for the Capitol City of Pointe-a-Pitre. The crossing was short and we were under the shelter of the outer islands, and although the trade winds were strong, only a heavy chop resulted in our area. Along the way, as we were sailing down the west side of the main island, we sighted a very old looking motor vessel with many people on board, who seemed to be under some distress. Upon investigation, we found it was a charter vessel which had broken down with about 10 French tourists on board. The vessel needed to be towed to Basse Terre as neither Art nor I could manage to breathe any life into the old gas engine. So we then transferred the passengers aboard the yacht and sailed on to Pointe-a-Pitre with the charter vessel in tow. The passengers were quite exuberant in thanking Mr. Eaton for our timely arrival and rescue, and although they were in no immediate danger, one would have thought we'd saved all of them from imminent disaster. The main spokesperson for the group turned out to be the president of Air France, who was vacationing in the area with friends and family. Upon arrival at Pointe-a-Pitre, he insisted that we all attend a large dinner in our honour at the Governor's Residence the following evening, so that they could properly show their appreciation. We spent the first evening cruising the streets of this French speaking city. Fortunately, Joe Turcott was fluent in the language, so he acted as our guide. A French warship happened to be in port at the time, and we were saluted at every turn by the sailors, since we were dressed in our officer type tropical uniforms.

The island is very beautiful with rolling hills and fertile farmland, and the people seemed prosperous, but the city was quite grubby and dirty, as are the British islands in the area. This is in complete contrast to the Dutch islands, which are spotless and clean.

The next afternoon, the Canadian Pacific ship the Empress

of Canada dropped anchor off the port and many launches began shuttling between the ship and the jetty, ferrying passengers to and fro. They all came close by to see who we were, as our Canadian flag fluttering at the back caught the attention of the mostly Canadian passengers. One launch came right alongside as Mr. Eaton and I were standing outside the wheelhouse, leaning over the rail. There was a lady standing high up in the bow, who called out to Mr. Eaton that she was a good friend of his wife, Signey. Could she come over to visit as soon as the launch landed? As the launch proceeded away to the jetty, Mr. Eaton turned to me red in the face and ordered, "Lawrence, start the engines. We will be departing immediately."

I, of course obeyed, calling Art to start the mains, which brought the crew topside with a rush. They had all been below dressing for the evening dinner to be held in our honour at Government House. Mr. Eaton announced to Captain Ed that we would be leaving right away for St. Martins. I guess a visit from one of his wife's friends was not what Mr. Eaton considered a good time and was something to be avoided at all costs.

Looking back, I suppose it was just as well, and the dinner would probably have been a very boring affair at best. I guess Mr. Eaton was just too shy to say no to the excited French official in the first place. Captain Ed did inform the harbour officials to convey Mr. Eaton's regrets and apologies to Government House, but "due to unforeseen events" we had to depart port in a hurry.

Our next stop was to be the island of St Martin's which is a small island, part British and part Dutch. We anchored off a village on the Dutch side and put one of our launches over the side. We had never done this before, and as the heavy launch hit the water, we were amazed at how far the Hildur listed back to the other side under the weight of the other one. This only encouraged Joe and me to work even harder on Art to get some lighter boats, to see if this would improve the yacht's stability in rough weather. Three of us went ashore with some American money to pick up a few cases of liquor for Mr. Eaton, and we had loaded many cases into the launch when Joe noticed that we were being over charged. $17 American for a 12 bottle case of good old Canadian VO rye, outrageous! We had only been charged $12 in Antigua. We argued with this robber, and as we had already loaded up, we told him to pack it back up the beach if $15 wasn't enough. He took the money with a broad smile which told us all that we needed to know, and we returned to the ship.

The next stop was Charlotte Amelia, on the American island of St. Thomas, which was totally overrun with tourists, cruise ship passengers, U.S. navy vessels and personnel. We spent a few days there stocking up on fresh supplies. Even milk was available, although it was made locally from powder. We were all given shore leave, and I found myself in one of those 'once in a lifetime' situations, where everything seems just perfect. I had made friends on the waterfront with some tourists from New York who were staying at one of the hilltop hotels. They invited Joe and me to join them for dinner that evening and everything was like a dream. We met on a huge outdoor dining area overlooking the harbour and city, and as it grew dark, the flickering lights ringed the harbour and ships and a full moon crept up out of the eastern sky. It was a warm and balmy evening, with just enough light wind to make it perfect. We had such a good time and I don't think any of us wanted the evening to end, but of course all things must come to a close, as we were due to set sail again the next day.

With fond memories and sad faces, we said farewell to St. Thomas, with a vow to visit again some day, a vow I'm sorry to say I've not yet managed to keep. Perhaps that's just as well, since some things in life are just so perfect the first time they can't be repeated or duplicated. We headed out into the Atlantic, leaving San Juan unvisited to port, as we looked longingly at the bright lights of this historic seaport. Mr. Eaton refused all pleadings to make a stop as the city had a casino. Our welfare and his morals dictated the choice of ports to visit. Instead, we once again entered Mona Pass, this time having quite a rough ride, as the strong current was flowing to seaward against a larger than normal Atlantic swell. Mona Pass is one of those places that has very much the Cape Mudge character and mentality, and can prove its ability to be truly miserable for mariners at any time the conditions are just right.

We cruised along the west coast of the Dominican Republic with no stop either at Santo Domingo, due to the presence of another casino. We stopped at Port-au-Prince in Haiti, arriving before daylight in this incredibly poor country. As it was my watch, Joe turned in with the rest of the crew, so I was left by myself in the wheelhouse waiting for daylight. As I sat there looking out, the thought occurred to me that this would be a good opportunity to put our garbage ashore on the large freight dock where we were moored. Shortly after I did so, this previously deserted dock came alive with noise and people who seemed to come out of nowhere. I turned on the searchlight to find a small riot had broken out over our garbage. I couldn't believe the violence I was seeing, and was worried it might spread on to the ship, so I turned on all the deck lights as a discouragement to anyone who might have had thoughts of boarding, and soon all returned to peace and quiet.

We left again the same day, as Captain Ed had been there before and persuaded Mr. Eaton we'd be better off elsewhere. We rounded Cape Dame Marie and set a course for the south end of Cuba, repeatedly over-flown by U.S. military aircraft to ask us our name, nationality and port of registry by Morse code. Joe Turcott was very good with the Aldus lamp, but grew weary of the constant requests. The conflict between the U.S. and Cuba was in full swing at that time, and we received no end of harassment from these aircraft. The island was ringed by old world war II destroyers that were anchored with a small crew on board to man their radar sets and keep a constant watch on shipping in the area. As we neared Guantanamo Bay, the U.S. military base, the encounters increased dramatically. Finally we were away from Cuba with a stop planned for Matthew's Town on Great Inagua Island.

The islands of the Bahamas are very low, which makes for difficult landfalls. Many of them had very good, manned lighthouses at their extremities, but sometimes the crews just weren't entirely reliable. Making landfalls during daylight presented unique problems, as the lighthouses were not visible during the daylight hours. So, as we rolled along towards Matthew's Town, we were not entirely sure of our position. Captains Joe and Ed both decided to take sextant shots to see if we could get an idea of how far we were from our destination.

I took their reading and worked out what should have been our position, and found that their two shots were almost identical, putting our position where we should have been within sight of Great Inagua Island. We all rushed to look out of the wheelhouse window, and we could see the tops of palm trees starting to come into view. I learned a valuable lesson I have used many times over the years. With all the navigational aids we have to help us, it still pays to look out the wheelhouse window and have one crew member responsible to keep visual watch at all times.

We spent a few days rolling around at anchor off Matthew's Town in the sweltering heat. Mr. Eaton loved places where he could get to know the local inhabitants. But on this occasion I can't honestly say the rest of us had any inclination to hang around too long, new horizons were calling. We departed early one morning for Nassau, with great relief to be under way again. The Hildur continued to roll to extremes with just a moderate following sea, and we all wished we could jettison the heavy motor launches right off the top deck to adjust the yacht's pitch, but the sails helped and we just rolled our way to Nassau, where we looked forward to spending a few days as tourists.

We entered Nassau harbour mid-afternoon and dropped anchor, hoisted our quarantine flag and waited for the customs launch. After clearing Customs, I went ashore to arrange for dockside moorage, and by late afternoon we were secure alongside. The difference between Nassau and Matthews Town was like comparing a gentle breeze with a hurricane. What a place! Many cruise ships were docked in port and it was wall to wall visitors. We stayed for four days and what a good time we had. Mr. Eaton didn't like the rowdy atmosphere and nightlife, so he just turned us loose to have a good time while he stayed on board most of the time.

Again the good times came to an end, and we set sail early one evening for Miami so we'd arrive early the next morning of the next day. We rolled our way across the Gulf Stream once again under moonlit skies, moderate seas and the never ending challenge of patrolling military aircraft. We entered the Miami ship channel early the next day as planned and proceeded to the quarantine station. Much to my surprise, the customs agents didn't have anything to say about the huge amount of liquor that had been put aboard in the West Indies. I did notice though that when they left the ship, they were carrying some gifts from Mr. Eaton.

Mr. Eaton and his guests were due to leave for Canada a couple of days later, so a retirement party for Captain Ed was planned for the following evening. The party was aboard ship and we had a great time listening to stories about his many years at sea. He told us he was from Martha's Vineyard, and related to us how his first assignment at sea had been as a young man with the U.S. Coast Guard. His first ship was under the command of a Captain Edward Eaton, so his career started with Captain Edward Eaton and ended coincidentally with John David Eaton.

As soon as Mr. Eaton and his guests left for home, it was off to the shipyard for some repairs and maintenance. We moved the yacht up the Miami River to a shipyard that was able to do the extensive refinishing of the beautiful teak rails. The salt from the ocean and the hot sun had eaten away the varnish work. The rails had to be completely stripped down to bare wood and refinished with many coats of new varnish.

Chapter 26

Joe knew a young lady from Victoria who worked for Trans Canada Airlines at their Miami Beach office, so he and I stopped by the office to pay her a visit our first Saturday in port.

Joan Squire happened to be the on duty and explained to us that Barbara had decided to stay in Canada rather than move to Miami for the winter. This meeting with Joan proved to be a new friendship for me. Joan was originally from London, Ontario, and along with several other Canadians, had gone to work at the airline's Miami Beach office for the winter tourist season, since this was a nice break from the chill weather of Ontario. They came south before Christmas and left for home about mid-April. Joan was engaged to be married upon her return to Canada, but due to our having many interests in common, we were to spend a lot of time together. She lived with several other women from Canada who also worked for the airline, and their residence became known as 'the Canadian compound'. It was located just off Collins Avenue, in the heart of Miami Beach.

After getting settled into the shipyard, I decided to go to see an eye specialist, as I was still being troubled by something in my left eye. The doctor I saw in Antigua had been unable to find anything wrong, but my eye was still red and irritated. The specialist in Miami used various dyes and scopes to try to locate the problem, but also without success. He had just about given up and was about to send me home, when the office receptionist called the doctor to take an important telephone call. With the doctor absent, she took a quick look into the scope and spotted a nearly invisible transparent insect wing stuck to my left eye. The doctor quickly removed it upon his return, and I had no further trouble.

We spent about two months docked in Miami that spring, during which time we explored the city and south Florida. Each day started early with routine work on the ship until lunchtime, then after lunch we'd decide on what to explore and go off, spending the afternoon taking in one of the many available attractions. One of my favourites was Marine Land, where there was a display of specimens of the many sharks that lived in the warm waters of the South Atlantic Ocean. If we had dinner on board, this would be at 5p.m., followed by a short nap before the evening activities. I'd usually head over to The Canadian Compound to meet Joan, who knew all of the best nightspots in Miami Beach. Sometimes Joe would come along and we'd go out as a foursome with a friend of Joan's from Canada who came down for a vacation. If Joan was working evenings, Pam and I would go out on our own. Sometimes we stayed out so late that we'd arrive back at the ship just in time for me to start the day's work at 7 a.m.

Captain Ed liked to go off to the Jai Alai matches at a nearby arena in the evenings, and I also very much enjoyed this sport, which was very popular at the time and is played much like racket ball. It's very fast and quite dangerous, as players can be badly injured or even killed if hit by the hard ball. Players use the narrow basket on a glove to throw a hard ball against the front wall of a court, called a cancha. The basket is called a cesta and the two foot length of the cesta gives the players tremendous leverage to hurl the ball at speeds of up to 150 miles an hour. A clear protective screen, similar to that used at a hockey arena, protects spectators' faces. The game can attract considerable betting among spectators.

We lived like we didn't have a care in the world, which we didn't, but eventually, there came the time when we all had to head back to Canada with Joan returning home to London, Ontario and her wedding to Ron Adams. Several of us drove her to the airport to say a sad goodbye because we knew we would miss her. Although we weren't due to sail for a few days yet, we knew things would never quite be the same again.

Departure day dawned bright and clear, with a favourable weather forecast as we slipped our lines and headed out through the Miami ship channel. Captain Ed had come down to say Goodbye and Joe finally took over as our new captain. We headed up the East Coast of Florida towards our next port of call, which was to be a small port near Great Point on the Potomac River. As always, it was good to be back at sea again, and we looked forward to new adventures ahead of us before we reached our final destination of Parry Sound, Ontario.

Joe was used to driving strong steel naval vessels under orders from a senior officer who had an operations schedule to meet. We, on the other hand, were on a small wooden ship and under no pressure at all to meet any deadlines or timetables, except in the most casual manner. We experienced some strong head winds and moderate seas as we traveled north and I suggested we should slow down a notch to ease up on the pounding the vessel was taking since we were in no hurry. Joe wasn't used to the wooden vessel regime or slowing down for anything, and this resulted in some minor damage which could have been avoided. Although we had some high seas off South Carolina, we soon rounded Cape Hatteras, the graveyard of the Atlantic as it's known, with calm winds and a perfectly flat ocean.

Other than some loose caulking forward, we basically had an uneventful trip, and a few days later we were moored alongside an American destroyer near Great Point. The skipper and a few of the officers were friends of Joe's, so we stayed to visit for a few days. I rented a car and we spent some time exploring the very lovely Virginia countryside. Jamestown was particularly interesting, as the location of some of the earliest European settlers in North America. I had my picture taken with a statue of Princess Pocahontas. Of course I didn't know at the time, but several years later I discovered my future wife was a ninth generation descendant of the famous princess. Jamestown and Williamsburg are both rebuilt villages showing how life was during the 17th century, complete with replicas of the ships the early settlers sailed from Europe. The shops are also from about two centuries ago, with the keepers and assistants and other residents all arrayed in olden day costumes of the period. It was a unique place to visit, and we all enjoyed our time there very much.

We next moved to the yacht club at Annapolis, a short distance up Chesapeake Bay in Maryland. Annapolis is the home of the U.S. Naval Academy where the training of young officers takes place. It's also just a short distance from Washington, D.C., so I decided to take advantage of the opportunity and visit there too.

The evening after our arrival, one of the deckhands and I were sitting relaxing at the local coffee shop, when we struck up a conversation with a couple of locals, who said they'd be happy to drive us up to D.C., and this turned out to be a most interesting trip, though I have to say we didn't get to see much of the U.S.'s capital city.

We fuelled up the car, a beat up old '56 Ford, and off we went at great speed over the hills to the District of Columbia. The kid driving was completely reckless, and we were happy to be in the back seat as we were sure he'd drive off the winding road at any minute. When we arrived, we asked to be dropped off so we could do some sightseeing and catch a bus back to the docks later. The driver asked us to go with them to their favourite bar for a beer, before they headed back to Annapolis. Of course we agreed, since it would have been churlish not to show our appreciation. The bar they took us to was the sleaziest place I'd ever seen. It featured a naked girl on a swing suspended from the high ceiling. She swung back and forth all evening without a break, and this tended to become quite hypnotic after a short period of time. As time wore on, a customer sitting at another table whispered to us that he'd overheard a conversation between our two 'friends' while we were away from the table, and apparently they were planning to rob us on the way back home. We had a few hundred dollars between us and this was not good news. So, when our friends returned to our table, we insisted we were going to leave. They quickly offered to take us back to Annapolis, as by now it was too late to get a bus. There was nothing to be done, so we both sat in the back seat again and were on the lookout for the first sign of trouble. When the driver stopped about halfway home at a dark and lonely part of the road, I quickly grabbed him around the neck from behind, and Ron pulled out his knife and flashed it to the other guy in the front seat. They instantly gave in and Ron kept his knife handy just in case, while they delivered us safely back to the dock without any further attempts at funny business. That was the end of my one and only visit to the capital of the U.S. I hope those kids learned a valuable lesson, that sailors usually carry knives as part of their everyday kit.

From Annapolis we sailed past Baltimore towards the Chesapeake and Delaware Canal, which would be a short cut for us, saving us from having to sail south around Cape Charles. Baltimore appeared as a grim looking waterfront with a huge cloud of smog smothering the city due to light winds. We sailed on through the canal in darkness and headed down Delaware Bay towards Cape May and the open Atlantic once again.

The trip along the New Jersey coast was warm and flat calm. We sighted the Ambrose lightship and set a course for the area where the passenger liner Andrea Doria was lost in 1956. After paying our respects to the great Italian ship, we turned through the Verrazano Narrows into Upper New York Bay. The famous bridge spanning the narrows was still under construction at the time, with just the massive main cables in place. The liner S.S. Constitution was under way outbound as we passed under the bridge. We moored at Bayonne New Jersey, to an old dock, as we were a day early for our berth at City Island. The next day we proceeded up the East River passing the Statue of Liberty, Battery Park, under the Brooklyn Bridge, past the United Nations building, and entered East Chester Bay to dock at City Island, located at the West end of Long Island Sound. We moored at a shipyard to carry out some repairs to fix the damage from the heavy seas we'd encountered on the start of our trip north.

We'd planned to be at City Island for at least two weeks, so we started off to explore the Big Apple. We were about 15 miles from the centre of Manhattan, but a subway went to within a long walk's distance from the shipyard. What a place! I think one could live in New York a year or more and never really come into tune with this almost living creature. A drive through the various districts was decided on as the best way to start. It was like driving through a small scale model of the world. Each nationality lived in separate area, dressed differently as their nationality dictated. Their shops and homes also reflected the culture, with most of the residents working within their own area and seldom venturing far from home. Five ethnic groups made up about four fifths of the total population.

Most people who visit this great city as tourists only see Manhattan and the views during a quick trip to one of the airports. I decided to take in as much of the city as possible. Joe suggested we take in a Broadway show, and we ended up taking in three. Even today I think those shows were among the best and most enjoyable events that I ever attended.

Joe was a member of the New York Yacht Club and had already visited the city several times during his career in the Navy, so he knew something about it. Each day we'd strike out to explore some new part. If all our activities were to be listed, I think it'd be quite impressive, but I'll just stick to some of the highlights.

Eaton's had an office in downtown Manhattan where they purchased items for the stores in Canada. The office also served as a financial centre for the yacht and crew. One day Joe had some correspondence that needed to be delivered downtown, so it was decided I should be the one to deliver it. Included was an invitation for several of the senior staff to attend a dinner party on board on the following weekend. Joe insisted I dress for the delivery in my naval style uniform with three stripes. Suitably attired, I made my way downtown on the subway, to an address on Madison Avenue, then up the elevator to a very posh office near the top floor. Joe had called ahead to alert them of my pending arrival, and I was duly met and treated like some kind of royalty by these fellow employees. I suspect none of them knew a yacht from an aircraft carrier, and with my gold braided uniform, maybe they thought I was admiral of the fleet.

After meeting all the staff at the office, I spent the rest of the morning touring the waterfront where the Queen Mary and several other large ocean liners were docked. I had never seen any of these gigantic luxury liners before and was most impressed with their size and beauty. Joe and a couple of the other crew met me in the afternoon at the Empire State Building and we took the tour up to the observation deck, where we could look down on the ships I'd just been visiting, as well as appreciate an unobstructed view of the Hudson River, Central Park and the New Jersey shore. Next we toured the Rockefeller Center, a well known and obvious tourist trap but well worth one visit.

We topped off the day with an evening Broadway show, followed by dinner. The show was called 'How to Succeed in Business, Without Really Trying', starring Rudi Valle, which was a major hit at the time. The Eaton office had kindly supplied us with free tickets, which normally cost $75 each, almost a weeks pay. What a day, but this was only the start of a couple more weeks of non-stop fun and some very late nights.

When I finally was able to shed my uniform and hit the bunk, I was more than ready for a long sleep. The next morning started early and it was off again for downtown, this time catching a ride with the manager of the City Island Yacht Club who drove us in via the Brooklyn Bridge.

This was to be our day to visit the United Nations Building, where a very charming Russian lady was our tour director. When she discovered we were Canadian, she quickly ushered us into the General Assembly, where our soon to be Prime Minister,

Lester Pearson, was making a speech. This was followed by a tour of Central Park and a much earlier return to the ship than the previous day since City Island was so far from the centre of Manhattan and presented a transportation problem after the subways shut down for the night. The alternative was to take a taxi, and this might sound simple, as many of the automobiles on downtown streets were taxis. We found out the true nature of New York cabs and cabbies though. First off, they talked non-stop from the moment one entered the vehicle. And the cabs didn't have radios, so one was obtained by stepping off the curb and flagging down a passing vehicle, which inevitably resulted in several cabs almost running you down in their rush to pick you up. Alternatively, one could stand there forever with no-one paying you a blind bit of attention. Fortunately the fares were very cheap, with the meter starting at about 10 cents and a ride of a mile or more resulting in a fare of about a dollar. A tip of at least double or triple the fare was obviously expected, and if it wasn't forthcoming, the language attracted would have been new even to a sailor. At busy times, if a cab stopped to let someone off, there was a rush of several patrons to be the first one to get in, sometimes overwhelming the poor passengers still trying to get out. Sharing a cab with someone was commonplace in those days, and was done simply for convenience, not any kind of consideration or kindness between patrons.

As today, taxi drivers made their money by as many short trips as possible, with the tips being the key to success. A ride back out to City Island would cost about $15 and take about 45 minutes. The desire of the cabbies for short rides resulted in us quite often being stranded during busy times when no-one was willing to take on a long haul back to the island, so we took to overcoming this hurdle on some occasions by reaching City Island in shorter stages. From downtown, we'd tell the driver we wanted to go to the Empire State Building. There we'd change our mind and decide to go on to Central Park. From there we'd usually have to give the driver a couple of dollars tip to bribe him to take us on to Yankee Stadium. This usually triggered some warm words about baseball and it never ceased to surprise me that even New Yorkers hated the Yankees. They were still boiling about the Brooklyn Dodgers and the New York Giants leaving for the west and were supporting the Mets to show their anger.

After a quick tour around the stadium and a further tip, we'd carry on to Fordham University, and there finally confess City Island was really our true destination. The language and abuse that brought about was so extreme it had to be experienced to be described, and one driver actually got out of his car and refused to go any further. Most often, we just turned off our hearing and provided a generous tip, along with an offer to tour the yacht once we got there. We actually made some temporary friends amongst the drivers with these yacht tours. One driver came by the following Sunday with his family, and asked if they could go on a tour too. Of course we immediately obliged and after a couple of weeks, we started to be become quite well known to the downtown drivers. Some of them avoided us at all costs, but others would take us if it were already very late. Some said they'd take us after business dropped off. As New York is known as the city that never sleeps, this resulted in some very late nights, including some exciting and interesting visits to after hours establishments.

Soon after arriving in New York, I had called up a couple of young ladies I knew who lived in the same apartment block as I did in Vancouver. They had worked for U.S. Immigration at the Vancouver Airport for a couple of years and were now at Idlewild Airport on nearby Long Island. They lived in Queens, so I rode the subway out to visit them one evening. We called some of our friends back home and had a great time just sitting around chatting. I remember the evening well as this was the first time I'd ever seen a long distance telephone call made by the new fangled method of direct dialling.

Rose and Betty said they'd like to go out on the town on the weekend, so I arranged for Joe and me to pick them up early Saturday evening. Joe suggested that dinner at the New York Yacht Club, followed by a Broadway show might be a nice way to get the evening under way, so off we went. The

NY Yacht Club was an interesting place, with numerous models and pictures of early sailing and large steam yachts. Paintings of famous people and past commodores also looked down on us from the walls. After dinner we next went to see A Funny Thing Happened, On The Way To The Forum, starring comic actor Zero Mostel. It was a great comedy and, thanks again to Eaton's New York office, the tickets were affordable. Next we decided to catch the late show at the Copacabana.

Joe was always one for practical or, sometimes, not so practical jokes. One time during the war his ship had been called back to Halifax unexpectedly with engine trouble. As his girlfriend wasn't expecting him back in port for many months, he decided he'd surprise her by calling up a moving company to have himself packaged up in a large box and delivered to her house.

On this occasion in New York, a party mood had overtaken us that evening as we drove to the Copacabana. Joe asked the cab driver to pull over at a drug store so he could go in, and he shortly reappeared with a big bag full of water pistols, and also a large jug of ammunition. As we drove through the heavy late evening traffic, we leaned out the window and squirted whoever happened to be standing on the curb waiting to cross. The cab driver was also supplied with his own pistol and joined in whenever possible. He obviously thoroughly enjoyed himself, to the extent of trying to talk us into staying with him longer so he could pick out likely targets for us. Soon though, so many people had been given a suitable dampening that we were getting low on water, so we get dropped off at the Copa, joining a long line of patrons waiting to bribe the Maitre De for a decent table. As our turn approached, a bouncer demanded that Joe, who was still clutching our bag of water pistols, either let him see the contents of the bag or lodge the package with the hat check desk. Joe said he couldn't let the important package out of his sight and insisted he had to keep it with him at all times. The argument that ensured continued for a couple of minutes, until we were firmly informed that either the contents of the bag must be revealed or we'd have to leave. This was the moment we'd all been waiting for and had carefully planned out on the street. Joe opened the bag, pulled out a water pistol and shot the bouncer point blank in the face, then we all joined in and completely soaked him and his nice black tuxedo. The management of course tried to have us thrown out for our bad behaviour but it had attracted such hilarity and we received such support from all the others in the line up that eventually, against their better judgement, they gave up and let us in, but only after we'd given most of our water pistols as rewards to our supporters.

The evening continued inside with wars between tables, as poor singer/star Connie Francis did her best to entertain us in competition with the good natured rowdiness. Rose and Betty said they'd been on duty at the immigration desk when Miss Francis flew in from Europe the previous day, reportedly somewhat under the influence of too much in flight Champagne.

This great evening ended early in the morning with us sending the ladies home to Queens in a cab. Joe and I then started our usual con job on the cab drivers to try to get one of them to take us out to City Island.

As daylight was once again dawning and the cabs were busy, we ended up taking the first subway of the day back to the yacht, where we spent most of the day in slumber.

One other night worth mentioning was The Night of the Monster Lobster. We always bought lobster whenever possible, as this was a novelty to those of us who were from the Canadian west coast. One of the crew had boasted that there wasn't enough lobster on all of City Island to satisfy his craving for these gourmet delicacies.

One afternoon, as I was walking down to the shipyard, I spotted in a seafood store what must have been one of the largest lobsters ever caught. I went in to ask about purchasing this giant creature, but was told by the store operator it wasn't for sale. He'd bought it for display purposes because of its great size and intended to have it mounted.

After we explained we were from the west and had never

come across anything quite like this, he gave in though, and agreed to sell it to me. It truly was gargantuan and I think I weighed twenty two pounds. The claws alone were fearsome.

When I got back to the yacht, I called out the crew who were awaiting dinner and told George the chef not to bother with dinner, as we were going to have lobster. We laid out newspaper on the galley table, and four of us, including the self proclaimed lobster glutton, went to work on this feast. Even the four of us couldn't eat it all despite the lobster eater's boasts, and George put the leftovers away for the rest of the crew. Joe and another crew member from the Maritimes said later they'd never even heard of a lobster that gigantic.

I had often heard of ticker tape parades taking place in New York, and I read in one of the newspapers there was going to be a parade for Gordon Cooper, one of the original seven American astronauts. On May 15 and 16 of 1963, Cooper had circled the earth 22 times in one of the Mercury spacecraft. This parade was going to be special, even for New York, where enormous deals take place almost daily. The parade was to be held right in downtown Manhattan at lunchtime, so office workers were able to take part. This was definitely an experience I wasn't going to miss, so I headed off once again to the center of the universe. The noise echoing between the tall buildings, the paper dumped down from the offices above, and the wall to wall crowds of people lining the streets were something to behold. Cooper was truly a national hero at that time and millions turned out that day to see him and join the celebrations.

A few days before we were due to leave, the management from the Eaton's office arrived in chauffeur driven limousines for the gala dinner on board. Joe and the galley staff were the only crew involved, so the rest of us just got all dressed up in our smart uniforms and stayed out of the way. They all had a good time and very much appreciated seeing the yacht for the first time. We turned in early after their departure, as the next day we were scheduled to start stripping down the vessel in preparation for our voyage through the canals to the Great Lakes.

Getting the Hildur ready mostly involved taking down the rigging and dropping the main and mizzen masts. Both masts were hinged a couple of feet above the deck so they could be raised or lowered by a hand pumped hydraulic ram, to allow the yacht to go under bridges. This all sounded fairly simple to those of us who hadn't done it before, but the whole process took all of two days, since all the rigging had to be secured so no damage would be done to the decks or cap rails. The main mast sat in a cradle and extended out about 30 feet beyond the bow of the yacht. As might be expected, this made the vessel very difficult to handle, and we certainly had some near disasters going through the locks and canals. My own thoughts were that it would have been just as easy to continue up the coast, enter the St Lawrence River then, travel through the Seaway, passing through locks and under bridges that had been designed to accommodate large ocean going vessels. Admittedly, that would have more than doubled the distance we'd have to travel, but as time wasn't an issue, I think it should have been considered.

Chapter 27

We started the day after we completed the decommissioning of the vessel, with Albany, New York, as the goal for our first day's run. What a spectacular trip it was. Down the East River, under the Brooklyn Bridge, then a hard starboard turn into the Hudson River. We passed various passenger liners at their berths, and sailed under the George Washington Bridge and others as we passed along the shore of Manhattan. It's always a surprise to see how soon a huge city turns into farms and pleasant countryside. Rural New York State is very picturesque, with rolling hills, farms and huge country estates. We passed West Point on our port side, where officers of the U.S. Army could be seen receiving their training. As we headed up river, our speed slowed as we started to encounter some river current.

We reached Albany as planned and moored for the night so we could enter the first lock in the canal system at daylight. Art and one of the deckhands were the only crew members who had previously made this trip, so the rest of us were in new territory. As we slowly entered the first of many locks in the Erie Canal, a most ornery canal master greeted us. He insisted he wouldn't accept us until we had hoisted our Stars and Stripes courtesy flag. Joe tried to explain to him that we were out of commission and so didn't feel a courtesy flag was necessary, but he stated that as long as we were flying a Canadian flag at the stern, we were showing disrespect to our host country if we didn't fly a courtesy flag as well.

"Take down the Canadian flag and stow it in a locker, out of sight," Joe told me. But that wasn't good enough for this guy, so I had to crawl out to the end of our main mast to attach our courtesy flag to one of the stays. With a look of smug satisfaction and a few mumbled words from ourselves, the lockmaster closed the gate and proceeded to fill the lock with water to raise us up to the first level of the Erie Canal.

The Erie is the grand daddy of canals in North America, running from Albany to Buffalo, New York. It opened for traffic in 1825 and cost about $7 million, which was a considerable amount of money at that time. The original canal was only about four feet deep, so, as traffic increased and barges grew bigger, the waterway also had to be deepened and increased in size to accommodate the larger vessels. The distance from Albany to Lake Ontario is almost 400 miles and the numerous locks raise vessels 565 feet above sea level. Before the opening of the St. Lawrence Seaway in 1957, the Erie Canal was of vital economic and navigational importance as the only access from the Great Lakes to the Atlantic Ocean for large craft.

This was truly the trip of a lifetime for me, as I had never seen such waterways on the west coast of Canada. We found navigating this busy, narrow waterway to be quite a challenge, as our vessel wasn't very manoeuvrable at the best of times. It was a thrill to me to be moving along the canal and be able to look down at a farm or village far below our level. Joe told us this story of when he was serving on the British Cruiser Malaya, which had been dispatched to proceed with all speed through the Suez Canal. When a ship sails at high speed through a narrow waterway, all control of steering can sometimes be lost, but the ship will still continue to steer in mid-channel by itself, regardless of the position of the rudder. The Malaya was travelling at 30 knots with a huge bow wave spreading out across the desert. Joe claimed the steering wheel could be put hard over in either direction with absolutely no effect on the course of the ship.

With our vessel and her slow speed and lowered mast hanging out over the bow, we were experiencing quite the opposite effect. The first vessel we encountered was a MacAllister tug with a fuel barge alongside. As the craft approached each other, the Hildur started swinging to port, with the risk of a collision. Joe immediately ordered "Hard a starboard, starboard engine full reverse!" But, as always, the Hildur had a mind of her own in close quarters, and continued to veer off to port. With both engines now full astern, we managed to avoid disaster by a matter of inches, with only our anchor light on the top of our extended mast knocked off as it touched the barge. This was far too close a call for us, and whenever we passed a vessel in close quarters in future is was at dead slow or with the engines completely stopped. This was a bit of a pain, but it was the only way we could safely navigate in these narrow waterways.

We always stopped overnight, as we just couldn't risk trying to steer this cantankerous and unruly vessel at night with limited visibility. We were usually very tired after a day of numerous locks with heavy traffic to avoid, and welcomed the overnight rest. Some of the ports we stayed at included Troy, Schenectady and Utica. I'm sure they would have been interesting to explore, but we were more interested in getting this voyage behind us. Joe taught me to play cribbage and we'd spend many hours on the boat deck playing cards and enjoying the scenery unfolding below us as we continued to be lifted ever higher and higher with each lock.

We left the Erie Canal at Lake Oneida so we could end up at Oswego rather than Buffalo. Art said there was a bridge at Oswego he was worried about for clearance, as the water level was higher than usual. With great good fortune, we squeezed under this bridge with about two inches to spare. With our canal voyage over, it was time to raise the masts and get the vessel back in shape before steaming to Toronto.

We stayed in Oswego for about a week and enjoyed this small town very much, due in no small part to a young couple, who were managing one of the marinas, befriending us. We'd spent each evening after work at their place of business, which included a fine dining room and bar. They were curious about the Canadian West Coast, as were many other patrons of the marina, and tried to impress us with stories about the storms and dangerous seas that can develop on the Great Lakes. To hold up our end of the conversation, Joe and I pretended these huge lakes were just lily ponds that deep sea sailors such as ourselves would hold in utmost contempt. Privately, he and I had both read up on piloting small vessels on these huge lakes and admitted to each other we were somewhat nervous about what might lay ahead. Amid all the banter though, we really became quite attached to the marina and its facilities and found it difficult to leave our new friends when our vessel was ready to go once again.

Mr. Eaton flew from Toronto to Oswego in the company Beaver aircraft, to be with us on the overnight trip across Lake Ontario to Toronto. We cleared Customs with all flags flying and started off with calm winds and flat water. The voyage went uneventfully until shortly after daybreak, when a light breeze developed. As we were nearing Toronto harbour, Joe decided we should hoist our spinnaker, so as to proceed into port under sail. Art immediately warned us that this just wouldn't work, but we were game to give it a try. The spinnaker pole was a wooden spar that took four of us to lift into place. With main, mizzen and spinnaker flying, Art shut down the engines, and we proceeded majestically under sail sideways towards Toronto Harbour. This was the last time we made a serious attempt to sail this beautiful barge. She behaved just as Art had warned us she would, churning along at about one knot, sideways. We moored at the foot of Spidina Avenue, cleared Customs and settled down to a couple of weeks shore time in Toronto.

I had been to Toronto when I was seven years old, and was surprised at how much I remembered from my earlier visit. I called up Joan as soon as we landed to see how she was doing in her new roll as a wife. She was quite excited to hear from me and suggested I come to London for a weekend visit. Also, her friend Pam had just moved to Toronto, so here I was back in Canada among friends again.

Joe had had his car shipped east from Victoria and it was in storage waiting for him to pick it up. What a machine! It was a 1955 Mercedes 300 SL coupe. I had seen it a few times in Victoria, but had never driven in it before. Joe gave me the job of getting it back in shape, and I started by changing the oil, and giving it a lube job and a detailed wash, wax and polish. Never before had I driven a car with so much raw power. It was a real head turner every time I parked, with people stopping to stare and standing around to admire it, which I didn't mind at all. The car was a two seater, black with bright red leather upholstery.

Joe and I drove to Niagara Falls one weekend, as neither one of us had been there before. It was a pleasant trip through what used to be, at one time some of the best fruit orchards in Canada. The car performed well on the highway, and we had a great time at this remarkable international tourist destination. The roaring falls were about what one would expect, with many tourists craning to have a look, and much commercialization. It was a beautiful sunny day so we had taken the top down and just cruised like a couple of carefree kids, which is of course what we were.

I met Pam at the airport one evening, to drive her to her new apartment in Toronto, and she said she was planning on going home to Tillsonberg where her family lived. She suggested we fly down together to London the next weekend so I could meet her relatives as well as Ron and Joan. They met us at the London airport and Ron and I hit it off right from the start. We stayed up until about 4 a.m. the next day, chatting up a storm until Joan, angry as an alley cat, came down stairs to break up our loud political discussion. Pam and I drove out to Tillsonberg the next day to visit with her family. Her father owned a fleet of school buses and had emigrated from England after the war. We had a nice time with the family and drove back to Toronto in Pam's car on the Sunday.

Soon after arriving in Toronto, I had called up Jeff Fielding, whom I had met through mutual friends in Vancouver. Jeff had lived most of his life in Toronto, and we spent a lot of time together in the city. He was a great host. We toured the city in Joe's car and had some good times during the balmy weather of early June. Each afternoon after work, Jeff would come down to the waterfront to take us on yet another sightseeing tour of this big metropolitan city. One day as I was stepping ashore, I was met by Dr. and Mrs. Nash, who were attending a medical convention in Toronto and came by to visit me. I kept busy during working hours with a new launch Mr. Eaton had acquired for his wife, as well as the constant chore of washing and repairing Joe's car. Mr. Eaton came by most days, and on a couple of occasions held lunch meetings with company executives on board the yacht. The managers would nearly always arrive in style by limousine, but Mr. Eaton preferred to ride in the Volkswagen driven by his friend Fred, who managed the executives' garage. Fred was something of a practical joker and had heard of Joe's reputation for pranks, so he tried to join in the fun with a few minor tricks of his own at our expense, so we set out to get even. After all, we had more time on our hands than he did.

Someone in the crew had a subscription for a men's fishing and hunting magazine. I don't remember who it was who first came up with the idea of signing Fred's name to all the numerous coupons that were on just about every page. We all set to work with a will, cutting out coupons to sign him up for safaris to Africa, hair loss formulas, lonely hearts clubs, language lessons, Cruises to the Arctic, body building classes and a whole host of other things. The opportunities seemed endless. We roared with laughter at each new sign up and were constantly going to the post office for more stamps. The best part was that by the time Fred started to receive his memberships by mail, we'd be long gone out of town and he'd have great difficulty retaliating. I hear later that the post office found itself delivering huge sacks of mail stuffed full with this junk when the results of our efforts took full hold.

Towards the end of June, we left the now sweltering heat of Toronto for Parry Sound, located at the east shore of Georgian Bay. Mr. Eaton came with us to be our guide, to make sure we didn't get lost among the lily pads. Our first stop was the Welland Canal, which would take us around Niagara Falls. This consisted of a huge lock designed for deep sea vessels, so there was no need to lower our masts, as we had done for the Erie Canal. We entered Lake Erie for the voyage through this very shallow lake with Windsor as our destination. The ship channel was rigged with buoys for navigation, so it was easy for us to follow the channel even though there was very heavy traffic in both directions. The crossing was with calm winds, clear skies and flat seas. We entered the Detroit River, passed under the Ambassador Bridge, and moored overnight at Windsor on the Canadian side of the river.

My Great Uncle Ameen and his family were living at Windsor and were expecting my arrival. My cousins picked me up at the dock for a visit with the family, and then it was off to Detroit for dinner and a pleasant time at a waterfront restaurant. On leaving Detroit to return to Canada though, we were warned by customs officials that a rather large race riot was under way and had spilled over into Windsor. When we got back to the dock, we discovered some of this mob was starting to threaten the yacht as a potential target for some of their nastier behaviour. Mr. Eaton was very upset by this turn of events and suggested we get under way as quickly as possible. We set out into the river at about 3 a.m., under dark skies and heavy fog. At this point, Mr. Eaton, who had been drinking rather more than usual, insisted he be in charge of navigation. This narrow stretch of river between Lake Erie and Lake St. Clair is a funnel for all the Great Lakes traffic, and on this particular occasion as a thick fog shrouded the area, the traffic seemed unusually heavy. With Mr. Eaton clearly upset by the night's rioting and with huge freighters all round us, I was most uneasy about having him in charge of my watch. Whenever I'd make a suggestion that we call Joe or make some course alteration, Mr E would send me below to the galley, to fetch him some more mixer or another lemon, both of which he seemed to consume in large quantities. As daylight approached, Joe took over and it was with some relief that I went below for some much needed rest.

By my next watch at noon, we had cleared the St. Clair River and were well into Lake Huron, with no wind, pleasantly calm water and no land in sight. All went well with the rest of the crossing into Georgian Bay.

On my next watch Mr. Eaton, who never seemed to rest, asked me to alter course and head for a nearby island. As we approached, he slowed the engines, which brought both Art and Joe into the wheelhouse with a great rush. We were running dead slow with Mr. Eaton at the radar, which happened to be working better following a complete overhaul in New York. Although it was still dark, we could see the outline of the trees and shore starting to show. Mr. Eaton asked me to turn on the searchlight. Right ahead of us was the looming shape of a rock formation in the perfect shape of a giant flowerpot. This was Flowerpot Island, which I believe is a provincial park. It was quite a sight, and I gained much admiration of Mr. Eaton's local knowledge of the area and his abilities to navigate in waters that were new to all the crew except Art and Gerry.

Finally we pulled into an anchorage in a small, quiet bay about a mile from the Eaton summer residence. We secured shorelines fore and aft across the bay. It was now July 1st, and we were scheduled to stay until the Labour Day weekend. After a quick look around, we decided this was going to be an uneventful summer, locked away in this deserted harbour. We were allotted one of the family launches for our use, and this was a great asset, as we were able to travel into Parry Sound, go fishing, or just explore wherever we wanted when we were not busy, which actually proved to be just about all the time.

We met some of the other summer residents who lived on the various islands, and settled in for a summer which in the end turned out to be quite a bit better than we'd first thought. We had the use of a couple of 14 foot International sailing dingys, which I used to teach some of the vacationing kids how to sail. We also had a couple of canoes, which were a new experience for me. Soon I caught on how to stay upright, but we didn't use either canoe very much. The motor launch that was our only means of real transportation was an old wooden vessel named

Bedelia. Painted a light green, it was powered by a Chrysler Crown engine, which gave her a speed of about 15 knots.

Ron Adams, Joan's new husband, had told me his parents had a summer cabin just outside Parry Sound and I was able to locate them by his description of the place, so I dropped by to introduce myself. They said they hoped Ron and Joan would be able to visit later in the summer, as did I. On my first visit to Parry Sound, I went to the doctor's office to get a final check on my eye. This was where I met Mary, a young lady who worked for the doctor. We spent many pleasant times together that summer fishing and cruising the many islands and bays.

July 15th was Joe's 45th birthday, as well as his official retirement from the navy. Naturally we took any excuse for a party, so we set out to find a suitable location. Mr. Eaton gave his blessing and suggested we try Amanda Lodge, which I had noticed located on an island about half way between our anchorage and Parry Sound. It looked somewhat run down but we stopped by to check it out anyway. An elderly couple owned the lodge and had apparently done so since about the beginning of time. Mr. and Mrs. Whitehead were most receptive to our plan for a party there and it was evident that they hadn't entertained any guests for a few years. The lodge had previously been popular with the rich and famous, but that was in a different era. The walls were covered with pictures of famous movie stars and business icons from that time.

This party was to be a surprise for Joe who was far from his many friends and former navy mates. Mr. Eaton declined our invitation to join us, but Mr. Powell and his wife said they would, and we invited a few other locals we had met and quietly got the lodge in good shape for the party ahead. When the day came, we poured a few tots of rum, navy style, into Joe and set off in the Bedelia for Amanda Lodge. The evening got off to a good start. After docking, we had to kill a rattlesnake lurking in the tall grass which bordered the trail from the dock to the lodge. We weren't too happy about having to do that, but this particular creature was quite threatening and let us know we weren't welcome which was demonstrated by the constant rattle of its tail.

Joe was somewhat taken aback by all this and was not showing too much enthusiasm about moving on up to the derelict looking old lodge with just a couple of his crew. All that changed though when he went in to find there were about 30 people waiting to greet us. The chef on the yacht had sent over food as well as a birthday cake, so with enough rum to float a battleship, the party was soon well under way.

Mr. Powell had practised law in Parry Sound for many years but had never been out to the lodge before. He indicated he was very impressed, as we all were, with the beautiful antique furniture and autographed photographs of famous people. Mrs. Whitehead dug out a very old 78 rpm record that some once famous singer had cut for her. The song was about returning once again to Amanda Lodge. With each rum toddy she consumed, the volume would be cranked up another notch. There was soon enough noise coming out to scare off any adventurous rattlesnakes seeking revenge, but after a few more rums Mrs. W drifted quietly off to sleep for a few hours.

All in all, the party was a great success, and went on until late Sunday afternoon, with catnaps taken as required. I think Mr. and Mrs. Whitehead had the best time of all, and both appeared to be most sad to see us finally taking our leave on the various boats.

We fired up the Bedelia with a full load of passengers and headed back to the yacht, dropping guests off along the way at their islands while singing sea shanties to help Joe over his blue mood from at last being out of the Navy after so many years.

I think the singing finally got to him and he warned us that if we sang one more, he'd leap overboard and drown himself. This of course prompted yet another of our tuneful renditions, whereupon Joe jumped over the side, fully dressed for the occasion in his naval uniform. The Bedelia was going flat out at the time, and Joe made quite a splash as he hit the water. I was at the wheel and decided to leave him to flounder around for a couple of minutes before turning around for the rescue. As we approached though, he tried to avoid us and almost succeeded in wading ashore on a small rocky island before we dragged him aboard and carried him on towards home.

Poor Joe was in a sad frame of mind for several days after that, and we wondered if the party had been such a good idea after all. But he was soon back to normal and expressed much appreciation for making his birthday and retirement a time to remember.

One interesting visitor who came aboard most every day at that time was the winter watchman and handy man who looked after the Eaton estate during the off season. His name was Axle Anderson and he had lived most of his life in Sudbury where he had worked in the mines. He told me a story on our first meeting of how he had almost gone west as a young man with his best friend, Bill Binnersley. I asked him a few questions about Bill and his family, and sure enough it was the same Binnersleys who lived at Heriot Bay on Quadra Island. Axle hadn't heard from Bill for over 30 years and was pleased to get all the news I could give him about his childhood friend and his family of boys. Axle had lived all his life in the wilds of Ontario and had never been as far south as Toronto.

Monotony was starting to be our constant companion by this time. By mid-August we'd only taken the yacht out from her moorings for one short trip. Mr. Eaton's regulars, Mr. Powell and Dr. Sharpe, joined us on this trip out to a deserted rock in Georgian Bay, and Mrs. Eaton was along also. This was the first and only time that she came aboard, as she considered the yacht an unfit place for ladies. Joe was kept busy for a few hours each week, instructing Mrs. Eaton on how to safely operate her new launch. Our life revolved around trips to Parry Sound after our duties to the yacht were completed each day.

Joe, myself and a couple of other crew members were on our way into Parry Sound one hot afternoon when it was suggested we stop at a shore side hotel for a cool drink. We ordered cokes and other soft drinks while Joe had his favourite rum and tonic. After finishing off our refreshments, Joe happened to say that he felt he could easily consume a gallon of rum tonics. We all looked at him and said we bet he couldn't. If he failed in this noble endeavour he would have to pay the bill for all of us. The bet was on and the bartender produced a gallon jug well spiked with rum. While all the patrons cheered him on he made a good dent in the gallon but decided that paying the bill was the best way out.

One day late in August Joe was called to come over to the Eaton house for a meeting. On his return he called all the crew together in the galley and announced that he'd just been fired, with the reason given that he had caused animosity among the staff. Later he asked me what my plans were, and I decided if Joe was going to leave, I would too. Art tried to talk me into staying, at least until we arrived back in Miami for the winter, but some developments back home that involved my sister and her children convinced me the time had come for me to get back home and start making some decent earnings again.

This was a major decision for me, as I was still being groomed for the marina development that Mr. Eaton had said was to be built at Park Royal in West Vancouver.

A friend who was the wife of one of the company pilots drove up from Toronto to pick us up. We stayed at their place for a few days to decide our future then, I went down to the Eaton office to pick up my pay and get a ticket back to Vancouver. When I returned, Joe told me he had a job offer to take over as skipper on the new Bluenose II, which was under construction in Nova Scotia. Joe said there was a position for me as mate, as this was one of his conditions if he were to take over the Bluenose. This put my plans to fly home on hold for a few days, but after several late nights of discussion, I decided my obligations at home had to come first for me, so Joe reluctantly turned down the offer. I felt sad, as this could have been an ideal position for Joe, who was such a good sailor as well as popular personality. Jeff Fielding drove us to the airport early one morning for me to catch a flight back to Vancouver. I never saw Joe or Jeff again, though Joe and I kept in touch by mail and mutual friends for many years.

After about a year of drifting, Joe became sailing master

at the Merchant Marine Academy at Kings Point, New York, just across the bay from City Island where we had moored the previous year. He stayed there for over 20 years and passed away at a fairly early age when his old war injuries caught up with him.

The flight home stopped in Winnipeg, where I gave my brother Jim a call at his office. Jim and family had just moved from California after 10 years living in Berkeley. He was surprised to hear from me and I quickly brought him up to date on my past year. The flight carried on to Vancouver, where Armond Giroday picked me up and took me to his place, where I stayed for a couple of days until I got settled. It was a beautiful West Coast summer's day and just great to be back home again. I called up Mike Nash, who came over to visit and bring me up to date on all our mutual friends. A few days later, I moved in with Jack Thompson at the family home on West 29th near Cambie. After getting unpacked, I picked up my car from Barry and headed over to the Island.

When I finally arrived home, Mum's greeting was typically short.

"I knew you'd come back," she said. I spent a few days on Quadra, visited with Bill and family and had a very pleasant picnic with them, and caught up on family affairs.

When I called Andy Tulloch, he said there was a job just waiting for me on the Sea Queen when she arrived in port later in the week. With this new job in my pocket, I headed down Island to Duncan and Victoria to call on John Lawrence and Dick Meadows, who was a close friend of Joe. Dick and I had lunch together, as Joe had wanted me to explain to Dick the circumstances of him being fired. Dick was an engineer in the navy and was just about to retire. He asked me what I thought he could do that would keep him connected with the marine industry. I suggested he look into starting a marine surveying business. He opened this business shortly after his retirement, and it turned out to be very successful.

Back in Vancouver again, I checked in with Andy and found the Sea Queen wasn't due back in port for a few days.

Jack and Mike held a rather long welcome home party for me that only ended when I finally sailed once again on the Sea Queen. Bill Zelly was skipper at the time and had had the first and only accident of his long career the previous trip. He was entering Kwakume Inlet and touched the rock located at the entrance, which is ironic because I can't remember how many times Bill had warned me about this rock whenever I was entering this inlet on my watch. It seemed strange he would end up hitting it when he was so familiar with that area, and I was quite surprised to see how much Bill had aged in the year since I had last seen him.

Although he lived on to be about 90, his many years of difficult work and stress were showing up in his ability to carry out his duties. He retired later that year, and I continued to visit him at his small home in Nanaimo for many more years.

Chapter 28

My first trip back at my old job was up to Growler Cove to tend the seiners working that area. Stan Palmer came aboard and once again I had to go over the events of the past year. It was good to see Stan again though, and we have remained friends and neighbours in the Campbell River area for all of our lives.

Our next trip was to start towing in some of the camp barges for winter storage, uneventful work as the weather was still fair, and we soon had all the camps in their winter homes located at Queensborough, just below New Westminster.

The Sea Queen was laid up for a few weeks, so Bill decided this was the time for him to retire after fifty two years as a skipper. I still feel honoured to have had the pleasure of having sailed with him, as he was a fine gentleman, as well as a highly skilled seaman. Much of my success in future years outside the scope of this record was due to the good training I received from Bill.

After a few days off, it was on to the Randy and other company boats that were under charter to Straits Towing for part of the winter season. Freight barges to Prince Rupert, chip barges to Tacoma, lime rock from Texada Island, and oil barges to Anacortes kept me busy on various boats that year. Suddenly it seems now, mid-November was on us and it was time to tow in the West Coast troll camps, so it was back on the Sea Queen again with Hans Larson as skipper.

I recall I was at Vancouver Shipyards getting the Sea Queen ready on November 22, 1963, when Don Cruickshanks, a manager with Tulloch Western, came down the dock and told me that President John F. Kennedy had been shot. I asked him if the young president had survived and Don said he thought so. So, with no further news, we set off for the west coast of the Island. Soon every radio was alive with the news that Kennedy was dead. When we reached Race Rocks, Hans decided to return to Vancouver, as gales out of the southeast were forecast. The barges we were to tow couldn't stand any rough seas at all, so we had to wait for better weather. Fortunately though, the forecast was soon revised, so we turned around again to pick up our tow at Ucluelet. We arrived back in Vancouver the day of the Kennedy funeral and I just managed to catch the last of it on the television at Jack's house. It was a historical time when the world seemed to come to a stop for a little while. Almost everyone of my generation remembers where they were when they were told of the assassination, and managed to see at least a part of the heart wrenching funeral, with John junior saluting his fallen father.

Mary and Pam, two of the girls I had met on my trip east, came to Vancouver for a visit that autumn. Pam and I went to a football game at old Empire Stadium, where we got completely soaked. I still miss that old stadium on a warm summer evening though. But when the rains of autumn start, it's a different story.

During that time Mike Nash had to go Winnipeg for a couple of weeks. His sister Betsy and her friend Mary Gale were due in town just as he was leaving, so he asked me if I'd look after them for him and help them find a place to live. I met them down near the Marine Building and we set off to find Betsy an apartment. I had only met Betsy once before, just as I was leaving for the east the previous winter. You may recall I wasn't too impressed to begin with. Well, Betsy ended up sharing an apartment with her friend Kay, who was also a nurse, and Betsy and I ended up looking after each for more than the next four decades at last count.

I made my last voyage on the Randy towing a gravel barge from Texada to the LaFarge cement plant on the main river. The crew was laid off until after Christmas, which was just fine with me as I intended to go back to school in January. I spent Christmas at home on Quadra Island with my family, which was to be a tradition for many years to come. After Christmas, I found an apartment on Cambie Street in Vancouver, and settled down to study once again to upgrade my knowledge of ship safety and fire fighting.

Betsy was working at St. Paul's Hospital, where her mother had trained as a nurse and her father had worked as a doctor. We saw each other most every weekend, and this friendship slowly blossomed and turned into a long lasting love.

After I finished my schooling in February I was offered a position on the M.V. Norango, which was owned by Frank Griffith.

This vessel had a varied history over her short life. Originally built as a North Sea trawler in 1958 at a shipyard in Scotland, the Norango's original owners ran into financial difficulties and construction had to be stopped for a while. Still uncompleted, the vessel was purchased and completed as a private yacht by Barbara Hutton, heir to the Woolworth fortune. After a couple of years, Miss Hutton had taken to new ways to deplete her fortune and put the Norango up for sale. I had first come across this fine little ship in Miami, where she was working as a walk on ferry carrying passengers between the islands in the Bahamas. Her name had been changed to Sea Search, but the new owners had maintained her very well. That particular phase of her life came to an end early in 1964, when Mr. Griffith bought her and sent her to the Canadian West Coast. The first stage of that voyage terminated partway through, in Acapulco, Mexico, with crew troubles and the death of the captain. Captain Bill Earnshaw was hired on as the replacement captain, and Doug Dakin became her chief engineer. They moved on to Mexico, took with them some new crew, and then sailed the vessel up to Vancouver.

I just happened to be down at Burrard Shipyard, located at that time on West Georgia Street just north of the Bayshore Inn, and was spending a few idle moments admiring the Norango, which had been dry docked for maintenance. I recognized her right away as the Sea Search I'd seen the previous year in Miami. Someone mentioned to me that the vessel was due to go to Alaska for the summer, and the owners were looking for crew. Doug Dakin was standing there with us. I had met him once before, as he was a good friend of Dr. Nash, so I asked him if he knew where I could apply for a position.

"I'm the chief engineer and I'm looking for engine room crew," he replied. I had just finished writing for a low grade diesel certificate, so I said I'd be interested if there were no positions as first or second mate available. As it turned out, I was hired on as second engineer and started work the next day. Our job was to get the vessel ready for charter to the Superior Oil company, which was exploring for oil in the Gulf of Alaska. We were to have a crew of 36 in total, most of them from the oil city of Houston, Texas. The vessel was well suited for this work after some major alterations had been carried out, but about halfway through the shipyard work, a major problem appeared. The area's shipyards were shut down by a workers' strike. As we had a deadline of May 15 to have the vessel ready, we were forced to move her down to Seattle to complete the partly finished work.

Next door to Burrard Shipyard was Benson's, where the nearly completed tugs Chieftain III and Dauntless II were being built. These fine new vessels belonged to Ron Wilson and Lance Higgs. Lance was to become my best friend a few years later, but that's another story for another time.

Before we headed south to Seattle, Mr. Griffith said he and his family would be using the vessel for a weekend cruise over to the Gulf Islands. We left Vancouver the afternoon of Friday March 25, 1964 with the family on board, and that evening anchored off an island near Swartz Bay which was owned by the Dueck family. I spent the weekend getting familiar with the engine room and the general layout of the machinery. I only mention the date because on the Sunday we heard the news by radio that there had been a massive earthquake off the coast of Alaska. This resulted in a big tsunami, a tidal wave which hit the outside coast of Vancouver Island and sent a huge surge rolling up the Alberni Inlet to smash into the city of Port Alberni. Much damage was done there along with several ports on the outer coast of the Island.

After this weekend cruise was over, we loaded up all the equipment that had been collected in Vancouver, took on fuel, cleared Customs and left for Lake Union Dry Dock near the Port of Seattle. I had been so busy since joining the vessel that this was really my first opportunity to have a good look around. The main lounge was huge, complete with a fireplace, rosewood furnishings and beautiful upholstery. The four main passenger staterooms were located below decks forward, complete units similar to an expensive hotel suite, with gold plated bathroom fixtures. The ship was fully air conditioned, and everything about her was of a very high standard. The crew's quarters and galley were aft on the main deck, with the Captain, 1st mate and chief engineer's quarters located on the boat deck behind a spacious wheel house.

I had never been through the lock into Lake Union before. We passed right in front of Jimmy Joseph's house located on the waterway and I asked Vick Fry, the first mate, to give Jim a good blast on the whistle as we passed. We docked without incident and made ready for the large amount of equipment to arrive from Houston by truck. Betsy drove down with my car the following weekend so I'd have transportation for what was to be a six week stay in Seattle.

The geophysical crew of 26 came in from Houston, with yet more equipment to be installed and stowed away. The superintendent of this oil survey crew was a Canadian, from Calgary of course, and we all worked well together, with Doug leaving most of the details for me to figure out. We had some minor work to do on the main engine, which we were able to complete in a couple of days. Much of the mechanical equipment was very heavy and had to be stowed aft on the boat deck. This could perhaps have resulted in some stability problems later on, but we were to discover that this was a most stable vessel, even with several tons of added weight topside.

Besides working to a tight deadline, we managed to have a good time during our stay in Seattle. We spent many evenings touring the sights of the city, which had just recently hosted a World's Fair. On weekends we'd take in some of the more lively nightspots, of which there were several. Birdland was by far our favourite. It was a new experience for the boys from Texas to be socializing with blacks, and it resulted in some lively discussions back on board, some of them lasting until after daylight.

I remember one of the Texans saying after a heated discussion, that if we kept up this dangerous trend in Canada, it might spread south and could even lead to having black people being allowed to live in every house. Most of us northerners laughed at this stupid comment, but he didn't, he was dead serious. We Canadian members of the crew soon learned to keep our political views under wraps, as we were greatly outnumbered.

During our stay at Lake Union, there was a small naval vessel moored at the yard with a couple of engineers on board. The vessel was being fitted with a very large electrical generating system for use on one of the South Pacific Islands. The electrician was one of those rare people who are a cut above the rest of us and never satisfied unless tinkering with the latest new toy, in this case the new large capacity generator. He'd come over for coffee after work to regale us with his latest experiment with the generators and how he was able to parallel with the other systems on other ships, including ours and, finally, the whole shipyard, so he said. One late evening after we'd come back on board, this electrical genius decided to come by to try to impress us with his latest tale of how he was now ready to try paralleling his generator with the electrical grid of the whole City of Seattle.

This was enough to convince me I needed to disconnect our shore power line, just in case of some mishap. I went below to the engine room, started up one of our 200 kilowatt generators, and hit the disconnect switch for our shore power. All went well on the naval vessel as he powered up his system and connected various parts of the city with his big ship's generator. Finally I received my vindication. The load became unbalanced and the whole area of Queen Ann Hill, a residential section of the city, was plunged into darkness as it lost its electricity. I suppose a switch or transformer blew out. All the streetlights went out and stayed that way, along with the power to the disgruntled residents, for some hours. Seattle City Power, according to newspaper accounts, was at a total loss as to what could have caused this very major and costly power failure. We all got a big laugh from it and our naval friend laid very low for a few days until, apparently he was able to come up with some new scheme to fill his idle evenings. He'd have done better just coming with us, as our evenings were very fun filled and entertaining.

After over a year of visiting numerous ports around the continent, I can very well see how the saying "a girl in every port" came into being. But soon it was time, yet again, for us to leave for our next port of call, which was to be Juneau, Alaska. Some of our crew had some very tense moments saying goodbye to young ladies who had come down to see us on our way. We sailed out through the locks once again, gave Jimmy and Leona another healthy blast on our whistle, and were on our way north. There were to be four vessels, in total, working together to carry out the geophysical work up in the Gulf of Alaska. We met the first vessel as we cleared Seattle; the yacht Principia, which was a well kept vessel from the 1920's. The others from Vancouver were the Calm C, which was a sister to the Sea Queen, and the Chenega, an ex-Union Steamships freighter which I had once pulled off the end of Cape Mudge after she had run aground.

By then, it was almost the end of May. The weather had warmed and it was through calm seas we made our way up the inside of Vancouver Island. I pointed out to some of the crew my birthplace on Quadra as we passed by. I had never been to Alaska before and it came to my mind that in the past year I had traveled from the tropics to the far north, with much experience gained along the way. Capable of cruising at 12 knots, we ran at 10 so the little fleet could stay together.

On reaching Juneau, we were met by some of the technical people from Superior Oil, who directed us to try out the exploration equipment outside the harbour. Each of the four vessels had specific tasks to carry out. The Principia carried fisheries observers to record any fish killed during the operation. The Calm C was used as a recovery vessel and to set off small underwater explosions. The Chenega was the dynamite and explosives store, carrying several hundred tons of dynamite and related equipment used for the underwater blasts. The Norango carried a long cable with microphones, which was towed behind us to record the shock waves caused by the detonations. The shock waves were recorded on a type of graph paper that showed the strata of the ocean floor down to a certain depth, as well as the exact location of the recordings. All this information was used to determine if the structure of the ocean bottom was of the type that could contain deposits of oil and natural gas, to give the geologists some idea of where best to do exploration drilling at some point in the future.

On board the Norango, we had sonar tracking and mapping devices, as well as Loran with a temporary 'slave' station located high on a mountaintop, which was looked after by a technician housed in a tent for the purpose. He spent many lonely days and nights on this mountain and on one occasion was attacked by a bear for his troubles. A helicopter supplied his only means of transportation, subject of course to weather conditions. Several times his tent was blown away by the fierce winds encountered at that elevated altitude. I don't think I'd have traded him positions without a good supply of comic books, with the addition of either a rifle or an assured source of friendlier bears.

We stayed several days in Juneau, which is the capital city of Alaska. I've been to some pretty wild ports in my travels, and I must say that at that time Juneau would certainly have ranked among my top three. The town is located on a mountainside which slopes steeply into the sea, and there was sizable mine shaft almost right in town, which was a major employer at that time. Since there was no road from the outside, access was by Alaska State Ferries or by air. The town population was about 20,000, and they rivalled both Minstrel Island and Alert Bay in their capacity to consume beer.

I went ashore only once, on the evening before our departure. The Texans brought a certain amount of glamour and an aura of the high life to town, so maybe this accounted for much of the completely wild night of partying that overtook what seemed to be the whole community. Luckily I decided not to get too involved, as I had numerous duties to look after for our departure, scheduled for early the next morning, that is, *if* our crew could be rounded up and recaptured. Even the captain and chief engineer proved difficult to get back aboard, since they'd been enjoying the hospitality of someone from the Alaska government.

Chapter 29

Somehow everyone showed up on board ship, and our flotilla departed Juneau about 4 a.m., under bright sunshine but with some very sleepy crew. As I came off watch at 6 a.m., we were headed out through Icy Strait with Yakutat as our destination. The day was cool under the sun and the scenery was astounding even to this fairly seasoned coastal sailor. The mountains were still covered with snow that sparkled in the bright light, and glaciers were seen winding their way down the valleys towards the bright blue ocean. We bucked a fresh northwester up past Cape Fairweather, with white spray washing our decks. By late afternoon all four vessels were at Yakutat, the first port where we saw evidence of the March 27th earthquake.

Apparently there had been an oil tanker delivering when the quake struck. One of the crew, the cook, was never seen again and a fire broke out as the fuelling lines parted. Some of the buildings were badly damaged, and there was evidence of a very high tidal surge.

The village had a crab processing plant as its major employer, and we were somewhat surprised to find most of the employees were university students from California. With a fleet with a total of some 60 people on board, we were like an invasion to this small village of a few hundred residents.

To me, as perhaps to most other people, the most outstanding feature about the north in high summer is the length of daylight each day. It was now early June and the sun would set at about 11 p.m., only to re-appear in a couple of hours. By 2 a.m., the sun was high in the sky, and after a few days one would have a difficult time knowing whether it was morning or afternoon, with the sun pouring down out of a bright clear sky all the time.

We fuelled up the fleet at Yakutat and headed out for our first day exploring oil in the Gulf of Alaska with some complicated kinks to be worked out of the systems. I was kept very busy with various tasks within my jurisdiction.

The exploration operation consisted of the Norango towing the long microphone cable through the water to a predetermined location. At that point the mountaintop Loran operator, if he wasn't being chewed on by some bear with a sore head, would order us to stop dead in the water and our exact location was recorded. The cable was then released to maintain its position, as Calm C set of an underwater charge of dynamite. The sonic shock waves from this were then recorded on a graph. We wound in the portion of the cable that had been released then, proceeded to our next location to start the process again. As there were some troubles with water leaking into the cable, we retreated to Yakutat or Icy Bay for repairs and modifications to the system several times.

There we discovered that the strain on the cable, as it was wound back on to a large drum aboard the vessel while we were moving through the water, was breaking the water tight joints. This resulted in water damage to the sensitive electronics housed within. It turned out that none of the Superior Oil crew except one had any experience with exploration on the water. The same system had been used on land, obviously with suitable success, but there the environment was much more forgiving. I discussed this problem with Ray, who had previous experience doing this work on the ocean, and we reckoned that if our vessel came to a complete stop as the cable was wound in after each explosion, that might take enough strain off the cable to solve the problem.

Sad to say though, we were unable to get the managers

to even try our idea, so the company had to go to the trouble and expense of sending up an expert all the way from Texas. That didn't work either, and the leaking continued, despite numerous experts and much lost time. Finally, someone high up in the company came up with the brilliant plan of stopping our vessel as the cable was wound in. After that we had no further problems! I got a big kick out of overhearing one of these 'experts' say if only they had listened to Ray.... He also mentioned that Ray had made other suggestions on previous projects that had been ignored, at the company's peril.

Although the weather was not a major problem in the gulf, we did experience a few storms the area is famous for. The wind would be mostly from the Northwest for a few days, and then die off completely. Then, if the prevailing swell flattened out for a day or so, look out! A strong Southeaster would sweep up the gulf and smaller vessels would take shelter at Yakutat or Icy Bay while we'd just head out to sea for 50 miles or more, to reach deeper water. Without any doubt, the Norango had the best sea going qualities of any vessel I had ever sailed on. We'd just lay dead in the water, broadside to the seas, which were often twenty feet in height, and ride it out. Even in those conditions we were quite comfortable, with not enough roll to shift a glass of water left on a table. The vessel seemed to just go easily and steadily up one side of each approaching wave, and down the other side, without any noticeable rolling. What a difference from the seagoing 'qualities' of the Hildur!

As we moved farther north with our explorations, we worked near Cape St. Elias, which had to be one of the most lonely, desolate landfalls I had ever seen. On our next trip to head in for fuel and supplies, Captain Earnshaw chose Cordova for the port of call, as it was now much closer than Yakutat.

I went ashore to see if I could get something done for a toothache that had been troubling me for a few weeks. None of the dentists would see me on such short notice, so I ended up at the pharmacy. The pharmacist, who was so large and tough looking that I thought she would have been more at home on a crab fishing boat than dispensing drugs, said I should go see a dentist. I explained to her my situation, whereupon she asked me to come with her to a back room. I immediately had visions of this rather huge mountain of a woman surrounded by pliers and other instruments of torment in a well kitted torture chamber, but I didn't have much choice but to go along with her. It didn't turn out to be an old fashioned dungeon after all and when we got there, she said she could give me something for my tooth, on the strict understanding that I promised as long as I lived never to tell anyone where I got it from. I readily agreed, more out of fear than honesty, as she handed me several small tablets, with firm instructions about dosage. To this day I have no idea what these tablets were, other than miracle drugs, because my tooth cleared up after taking just one tablet and has never bothered me since.

Cordova, which is near the southern terminal of the Trans Alaska pipeline, was what one would expect from a frontier Alaska town. The place was busting at the seams with the fishing fleet in port, and what seemed like a bar on every corner. We stayed in port just long enough to take on supplies then, headed back once more to what was already becoming very tedious work following a grid pattern of exploration over towards Kodiak. I usually called Betsy each time I had access to a telephone, and on one occasion she told me Andy Tulloch was trying to reach me. I called Andy right away, and he asked me to come to see him as soon as I got back to Vancouver.

By mid-August, as we completed our assignment, a message came from Mr. Griffith to prepare to go to Japan, where we would have the exploration equipment removed. The plan was that the Griffith family would meet us there and stay aboard while they attended the Olympic Games. Unfortunately this didn't work out, as Superior Oil wanted their equipment nearer to home. So, with some regrets, we started south for Victoria where the vessel was to be docked. The weather warmed nicely and the daylight grew shorter as we made our way south.

Docked securely in Victoria, I made my way by bus to catch the ferry to Vancouver. Betsy met me at the ferry, and it was great to be with her again after four months away from each other. I went to see Mr. Griffith the next day and he thanked me for my service while I was waiting for my paycheque. Then I crossed the street to Bow Mac, and bought a new 1964 Pontiac from my friend John McDermid.

A couple of days later Betsy and I made a trip over to the Island so the rest of my family and friends could meet Betsy, who had agreed to be my future wife.

Chapter 30

About a week later I finally called Andy, who asked me to come down to his office to see him and Ed Moir. Andy was reinventing the company once again, while Ed, his partner, was taking over part of the operation with his sons. This is difficult to believe, but when I left their office, I was working for the Moir's new company as skipper on the Amboyna, right back to where I had started five years before, in 1959.

So here we were, going round and round again in the Gulf of Georgia, tending the fish camps I was so familiar with. But I didn't plan on staying beyond the end of the fishing in October, as I had decided to start my own business.

I thoroughly enjoyed those two final months making the rounds twice a week, meeting old friends and helping the Moirs get their new company, Norpac Fisheries Ltd., up and running as smoothly as possible. On the last trip I made on the Amboyna as skipper, Pete Sainas joined us as our new deckhand. Pete later worked his way up to skipper and served on this faithful old vessel until 1981. Betsy came with us on one trip around the gulf, and we had a great time while I introduced the people at the various ports to my future wife.

The big event that fall was that Betsy and I were married on October 25, 1964, with my brother Bill as best man, and Mike Nash and Jack Thompson in the wedding party along with Betsy's friend Mary Gail Achtem and Betsy's three sisters.

Betsy had just one day off before she had to be back to work at St Paul's Hospital.

After a few weeks, we moved to Vancouver Island which has been our home base ever since.

This marks a suitable place for me to draw to a close some of my memories of the earlier part of my life. There was much more life to come and many more adventures, but that will perhaps be for another time. Looking back at those days, I think there's really only one piece of advice I believe I steered by and which I think might be helpful to others. As you only have one day to live, live it to the fullest. That's what I've always tried to do.

About the author

The author, although well travelled, has always drifted home to the West Coast of Canada. Forty years were spent making a living from the ocean, first as a mariner working for various employers until age 24, then as a tug boat owner and partner of a fish processing company. Volunteer work as Chamber of Commerce director and later president, twinning society chairman and youth sports volunteer has led to an active interest in community affairs. The father of four grown children, Lawrence resides at Campbell River, Canada with his wife Betsy at a seaside residence within sight of his birthplace on Quadra Island. The author has written several short stories but Child of the Storm is his first attempt at a full length book.